D0849687

LIFE IN TWO WORLDS

LIFE IN TWO WORLDS

A Coach's Journey from the
Reservation to the NHL and Back

TED NOLAN

with MEG MASTERS

VIKING

VIKING

an imprint of Penguin Canada, a division of Penguin Random House Canada Limited

Canada • USA • UK • Ireland • Australia • New Zealand • India • South Africa • China

First published 2023

www.penguinrandomhouse.ca

LIBRARY AND ARCHIVES CANADA CATALOGUING IN PUBLICATION

Title: Life in two worlds : a coach's journey from the reserve to the
NHL and back / Ted Nolan with Meg Masters.
Names: Nolan, Ted, 1958- author. | Masters, Meg, author.
Identifiers: Canadiana (print) 20230150098 | Canadiana (ebook) 2023015025X |
ISBN 9780735244955 (hardcover) | ISBN 9780735248038 (hardcover ;
signed edition) | ISBN 9780735244962 (EPUB)
Subjects: LCSH: Nolan, Ted, 1958- | LCSH: Hockey coaches—Canada—Biography. |
LCSH: Hockey players—Canada—Biography. | LCSH: First Nations
hockey players—Biography. | LCGFT: Autobiographies.
Classification: LCC GV848.5.N65 A3 2023 | DDC 796.962092—dc23

Book design by Matthew Flute
Cover design by Matthew Flute
Cover image: Ted with the Sabres,
photo by Bruce Bennett/Bruce Bennett Studios via Getty Images

Printed in the United States of America

10 9 8 7 6 5 4 3 2 1

Penguin
Random House
VIKING CANADA

To Mom and Dad
The words I never had a chance to say:
"Thank you and I love you."
Your son, Teddy

CONTENTS

PREFACE

I OPENED THE DOOR AND FELT A STAB OF ANXIETY. A delivery man was on the steps of my Garden River home, a clipboard in one hand and a box tucked under his arm. I knew what was in that box, but I'd pushed any thought of its arrival far from my mind.

It was the Jack Adams trophy. I'd won it about a year before at the NHL annual awards ceremony. The Jack Adams, voted on by members of the National Hockey League Broadcasters' Association, is awarded to the NHL coach of the year. I'd been given the honour after my second year coaching in the league. As the head coach of the Buffalo Sabres, I'd been in competition with the legendary Scotty Bowman, who had just led the Detroit Red Wings to the Stanley Cup. My win was, by all accounts, an incredible achievement for a coaching newcomer, an event I greeted with tears of pride.

I signed the delivery form, thanked the driver and took the box from him. Once I'd closed the door, I put it down on the entry-way floor.

Then I stood for a few seconds, staring at it, resting there between two sets of stairs—one leading up to my living room, one down to my basement. A rush of emotions came at me. Finally, they began to ebb, leaving just one: pure anger.

I lifted my foot and, with all the strength I had, kicked the box, sending it hurtling down the basement stairs. I heard it land with a loud metallic crash. Then I turned and went upstairs, determined to forget everything about it.

1

GARDEN RIVER

"ALWAYS BE PROUD OF WHO YOU ARE."

It's been over forty-five years since the last time I heard my father say those words, and yet I can hear his voice as clear as if he was standing by my side. No doubt, I remember it so well because Stan Stewart Nolan said this hundreds of times.

When I was very young, I didn't think much about why he said it. And it seemed an easy enough instruction. After all, I was part of a great family. Stan and Rose Nolan had twelve children: five daughters and seven sons. I was the third youngest. Despite our numbers, my parents managed to make us all feel loved, special and appreciated. The youngest of us received plenty of kind attention from our older siblings as well—our family was extremely close. We also lived in a great place. The Garden River First Nation Reserve is located in the middle of the 1850 Robinson-Huron Treaty area of the Anishinabek Nation and is fifty-two thousand acres of dense pine, stretching along the St. Marys River in beautiful Northern Ontario. My mother's family had lived there for generations and had always been a big part of that community—my grandfather had been the Chief, as had my mother's uncle Jack. My father too was a leader in our community, the band manager and the welfare officer for a number of years, as well as the manager of a small lumber mill on the reserve. My mother was just as involved in the life of Garden River, devoting herself to all sorts of local cultural activities.

There was so much to be proud of. I hardly needed reminding by Dad.

Later, I would realize that how I looked at myself, my family and my community was a little different than how the rest of the world might regard us. I would come to understand that Stan Nolan's words, "Always be proud of who you are," were probably repeated so often because he knew how difficult that could be made for us by outside forces. And I would come to appreciate that a robust sense of self-respect was the best protection any of us could have against what faced us in the future. But it would take some time for me to recognize my father's words as the gift they were.

♦

When I think of my father, that's what I remember best: his words and his voice. That voice wasn't loud or harsh, and yet there was a calm firmness that made you listen. And when you did, you heard not only about pride but also about hard work.

My dad was a relative newcomer to Garden River. I believe he grew up somewhere near Wawa, but I'm not entirely certain. When he met and married my mom, he moved to her reserve, where my mother's dad, the Chief at the time, made him a member. In return, Dad devoted himself to the community.

It was in the role of welfare officer that my dad made loud and clear to many in Garden River his intense belief in the value of hard work. At home, we learned this early. He had us chopping wood, stoking the fire, emptying the slop pail and doing other tasks around the house as soon as we were able. If he didn't think we were working hard enough, he'd give us an earful. At the welfare office, he often told those looking for aid that he expected them to do some community work in return, whether it was chopping wood or shovelling snow.

"Don't you ever rely on this government, Ted," he used to tell me.

That you had to earn your way in the world was central to my dad's way of thinking, and when you couldn't earn what you needed, you had to learn to do the best you could with what you did have. Self-reliance and perseverance—those were Stan Nolan's golden rules.

An imposing man, six feet tall and broad framed, Dad was a strict disciplinarian who didn't tolerate nonsense. We'd get a smack if we acted up in front of him, and if he heard we'd made trouble at school or elsewhere, we'd get the same. But we always knew that Dad's punishments were not about showing his authority or being in control. Instead, he made it clear to us that being disciplined like this was a way to remind us that we needed to have respect for others, and just as importantly, we needed to have respect for ourselves. Bad behaviour dishonoured those who exhibited it. Whenever he sent us off to wash our faces or tuck in our shirts, he'd remind us, "We may be poor, but we don't have to look like it."

One of Dad's other passionate beliefs was the importance of telling the truth. Honesty is one of the Seven Grandfather teachings of the Ojibway culture: debwewin. And in many ways, it was linked to my father's attitude about self-respect. To truly act with self-respect, it was essential that you speak your truth. Telling people what they wanted to hear, pretending you thought or felt differently than you did, was no way to live, according to my father.

Not until years later did I realize how deeply and thoroughly I had embraced these two ideas—respect and truthfulness—how they strengthened me even as they made some of my interactions with others challenging.

♦

While it's my father's voice I think of when I remember him, the first thing that comes to mind about my mother is her eyes.

My mother, Rose, was more gentle but no less firm in sharing her beliefs and opinions with us. Never once in my life did I hear her raise her voice or lash out in any way. Calm and steady, she layered her love with reassuring advice: "Just do your best." And if we misbehaved, we read her thoughts in those expressive eyes of hers: *I'm disappointed.*

She was affectionate and nurturing, with a magnetism that drew our family together. And despite the fact that there were fourteen of us, not including the grandchildren that were around even when I was young, she was full of energy. Her primary focus was always her family, but her passion extended to her larger community and her Ojibway heritage and beliefs as well.

My mother was a deeply spiritual person. She and Dad raised us children in the Anglican faith. Almost every Sunday, we attended the little church that was just down the road from us, bringing a penny for the collection plate. On Christmas Eve, we'd travel to the bigger Garden River church, which sat at the junction of the St. Marys and Garden rivers. At church, I learned about God and about the importance of faith. But when we got home, our prayers were a little different than those we practised with the minister. Instead of telling us to hold our hands together and bow our heads, my mother would bring out a bowl of sage, cedar, tobacco or sweetgrass, light it and then hold the bowl in front of us, encouraging us to wave the fragrant smoke over our heads while thanking the Creator. This smudging ceremony, she explained, would allow us to release negative thoughts and feelings, and would cleanse us and bring positive energy into our lives. When I asked my mother if the Creator was the same as God, she nodded. God was simply the white people's name for the Creator. In this way, my mother showed us that Christian teachings could be combined with a strong belief in traditional medicine and wisdom. She also often sought out the advice of our local Medicine Man when one of the family wasn't feeling well or was struggling in some way. And over every doorway in the house, she hung bunches of everlasting flowers to ward off spirits.

In addition to embracing traditional spiritual practices, my mother was devoted to our Ojibway history and culture, attending local folk-art festivals and overseeing our annual performance of the Hiawatha play on the banks of the Garden River.

The Garden River First Nation had been staging annual performances of this play, based on Henry Wadsworth Longfellow's epic poem *The Song of Hiawatha*, since 1901. While Longfellow didn't feel it necessary, apparently, to stick to the known facts about the pre-colonial Mohawk co-founder of the Iroquois Confederacy (including making him Ojibway, not Mohawk), the poem was meant to celebrate First Nations history and culture. In 1900, a Garden River Chief, George Kabaosa, adapted the poem into a play that reflected our own stories and accounts of our past and present and featured our Ojibway language. Many folks from the Soo and surrounding area would come each year to watch it, and the Garden River troupe would sometimes travel to various cities in Canada and the States to put on performances for wider audiences. When I got to be about eight, I started to play the central role of Little Hiawatha. I wouldn't have said I was a kid with the acting bug or a flair for drama, but something about stepping into my First Nations past on that stage brought me to life. I loved every minute of it.

The Pow Wow circuit was another passion of my mother's. She organized our Garden River Pow Wows and was one of a group of local First Nations folk who travelled across the province and the country to attend them in other communities. About the time I took on the role of Little Hiawatha, I started going with her.

Pow Wows in the sixties and seventies were a part of the re-emergence of Indigenous culture that had been suppressed for generations, officially by the Indian Act, which had outlawed certain types of First Nations practices and celebrations, and unofficially by the disapproval of settler societies and religious orders. First Nations peoples across the country were not only hosting their own celebrations but were also connecting with and learning from other First Nations by attending their Pow Wows.

At the Pow Wows, we guests slept outdoors in tents and spent the days and evenings talking, dancing and singing with the rest of the participants. One of the traditions I loved was the forty-nine songs. The legend went that a First Nations community had sent one hundred warriors to battle but only fifty-one returned. The forty-nine songs were sung for those who didn't return. We'd gather together and sing, stopping between each song to talk and tell stories. Storytelling was always a big part of these gatherings. It was the way we shared our spiritual beliefs, our histories and our traditions. And since people came to Pow Wows from across the continent (at one Pow Wow in the

Northwestern United States, I met Indigenous folks from Mexico), I learned that First Nations culture was vast and varied.

When I was about ten, my mom organized a group bus trip all the way to Morley, Alberta, for a huge Pow Wow hosted by the Stoney Nakoda Nation. Over the course of several days, there were many ceremonies and festivities, including Sundances and a Sweat Lodge. This was my first experience participating in a Sweat Lodge ceremony. Sweat Lodges were not a big part of Garden River culture when I was young, although their use was widespread in the First Nations communities across North American, and I'd seen them at other Pow Wows. Inside a circular tent covered with hides or a tarp or even pine boughs, a fire is built, which eventually produces an intense heat. People gather inside to sit on the ground and pray, asking the Creator for wisdom, for forgiveness, for health and for the well-being of others. The heat seems to focus you, to lift you out of yourself. Leaving the Lodge and entering the cool air again feels like a rebirth. It was an amazing experience. The other highlight for me at the Stoney Nakoda Pow Wow was the buffalo hunting demonstrations, in which the hunters brought down an enormous beast with only bows and arrows. The hunt was followed by a huge feast.

Attending Pow Wows also gave me the opportunity to participate in First Nations dance traditions. While I enjoyed the group dances that we all performed at the Pow Wows, what I loved best was solo, or "fancy," dancing. With this style, the movements are more pronounced and athletic than those in circle dances—dancers spin faster, leap higher and bend deeper. They dance backwards, on one foot or in a squatting position. And the finale of a fancy dance is dramatic. The drummers pound out seven strong beats, and for each beat, the dancer tries to make a big, impressive move—and then stops his body on a dime when the final beat is sounded. I loved the strength, flexibility, creativity and energy that fancy dancing demanded, and I began to perform regularly on the Pow Wow circuit.

The Pow Wow circuit brought me a sense of pride and belonging that has never left me. I was overwhelmed by how joyfully we were welcomed by people we didn't know, how quickly we were made to feel at home on unfamiliar reserves. At every Pow Wow I attended, people would come to check on the visitors: Did we have enough to eat? Did we have enough firewood? Was everything okay? We were *wanted* in these places. And that feeling reinforced the sense that my family and I held a deep connection to communities that stretched across the province, the country, and the continent. My time attending Pow Wows taught me that my First Nations world was much bigger and more richly diverse than I could ever have imagined back in Garden River.

And those Pow Wow days were some of the happiest times of my childhood.

◆

My eldest sibling, Rod, was almost nineteen years older than me, and my eldest sister, Katie, had just turned sixteen when I was born on April 7, 1958. The age range meant that I don't remember us all living together—Rod, Katie, Rita and Rick were already out of the house when I was a young boy. As I got older, Tom, Barb, Arlene and Terry moved out as well, so there was just Joe, me, Steve and the baby, Janice. But the difference in our years also meant there were many loving and caring adults in my world—older brothers and sisters who joined parents, grandparents, uncles and an aunt in showering us younger siblings with affection. Our big family made hunting for friends unnecessary. I spent most of my time with Steve, who was two years younger. It wasn't until I started school that I really made friends from other parts of the reserve, and even then, my family members were my favourite companions.

Despite the size of my family, our house was tiny—just one room that served as kitchen and living room, and three or four small, doorless bedrooms.

By the time my memory kicks in, our house had electricity, although this would have been a fairly new addition in the sixties. We didn't, however, have running water. Neither did most of the houses on the reserve. Instead, there was an outhouse and a pump for the well several yards from our back door. We used a slop bucket during the cold winter nights. To wash our faces and hands, we had a small basin on a little table. To have a bath, we dragged a large tin tub into the kitchen and filled it with water we heated on the wood stove. Not only did my mom cook on that wood stove, it also served as our only source of heat for most of my early childhood. And when one of us forgot to stoke it properly before bed, we'd wake up in the morning to a house so cold our breath hung in the air like clouds.

Our little home was no better at keeping the wet weather out than it was at protecting us from frigid temperatures and the icy winds that blew in around the door and window frames. When it rained, we'd pull a few large pots and pans from the cupboards, lining them up on the warped wood floors in an effort to catch the water that dripped from the ceiling. And it wasn't until I was in my late teens that we got an oil furnace and a party-line phone (our ring was one long and two short).

Our house may have been modest, but it was positively roomy compared to the little shack that stood about forty feet from our door. Not much bigger than a woodshed, with only a bedroom and a small area that could be used as a kitchen, it served as the first home for a succession of my older siblings and their spouses.

Our home and the shack were located about a quarter of a mile north of the point where Garden River and the much bigger St. Marys River met, and were on the main artery through the Garden River reserve, which also happened to be the two-lane Trans-Canada Highway. (The highway was relocated a mile or so north of this road in 2007.) That meant a steady stream of traffic in front of our yard, but it also meant we were close to the heart of our community. Running along the highway were our band office, baseball field and outdoor hockey rink. The Pow Wow grounds were directly across the highway from our house, and the small Anglican church was just down the road.

Extended family were close—my aunt Fanny lived two doors down, my uncle John right next door to her. We had neighbours on the other side of us, but most of the families were spread throughout the reserve.

My family always managed to get by, but many of the basics were often in short supply. Despite living in Northern Ontario, with its deep-freeze winters and mountains of snow, none of us kids ever owned warm winter boots. Instead, we wore those red-soled black rubber ones and tried to keep the cold out with as many pairs of socks as we could fit inside. The same was true of jackets. There wasn't one down jacket or well-insulated parka in the whole house. We layered sweaters and bush shirts and whatever coats came our way. Not that we had a lot of clothes to layer. We each had just one pair of jeans and a single pullover. If our sweaters got dirty before wash day, we turned them inside out. My father always reminded us that there was no point in feeling sorry for ourselves—the best move was to make do with what we had. With those words in mind, when I was about ten, I solved the problem of frostbitten ears by making a hat for myself by tying two grey wool socks together. The fact that no one teased me about it must be a testament to the number of cold ears around the reserve.

Food was often in even shorter supply. Without a car or driver's licences, my parents usually waited to go grocery shopping until a friend or relative was driving into the nearby farming community of Echo Bay. There, we would head into the general store to buy huge chunks of bologna, cans of Klik luncheon meat, big bags of puffed wheat cereal, boxes of powdered milk and loaves of soft white bread. When we got home, the cupboards would be full—for a time.

We supplemented our groceries by fishing and hunting, although my father was never a very enthusiastic hunter. Friends and relatives often shared their game with us, but even with this, our bellies weren't always full. When my mother made a pot of stew or soup, everyone would help themselves when they were hungry instead of sitting down for meals together. Same went for the food in the cupboard. It seemed like no time at all after a visit to Echo Bay that empty shelves would greet us when we opened the cupboard doors. There might not even be a slice of bread for the lard and mustard sandwiches that were my occasional lunch. From an early age, I figured out what to do at those times. I'd wander over to see Aunt Fanny, knowing that a smile went a long way, especially with a kind-hearted woman. I also knew Aunt Fanny was a great baker and always had a loaf of fresh bread in the house.

"Are you hungry, Teddy?" she'd ask, when I showed up. And at my nod, she'd pull out a loaf and make a pot of tea for us.

We kids never thought twice about being out and about by ourselves like that. My parents didn't keep tabs on us—as long as we got our chores done and made it to school every day, we could pretty much do as we pleased. We took off in the morning and came home when we were hungry. We played outside at night until we were tired enough to go to bed.

Yet, despite our unstructured life, there was never a moment when we Nolan children weren't aware of how much our parents loved and cared for us.

♦

While my mother made sure we had a good grounding in our Ojibway heritage, the one thing she refused to share with us was the language.

She and my father often talked with each other and their friends and siblings in Ojibway. In fact, my mother's mother couldn't speak a word of English. But when my parents addressed any of the younger generation, they immediately switched to English. I couldn't understand this. I could see how my mother lit up when she began to talk in her first language, how she came alive when those words flowed from her tongue. Why didn't she want to share that joy with us? One day, I asked her about that. Why wouldn't she teach us?

Her eyes were immediately clouded with sadness, and she seemed to struggle with how to answer me. Finally, she began to speak in halting sentences. "I don't want you ever to be punished for speaking Ojibway," she said, "like kids were punished in residential school." She paused and then said quietly, "They beat kids. One girl had her tongue nailed to a board."

When I went to bed that night, I couldn't get that picture out of my head (to this day, I can't). But as gruesome as it was, I never doubted it. I'd overheard many adults recount horrific experiences that happened to them in the schools when they were young children.

My mother was such a welcoming soul that our house was like an official meeting place on the reserve. Family and friends would drop in any time of the day or night—there were always people sitting at the table with big mugs of tea, chatting. On weekend evenings especially, my parents would put on the radio and bring out a deck of cards. As Hank Williams songs filled the air, people would arrive with six-packs of beer or a bottle of Catawba sherry. Within minutes, the stories would start. The early-evening tales were often funny ones, but slowly the laughter faded and the conversation grew quieter. The games were abandoned and the storytelling took over completely. My brothers and sisters and I would lie in bed, trying to drift off as voices cracked, words broken by sobs, the sentences trailing off. We heard how children were snatched away from their parents and forced into residential schools, how the Indian agent controlled everything on the reserve, how our Elders had been mistreated in the outside world. Eventually, much of the conversation became hard to follow, as words slurred and tears fell.

From a very early age, I realized that our kitchen was a place of communion. A place where people gathered to connect with one another, and often to drink. The drinking wasn't a way to celebrate. It was a way to forget—and to grieve. I couldn't have explained that back then, but I knew it as sure as I knew anything.

Sometimes, when we children got up in the morning, my parents' guests would still be in the kitchen, slumped over the table or dozing on the hard chairs. Eventually, some might rouse themselves and wander off, either to return a little later or to be replaced by another acquaintance. Some would just stay put as one day turned into the next. More than once, Monday morning rolled around, and my brothers and sisters and I had to pick our way around a sleeping guest in the kitchen to grab a piece of fry bread before we headed to school.

My mother's uncle Jack was often at that kitchen table, sometimes showing up on Friday evening and not leaving until Monday morning. In fact, I never saw him rise from his chair and used to wonder if he'd somehow figured out how to survive without peeing.

Unlike my parents, who seemed able to escape their sorrows with a few drinks and then balance those good times with work and other responsibilities, my mother's brothers, Earl and John, who'd both survived the battlefields of World War II as well other traumas, had fallen into full-blown addiction by the time I knew them. They would go on six-month drinking jags, which eventually led to blackouts and the DTs (delirium tremens), making them so incapacitated they were forced to stop. When I was six or seven, my mother started bringing me with her to help when my uncles were "sick" from withdrawal. As they lay there shaking, we would mop their sweating brows and hold buckets for them when they vomited or started to dry heave. As soon as the detox was over, however, they'd start drinking again.

It wasn't just my uncles whose tortured pasts led to harmful behaviour, of course. While I never saw either of my parents being violent, I was always aware that it was a part of our world. Sometimes, during those long-night gatherings in our kitchen, fights would break out. When the voices woke me, one of my older sisters would comfort me until I was able to fall asleep again. More than once, I saw my older sisters with bruised faces or busted lips themselves. And as I got older, I understood that many folks in the community were not only violent with their partners but also unfaithful.

Everyone around me seemed to accept that all of this was just a part of life, the sort of sadness that is bound to arise in a community with a painful past. Not once did I hear words of blame or judgment shared among the people in Garden River. As the years went on, I came to understand that when a community is judged by the whole outside world, it seems especially important not to inflict that same judgment at home.

But when I was young, I was a real softy, and I sometimes struggled with it all. My father and brothers taught me one way to handle my distress. If they caught me crying about anything—a skinned knee or something more troubling—the conversation would go something like this:

"Why are you crying?"

"Because it hurts."

"Of course it hurts. Life hurts. Nothing you can do about it. No point crying."

They would tell me to eat the pain, push it down out of sight. So I learned not to show my feelings, to put a smile on my face and behave as if nothing had happened.

And if I couldn't do that, I'd escape into physical activity.

When the sad stories, the drinking or the bruised faces began to weigh on me, I'd search out my brothers or friends to join me in a game of catch. And if there was no one to throw a ball with, I'd go for a run down the Garden River roads and trails. I'd run and I'd run, until my mind quieted and all I was aware of was the feel of the gravel under my feet and the air rushing past my face.

◆

I don't believe either of my parents ever attended residential school, but I'm not entirely sure. Unlike some of their other family and friends, they were careful not to talk with us children about their own difficult experiences. Maybe my mother didn't want accounts of her past to make us think negatively about our own schools. She was a strong believer in the importance of education and felt that to succeed we needed to learn the ways of the white world. (She even sat on the Sault Ste. Marie school board for a couple of years.)

But it was pretty clear how my parents felt about these terrible places. One day, I asked my mother why my brothers and sisters and I didn't have to go to residential school.

She pointed to my father's hunting rifle leaning against the doorframe. "Your father would never allow that, Teddy," she said.

As I got older, I realized that a rifle wouldn't have helped the parents of past generations. When school officials showed up on reserves, they were often accompanied by the RCMP or other police forces—particularly if the parents had resisted in the past. By the sixties, in my part of the world, forced removal to residential school wasn't happening in that way. The same could not be said of forced removal by child welfare workers—a practice now known as the "sixties scoop," although my immediate family avoided that tragedy.

So my siblings and I attended a day school on the reserve until we were about nine, after which we bused into Sault Ste. Marie for grade five and beyond.

For me, school wasn't the deeply traumatic experience it had been for so many older people in my community—but I wouldn't say it was a good time either. The day school on the reserve was a one-room building, staffed exclusively with white men and women, many of whom didn't seem to care for the assignment. Mostly, I remember their cool indifference—which was a heck of a lot easier than the attention they gave us. One of my sisters clearly remembers the nurse who visited the school and gave us our vaccinations without ever changing the needle. Once, one of the teachers offered us what were clearly dog biscuits as an afternoon snack. I refused to eat any, although a few hungry kids did. And when we weren't paying attention or got too noisy, we'd be dragged by our ears into the corner or, worse, forced to hold out our hands so that a thick leather strap about the length of a beaver tail could be brought down on our open palms. The whipping didn't stop until beads of blood appeared. One of my pals told me that if I put one or two strands of hair across my hand, the blood would spring up quicker. Unfortunately, I had many chances to try this out—and it never seemed to work. The day the school closed permanently, I'd finished grade four, and I wasn't sorry to walk out through the doors for the last time. I was worried, however, about what lay ahead—and about leaving the familiarity of Garden River.

The move to the city schools did indeed turn out to be a tough adjustment. For one thing, there were the long bus rides back and forth each day. More than once, when we were fooling around on the school bus, the driver pulled over on the side of highway and forced the most boisterous off the bus. The only thing we could do was walk the miles and miles left to go. Several times, my ten- or eleven-year-old self spent two or three hours trudging along the gravel shoulder of the Trans-Canada Highway as enormous transport trucks sped past me at one hundred kilometres an hour or more. It's a miracle I made it home every time. And—shocking to think about now—none of our parents ever complained to the school or the bus company. As often as not, in fact, my dad would greet my late arrival with a licking. We kids were supposed to know better and not give the drivers any excuse to punish us.

The size of the city was also a challenge. Sault Ste. Marie, with a population of about eighty thousand back then, wasn't a big place as far as cities go. But to us, coming from a community of a few hundred people, it was huge. It was also unfamiliar. We seldom went there to shop, favouring the tiny Echo Bay instead. One time, when I was about seven, my mother took me into town for a haircut, an experience that sure dampened any interest I had in going into the Soo for anything. After I got settled into the barbershop chair, my mother went to do errands. The barber disappeared in the back for a minute and came out with a bowl. He placed it on my head and began to follow the rim with his scissors, chuckling the whole time. "There you go," he said, smirking, when he took the bowl off.

I got out of the chair as quickly as I could and went outside to wait for my mother. When she came up the sidewalk a few minutes later, my humiliation was swept aside by heartache. Her eyes welled with tears as she reached out and touched my hair. In the coming hours and days, we didn't talk about my haircut, but every time my mother glanced at me, an expression of pain crossed her face. It was the same expression I noticed when I'd asked her about her Ojibway language or about residential school.

It would take weeks for my hair to grow out, but it felt like an eternity, knowing that until the bowl-shaped cut was gone, my mother was hurting—hurting for me.

The incident also deeply upset me because it reminded me of the stories I'd heard of the haircutting and other brutal treatments that kids had suffered at the residential schools. The barber knew my mother would be back soon, but he still did what he did. What cruelties might he have committed if I was alone? If no one would be picking me up or checking on me?

My only other childhood memories of the Soo were the long and tedious afternoons and evenings my brothers, sisters and I spent in the Caswell Hotel parking lot. From time to time, my parents would get together with friends in the basement beer parlour at the Caswell. If none of the older kids were around to watch us, they'd bring us younger ones with them. Since we couldn't go into the bar, we would stay outside, playing in the car or in the parking lot. One of my parents would pop out from time to time to check on us and give us money to buy a bag of chips or a bottle of pop at the store down the road. We entertained ourselves as best we could, but I was always eager for closing time so we could get back home.

♦

The first school I attended in the Soo was a tough place, and probably not the best introduction to the white educational world. The First Nations kids tended to stick together, but that didn't keep us out of reach of the many bullies. One day, as some friends and I were playing on the bleachers in the schoolyard, a fellow came up to me and elbowed me so hard in the face I fell about six feet to the ground. When I got up, blood was streaming from my nose.

We Nolan boys were pretty tough ourselves. My older brothers looked out for Steve and me whenever they could. Joe was at the new school with me, but he wasn't around all the time, and I knew I had to take care of the bully myself. At recess, I found the kid and made sure he wouldn't target me again.

It was a little harder responding to the teachers and staff. The First Nations kids were subjected to regular physical inspections. (I don't remember white kids ever joining us when we were forced to line up for this.) The teachers or school nurse would examine our hands to make sure they were clean. If they didn't like what they found, they'd dig under our nails with a sharp file. We'd also have to endure the dreaded "lice check." At home, my mother frequently checked our heads for lice. Occasionally, she'd pick out a few nits or a louse. But before the school checks started, I'd never realized that having lice might be a source of disgrace. The nurse would dig the comb across our scalps so hard it brought tears to our eyes, as if it was as much a punishment as a "health" measure. Everything about it suggested we had done something wrong.

And then there was the atmosphere in the lunchroom. One day, tomato soup was being served. I hated tomato soup. The teacher supervising the lunchroom came over to our table, a long ruler resting on his shoulder. He asked me why I wasn't eating, and I told him.

"Well, you're going to eat it," he said. Then he put his hand on my head and shoved my face down into my soup bowl.

Worse was my classroom teacher. When I first arrived in the school, she told me to sit in the second row, in the middle, and there were days when she would ask the kid sitting in front of me to move to another desk. I dreaded this happening. She would then sit down on top of the empty desk, facing directly towards me. She would spread her legs wide, her skirt sliding high up her thighs. She wouldn't be wearing any underwear. I would try to keep my head down and stare at my worksheet, but she always asked me a question or addressed me in some way, forcing me to look up. As soon as I did, my eyes would momentarily catch sight of what she wanted me to see. If she thought anyone around us had noticed, she'd grab me by the collar and lead me to the corner. She'd pretend she was reprimanding me, but she always gave me a wink while doing it.

There were a number of those bad days. And every time, I felt dirty—dirty and humiliated and angry. And afraid. Even at ten years old, I knew that this was very wrong, and whatever she was playing at, I was at risk of losing much more than a morning of desk work.

I guess I wasn't the only Garden River kid having a miserable time at that school. The next year, we were all sent to a different public school. (The Catholic kids from Garden River were sent to Catholic schools.) There, for the first time in my life, I had teachers who seemed to care about me and treated us First Nations kids just like the other students. Two in particular—Mrs. Forbes and Mrs. Payette—took me under their wings. Mrs. Payette even asked me to be her helper when she went to the public library every Friday afternoon to pick out books for the classroom. I was never much of a student, and those years didn't turn me into an academic by any stretch, but the kindness of those teachers, as well as my mother's passionate belief in the importance of education, kept me from dropping out in the early years of high school, as so many First Nations kids did. And they made me trust that I could do okay at school if I ever wanted to apply myself.

◆

Despite the sometimes frightening and painful aspects of my early years, my memories of that time are overwhelmingly happy ones. Not only was every day filled with affection and gestures of love from my mother, father, brothers and sisters, but most days also gave me the joy of spending time outdoors with my brothers and friends. My friends and I built a log cabin in our yard, felling the trees ourselves, stripping the bark and notching the logs by hand. We spent long days fishing by the river and had the freedom to head out into the bush for overnight camping trips when we were quite young. We'd build ourselves lean-tos to sleep in and do our best to live off the land—either fishing, hunting or trapping our dinners. We usually caught rabbit, partridge or even squirrels, skinning and roasting them over a fire, although we always brought along a few potatoes in case we weren't lucky.

My father gave me a .22 rifle when I was about ten years old. Later, he would give me his old British .303 for deer and moose, but, like him, I was never very interested in hunting big game. Deer are just too beautiful to shoot.

Being mostly self-taught in outdoor living had its limitations. One day, my friends and I trapped a beaver. We knew that a trader visited Garden River from time to time, purchasing whatever pelts were for sale. We figured we could make a little money next time he came by. We skinned the beaver and made a frame out of some cedar branches. Then we stretched the pelt across the frame and stashed it in the basement of the day-school building to let it dry. Of course, none of us really knew what we were doing. When we came back to retrieve our treasure, the pelt had come away from the branches and shrunk up to a little lump of fur about the size of a baseball mitt. After that, we gave up on beaver pelts, although eventually we did manage to make some money selling muskrat skins to the trader and sturgeon to a restaurant in the Soo.

Another time, we caught a salmon that was about to spawn. One of my buddies had heard of an expensive delicacy called "caviar." The rest of us were surprised to learn it was raw fish eggs, just like we had in front of us. Excited, we each took a fingerful of eggs and popped it in our mouths—then promptly spat it out. Rich people, we decided, had weird tastes.

And, of course, there were sports.

My dad helped build the first baseball diamond on the reserve, and by the time I was a kid, we had a men's team, coached by my brother Rick, that travelled to tournaments all across the country. Rick and my dad taught us younger boys not only how to hit and catch but also the strategy of the game.

Baseball was my true love. I played as often as I could, joining the men as soon I was about twelve or thirteen and participating in ball tournaments right into adulthood. But when I was a child, we didn't have teams for players my age on the reserve, and it was hard to have a game with just a couple of kids. There was another sport, however, that seemed perfect for either a big group or just a couple of brothers with time to kill on a Saturday afternoon. All we needed were a few pairs of old skates, some sticks and the constant sub-zero temperatures of a northern winter. Hockey, we discovered, was a game we could make our own.

2

HOCKEY

IF THERE WAS ONE PLACE YOU COULD BE SURE TO FIND ME in the depths of winter, it was the Garden River hockey rink. Just as he had with the baseball diamond, my dad worked with other men in the community to build the rink from scratch. They constructed low walls, then put water down with a hose and used shovels to scrape it smooth. Posts with electric lights strung between them lined the perimeter. Rick, an even more passionate sportsman than our dad, was always out there, and when I was really little, I loved to watch him play with the rest of the Garden River Braves team. The only problem was that if the older boys were playing, us younger kids couldn't get on the ice. Day after day, I would put on my old second-hand skates anyways and walk over, waiting for my chance. One day, when I was about seven years old, frustrated with waiting, I thought about how my father and the others had made the rink. *I can do that too*, I thought. *I can make a rink. It's just water.*

When I got up the next morning, I put on four pairs of socks and my cracked rubber boots and headed outside to the pump. I'd brought along a bucket. I filled it with water and then dumped it out on a flat patch of snow in the yard. I went back and forth and back and forth all day until there was a fairly large puddle freezing up in the deep cold.

One pail at a time, I kept at my task the next day. My dad, noticing there was a lump of snow and ice in one corner of the "rink," came out with an axe to chip it away. Other than that, I laboured on my own. After a few days, I was done. I had my very own hockey rink.

In no time, my brothers and various friends and cousins began meeting in our yard to play endless games of shinny.

In those early days, Joe was our coach. And he was one tough task-master. The first rule was always no whining or complaining, even if you got hurt.

"Anyone starts bleeding," he'd say, "we use that to make the red line."

And sure enough, we did. Steve's nosebleed was his one and only contribution to making or maintaining the ice.

But he and I spent hours and hours outside in our hand-me-down skates and the cheap wooden sticks my dad would occasionally pick up for us at the local gas station. Even if we'd spent the whole day playing shinny, I would always try to get back out at night and skate by the glow of light coming from our kitchen window or, better yet, a crisp, clear moon. On those cold evenings out on the ice, everything would fall away: the sad stories that filled our kitchen, the gnawing of an empty stomach, the tingling of frozen feet, the frightening games of a teacher. There was nothing to worry about, nothing even to think about. It was like running—but better. It was as if I had been transported to a place of perfect peace and freedom. It was magic. Pure magic.

♦

Dad could clearly see how much Steve and I loved playing hockey. When I was about ten, he scraped together a bit of money and took us to the Soo to register for house league so we could play on a real team.

The first time I saw the Soo arena, I was dumbfounded. It was a huge building made entirely of metal—like a big tin can. When we got inside, the wonders continued. A little canteen stood near the entrance, and the smell of popcorn filled the crisp air. There were rooms with brightly painted benches, just for getting dressed and undressed in. And the rink itself was another surprise. An enormous machine, a Zamboni, was gliding around it, leaving the ice smooth and slick and entirely free of snow. It felt like being in another world.

At our very first practice, however, it became clear there were going to be a few challenges bigger than finding money for the registration fee.

Steve and I each had a pair of skates, but they were much too big. They stayed on our feet only because they were stuffed with socks and laced up as tight as they would go. (When I was really little, my skates were so big, I'd worn my rubber boots inside of them.) I'd also become quite good at stick "repairs," joining broken shafts together with glue and finishing nails and wrapping the wood in electrical tape, but for this practice I'd only been able to find one in good enough shape to hold up, so Steve and I had to share. We had just one helmet between us (again, so big it bounced around on our heads, providing almost no real protection) and one pair of gloves.

The equipment shortage meant that when one of us played, the other had to sit out. During the final skate-around at the end of the first practice, however, I told Steve to keep the gloves on and got on the ice with bare hands. Just before everyone skated off the ice, I fell, and another boy skated right over two fingers of my left hand. I picked myself up and, holding my hand against my chest, followed the rest of the players off the ice.

My fingers were bleeding badly, so Steve and I went straight to the bathroom. There, we tried to wrap up my hand with toilet paper and paper towels. Then we went out into the arena lobby to wait for our ride home.

We had no idea when my dad would arrive, as he had to hitch a ride with someone coming into town. For five long hours, we sat on a hard bench in the arena lobby, my throbbing hand in a wad of blood-soaked paper towels, as kids and adults walked past. Some glanced our way, but most hardly seemed to notice or care we were there. When Dad finally did arrive, he took me straight to the hospital. I needed four stitches.

After the next practice, one of the men who was managing the team seemed to realize that Steve and I didn't have the necessary equipment. He told us that the team provided goaltending gloves and pads. Being two years older, I was the stronger player, so it was decided that Steve would be the one playing in net. That's how he became a goalie and I became a winger.

I was glad to be playing out, as I loved to skate and shoot. But I found the hard, smooth surface of the indoor ice much more difficult to manage than the sometimes rough and patchy surface of our back-yard ice or the Garden River rink. My skate blades were so dull, I slid and slipped as I tried to move. One day, walking past one of the rooms in the arena, I noticed a man holding a skate blade up to a whirring machine. Sparks were flying from the blade. I must have asked some-one what was going on, and I learned that skate blades could be sharp-ened. I wondered if that would help me. On the way home that day, I thought about the only other time I had seen sparks coming from blades—when I walked along the asphalt highway in my skates to get to the Garden River rink. After supper that night, I laced on my skates and then ran back and forth across the road, a shower of sparks flying around my feet. At the next practice, I was surprised to find it hadn't helped at all.

Eventually, my father found a hardware store that would sharpen our skates inexpensively. I was able to skate with a little more control, but I sometimes found myself missing the slipperiness of my old blades.

The biggest remaining challenge of playing league hockey was simply getting into town. Because of our age difference, Steve and I were soon put on two different teams, which made the logistics even tougher.

When I got to be thirteen or fourteen, I'd occasionally hitchhike to the Soo or back when no rides were available. But when I was younger, I had to rely on one of my older siblings or their spouses to get to and from the arena. That often meant waiting for hours after the game— and being dropped off hours early. And occasionally, I had to miss games or practices altogether.

One time, when I was in my early teens, my team had an exhibition game in Sault Ste. Marie, Michigan, and my brother Tom drove me and my dad down. When we got to the rink, the coach pulled me out of the dressing room. "Ted, since you missed the last practice," he said, "you're benched for this game."

When my dad heard about that, he was furious. It angered him that no one had asked what it took for me to get to the game, or asked why I'd missed the practice. He knew how devoted I was to hockey. He watched me go out to my backyard rink night after night, even when there was no one to play with. He saw me make "pylons" out of piles of snow so I could repeat the drills I'd seen the rep teams do at their practices. He knew I probably spent more time practising than any player in the house league.

"You're not playing on that team anymore," he said to me.

I didn't want to quit, but he was adamant. It wasn't until we found another team for me that I could get back on the ice that season.

I don't think my father's response to the benching was just about the unfairness and bias he perceived. It was also about the attitude of the coach. My father wasn't reluctant to voice his disappointment when we kids acted up or weren't working hard at our chores. But to him, playing sports was simply about enjoyment, including the joy of a hard-fought battle. He never once admonished us for making mistakes or critiqued our play in any way. The only thing he ever said after games was, "Well, did you have fun?" I suspect he thought the coach had lost sight of that priority, among other things.

Steve and I stayed playing recreational league hockey even as we got older and most of the best players migrated to competitive leagues where rep teams played similar clubs from other cities. My family couldn't afford the extra fees and travel costs for that level. That didn't stop me from continuing to work on my game. I practised in the backyard and on the Garden River rink. If the ice wasn't good on the rink or the Braves were using it, I'd sometimes skate thirty kilometres along the ice-filled ditches that ran alongside the railroad tracks until I got to the rink at the Rankin First Nations Reserve.

Finally, when I was about fifteen, I got an invitation to play on a team that was one step up from house league: a midget division club in Sault Major Hockey called the Elks.

Since the team played clubs from nearby towns—the Soo; Sault Ste. Marie, Michigan; and other small towns in the area—one of their managers, a fellow named Bill LeClair, said he would be happy to pick me up on the reserve and take me to games and practices.

Bill was one of those people who change the direction of your life. Not only did he put me on the more skilled team, he also took me under his wing for a time. I had my first meal in a restaurant with Bill. After one game, on our drive home, he took me for dinner. When the menus came, I guess he could see I wasn't sure what to make of the long list of items. He explained to me what "appetizers" were, what all the forks were for, and even that many people ate dessert after every meal, which seemed a real extravagance to me. And he would continue to be in my corner during what would be one of the most difficult years of my life.

◆

One day in early January 1975, when I was sixteen, Steve and I awoke to the sound of a commotion outside our bedroom doorway. When I sat up in bed, I saw a big white vehicle parked on our lawn. I threw the covers off and scrambled off the mattress. As soon as Steve and I were out of our room, we could see two white men in uniforms leaning over my father as he lay on his bed. One of them was pumping Dad's chest with both hands. My mother rushed over to us and told us to go back to bed. Dad was sick. Everything would be okay. A few moments later, the men were wheeling my father towards the ambulance.

Dad was in the hospital for a day or two, and my mother was with him all that time. Steve and I were playing hockey outside when she finally returned home. She was alone. I knew immediately that my dad was gone. The realization made me feel as if my heart had stopped, like part of me had been ripped away. Like part of my life had just ended. Faith in the Creator had always been a comfort to me, but now I was furious at God for what he had done.

For the next several hours, people came and went, but I didn't want to talk to anyone. Instead, I retreated to my bed and lay there, sick with shock and grief. That's where my eldest brother, Rod, found me when he showed up.

"Teddy," Rod said, "I have something for you."

He was holding out Dad's wristwatch.

"I think he would have wanted you to have this."

As I took it from him, my eyes filled with tears. It was just a watch, but when I fastened it around my wrist, I felt comforted, somehow closer to my father now I had something of his touching my skin. I didn't say anything, but I was immensely grateful to Rod for the gesture. He was the oldest. He could have kept the watch for himself.

Rod had always been a special brother to me, and while many of my oldest siblings had often acted like surrogate parents, a number of them were now struggling and couldn't be there for their younger brothers and sisters. Joe was one of those. He had started down a dark road, drinking and developing a hard edge with some of us. A few hours after Rod had given me my father's watch, Joe showed up in my room. He wasn't there to comfort me the way Rod had.

"Where's Dad's watch?" he said. "Let me see it."

I held out my arm to show him. Joe grabbed my hand and slipped the watch off my wrist.

"Rod shouldn't have given you this," he said. "It should have gone to me."

Then he turned and left the room. My heart broke, watching my small inheritance disappear. I would never see the watch again.

My father's casket lay in our tiny house for three or four days, a period of time that felt like years to me, as people came by to pay their respects. We held ceremonies outside and lit sacred fires to guide him to the next life. But to my young self, this sort of spiritual goodbye just wasn't enough. I felt as if my father had been snatched from me. I didn't realize it at the time, but this would become a pattern in my life—family members leaving this world quickly, often without warning, often when I was far away or so immersed in my own challenges that properly mourning and marking the loss was impossible. And yet those losses were always there, like deep, untended wounds. My dad's death would haunt me for years.

The next months were hard. I went to school; I played hockey with the Elks and softball with the reserve team. When summer came, my brother Tom, who was working at the band office, got me a job leading summer activities for kids. Rick, who'd always been a second father to me and the younger kids, teaching us to play hockey and baseball and watching over us, stepped in to help the family. I tried to help at home as much as I could too, but the whole time I missed my father more than I can put into words.

Near the end of the summer, Bill LeClair came to speak to me.

Earlier in the year, he'd tried to talk to me a little about my future. "Ted," he'd said, "you could play this game if you worked at it. Quit partying and hanging out with your friends all the time. Exercise. Work on your skills." He was encouraging me to take the long view. "Give yourself five years. You never know."

Bill's assumption that I was partying a lot was probably based on what he had seen in my home and around the reserve when he came to pick me up for hockey games. I'm sure he suspected that growing up a world where adults were still at the bottle-filled kitchen table when the sun came up might lead a young person to start drinking early. And he wasn't wrong.

Like all my friends, I'd started going to parties on the reserve before I even entered my teens. But by the time I was fifteen or sixteen, I'd realized I actually liked the company of the guys in their twenties and thirties better than that of my teenaged pals. I preferred their stories and their serious thoughts about life, history and politics to the goofy fooling around of the girl-obsessed younger guys. Listening to the men, I felt I was coming to understand more of the outside world, and in particular how hard it was to prove you belonged there. You had to be cleaner, neater and better dressed than the white guys, my older friends told me. You had to work harder. You had to keep your thoughts and feelings to yourself. And on the practical front, you needed to have a car to get to work on time or you'd be accused of being lazy. The trick was to avoid that accusation long enough to save money for the car to begin with. And despite your best efforts, the chances of getting fired or not getting hired in the first place were huge.

No matter who I was hanging out with, however, or what we were talking about, the nights out always featured plenty of beer. And while the older guys seemed more measured with their drinking, I soon saw that this posed its own danger.

At one party, one of the older guys took me aside to give me some advice.

"The way to drink," he explained, "is to go at it slow and steady. Always pace yourself, Teddy. That way, you can get drunk and stay drunk without losing control."

My reaction was immediate. *To hell with that*, I thought. *Advice on how to become a better drunk?* I was never, ever going to destroy my life like that. Being able to stay drunk was not a lesson I was interested in learning.

So perhaps Bill's words were especially meaningful to me. I had certainly remembered them, even if I didn't follow them right away.

But this time, when Bill came to speak to me, he wanted to talk about something more immediate. The local Junior A team, the Soo Greyhounds, would be holding tryouts in a couple of weeks, he said. He knew Jim McAuley, who was part of the management team, and Bill had asked him if I could attend as a walk-on. Jim had said yes.

I had no idea how big a favour it was that Bill had requested. I didn't realize that the other guys who would be attending were coming from across the province and had been hand-picked and formally invited by the team management.

It's hard to capture how unaware I was of the hockey world outside of the purely recreational leagues. For one thing, while I loved playing the game, the NHL had never loomed large in my life the way it did for so many hockey-loving kids. Of course, I knew about the big teams—most of my family members were devoted to the Canadiens, and I loved the Indian-head jersey of the Black Hawks, so I called myself a Chicago fan. That said, we didn't listen to *Hockey Night in Canada* on the radio—the airwaves were strictly for music for me and most of my family. When we finally got a TV, my dad tuned in to *Hockey Night in Canada*, but not religiously. Steve, Joe and I would watch with him, but I was just as likely to be outside on our rink if the ice was good. As the years rolled by, I became aware of the stars of the day and the greats of the past. I grew to admire the Broad Street Bullies—the Philadelphia Flyers. Not because they were fighters, but because they'd won two Stanley Cups even though people thought they weren't the most talented team. And while hockey, as far as I was concerned, was about playing, not watching, I never really connected what I was doing on the ice with the pros. When we were little, Steve and I might have pretended to be NHLers on our backyard rink, but to us that was a bit like pretending to be a superhero—it wasn't something a real person, or at least a First Nations one, could actually do. And that didn't change as we got older.

Even in my teens, I was still only playing recreational hockey, so I wasn't hearing my teammates or their parents talk about how a young player might move from, say, triple-A to junior to a professional contract. In other words, when Bill LeClair told me I had a future, I really had no idea what he was talking about.

Looking back, I'm amazed Bill went to bat for me the way he did—that he saw something in me worth promoting. After all, among the long list of things I was clueless about were the finer points of hockey. I'd never attended a hockey school or clinic or been given a minute of personalized training. I learned by watching other kids on the rinks and trying to imitate their moves as best I could. But I missed a lot of the subtleties. Since I learned to skate on blades duller than butter knives, I'd had to propel myself around with pure power, moving my feet in more or less a straight line, like a cross-country skier. I'd never figured out crossovers, so I used my weight and momentum to make wide, gliding turns—and in one direction only. I didn't know to bend my knees as I skated, and I couldn't stop quickly—instead, I dug in the toe of my blades as hard as I could or bounced off the boards to slow myself. I didn't have a bad shot, but most of my game relied on an unpolished combination of effort and strength.

When I came home and told my family about attending the Greyhounds tryout, my brother Terry must have been aware of the uphill battle I faced. He also knew I had never really played contact hockey. So he thought he could give me a little edge.

By this time, Terry was coming to the end of what had been a promising boxing career. He'd left home when he was only fifteen or sixteen and landed in Toronto, where he discovered the sport. At the age of seventeen, known as "Kid," he made it all the way to the Golden Gloves middleweight finals in Buffalo, New York, winning six straight fights by knockout to get there. But over the years, Terry let his love of a good time affect his performance, and he had never been able to recapture that early glory.

In the early days, whenever he was home, he spent time showing us younger boys what he knew. We learned how to position our bodies and shift our weight when we punched, using both fists for an added advantage. So we could protect ourselves on the schoolyard or any-place we might need to.

Now, however, he was stressing another benefit of a good fight.

"You got to get their attention, Teddy," he said. "Show them. Make sure they know you are there."

It turned out to be quite the miscalculation.

I didn't take his advice during practice, but in an exhibition game I played with the Greyhounds that week, the other team's goalie raced out of the net to meet the puck just as I was going in. Unaware that hitting a goaltender was a big taboo, I figured running right through him would be a great way to get noticed. I was right, but not in the way I imagined. Before I knew it, five players were pummelling the daylights out of me.

"Well, they knew I played that one," I said to Terry after the game.

At the end of the week, the successful candidates were announced. Not surprisingly, I wasn't one of them.

But a few days later, I heard from Bill LeClair. The coach and general manager from a Tier 2 Junior A team in Kenora had been watching the tryouts, and he'd noticed me. He thought he could use me on their team and was holding a spot for me at their training camp. If I did well there, I might have a home with the Manitoba Junior Hockey League and the Kenora Thistles.

The idea of moving away to play hockey came as a shock. I'd tried out for the Greyhounds because Bill had made the effort to get me that opportunity. Playing this level of hockey had never been on my mind. I was thinking I would finish high school and then maybe apply to be an officer with the OPP (Ontario Provincial Police). I liked the idea of being a familiar and friendly face on the force for First Nations people. I thought I might be able to help my community that way. If I had made the Greyhounds, it might have delayed the plan a bit, but I could still live at home and have a little fun playing the game at a more challenging level. But moving away, *for any reason*? That was something that had never crossed my mind.

Yet, I could tell Bill thought this was a great opportunity. And so did all my family and friends. Once the surprise wore off, I too began to get excited. It was thrilling to think people wanted me to come from so far away just to play hockey with them—like I'd been given an invitation to some amazing party. From my older friends and all those folks around the kitchen table, I'd learned how seldom my people got invited to show what we could do in the white world. I'd never had the thirst to pursue hockey in a serious way, but now that I was being given this chance, I knew—with a doubt—I had to take it.

3

KENORA

KENORA SURPRISED ME. The city, traditional territory of the Anishinaabe and Métis of Treaty 3, sits on the edge of a beautiful lake, surrounded by many other lakes and the deep green boreal forest. It's small, much smaller than Sault Ste. Marie (about eleven thousand people in the mid-seventies), yet on its streets I saw a huge number of First Nations men and women—more than I had ever seen in the Soo or any other town. It was both a shock and a big comfort. *This is going to be great*, I thought, as I walked into the Kenricia Hotel. *My people are here*. Kenora, it seemed, was a place that might be a home away from home.

Strangely, there were men in my life who had probably visited Kenora just the year before I arrived and could have told me how wrong I was about that. But I hadn't talked with them in a while, so I had no warning whatsoever about what was really in store for me.

♦

When I was about thirteen, my family and I went to Terry's wedding in Toronto. At the church, I noticed a striking man in a suit with a long black braid hanging down his back. He looked strong and majestic, like a young Sitting Bull. My hair had always been too curly for braids, but I would have liked to show pride in my heritage with a look like that. At the reception later that evening, I noticed the man again. He was sitting and talking with some of Terry's other new friends. Perhaps the fellow saw me staring at him, because some time later, as I was doing a traditional group dance on the dance floor, I felt a hand on my shoulder. The man was inviting me to join him and his friends at their table.

Apparently, Terry had become involved with the American Indian Movement (AIM), an organization formed a few years previously to address issues such as First Nations' struggles with unemployment, poverty, treaty rights and treatment by police and other settler authorities. They were also fighting to protect First Nations culture. Alex Akewense, the man with the braid, and some of the others at the table were members of the organization. I had been looking forward to spending the entire evening on the dance floor, but once Alex and his friends began to talk, I was glued to my chair.

The bond my family and I made with Terry's new friends at that wedding would last for years. Alex and other activists stopped by Garden River whenever they were in the area. We'd always share our meals and invite them to pitch their tents on our property. I loved their visits and the hours we spent talking about what they and other

First Nations activists were working for. Their ideas resonated with what I'd already been told, and built upon the growing pride I felt for my First Nations heritage. (At thirteen or fourteen, I'd gone to see the movie *Billy Jack* and had been thrilled to see, for the very first time, a story about one of our own, with Indigenous actors, on the screen.)

My mother had always warned us not to trust the joganosh, the white people. And I'd heard plenty on the Pow Wow trail to support her advice. From the accounts of broken treaties, the Indian Act's restrictions on First Nations freedoms and autonomy, and of course, the terrible residential school experiences, I'd come to understand that I shared a shattered past with the rest of my First Nations community. Alex and his friends gave me an even wider context, educating me not only about injustices across North America—historical and current—but also about First Nations' attempts to protest those injustices. My brothers had shown me how to defend myself in the schoolyard, but listening to Alex and others made me realize that another way to protect ourselves was to prevent attacks by gaining acceptance. They made it clear, however, that the world wasn't likely to accept any of us for who we were unless we fought for that acceptance. I wasn't much of a student, nor a big reader, but this wasn't the history they taught in our public schools. The stories Alex and his friends told were *our* history, and I couldn't get enough of it. From them, I learned about a number of the AIM founders, including Russell Means and Dennis Banks, whose works and words made a huge impression on me.

They also talked a lot about the civil rights work being done in the States. I knew of Martin Luther King Jr., but now I also heard about Malcolm X. What I particularly liked about MLK and Malcolm X was their resolve. Just like my other heroes, Sitting Bull, Tecumseh and Big Bear, they were hated and persecuted, but they never backed down, changed who they were or wavered from their principles. And they were men of action.

I was endlessly intrigued by the Black Power movement. It struck me then that the Black and Indigenous populations of North America had so much in common. Just like so many First Nations activists, these Black civil rights leaders were responding to white settler populations that were always telling us how to live and what we needed rather than asking us what we wanted.

From Alex and his friends, I learned not only about ongoing civil rights work but also about First Nations' own acts of protest and civil disobedience, including the Alcatraz occupation, which began in 1969; the protest at Mount Rushmore in 1971; the cross-country Trail of Broken Treaties Caravan, with its occupation of the Bureau of Indian Affairs in Washington in 1972; and the Oglala Lakota and AIM forces' occupation of the town of Wounded Knee, the site of the infamous nineteenth-century massacre in 1973.

But what I'd missed was an important action that had happened a little closer to home.

In early July 1974, Louis Cameron, the founding leader of a group called the Ojibway Warriors Society, met with a group of other First Nations people to talk about how to draw attention to the various crises facing the local Ojibway community in the Kenora area. A huge number of the people were dealing with extreme poverty and the long-term effects of Minamata disease, caused by a mining company's dumping of mercury in rivers near the Grassy Narrows and Whitedog First Nations reserves. Accidents, murder, suicide and neglect also contributed to the shockingly low life expectancy of the local Indigenous population. Ninety percent of the Kenora-area First Nations population had been labelled "unemployed." Cameron and his group wanted to draw attention to these horrifying realities and to his demands to abolish the Indian Act and close the Department of Indian Affairs, as it was then known. He and others suggested a non-violent occupation of Anicinabe Park in Kenora, land that had been stolen from the local First Nations community by the city fifteen years earlier. They invited Indigenous folks from across Canada and the United States, as well as several First Nations organizations, including AIM, to join them. In the end, about eighty people, some armed, set up camp in the park and stayed for thirty-nine days. The protesters left after negotiations with the federal government, which were facilitated with the help of Dennis Banks, who had come up from the States during a break in his trial for his role at the Wounded Knee protest.

While the occupation was largely peaceful, many in the white community were incensed that they couldn't use "their" park over the summer—and by the show of First Nations strength and solidarity. More than a few times during the protest, townsfolk beat up Indigenous people in the streets of Kenora.

Louis Cameron has said that the First Nations' fight was always with the governments of Ontario and Canada, never with the people of the city. He suggested that the governments pitted First Nations and the settler population against one another, hoping the white citizens would force an end to the occupation on their own. I can't say whether he was right about this, but I can say that by the time I arrived in town a little more than a year later, bitterness and resentment hung in the air like smoke. In no time, I was choking on it.

♦

I didn't travel to Kenora alone. Two other Sault Ste. Marie players were trying out for the team, and although I didn't really know them, I was grateful for the company on my first ever plane trip. At the

Kenora airport, we were met by the team's general manager, who gave us each a schedule for the training camp and then loaded us in his car to take us to the little downtown hotel where we'd be staying for the duration of the tryouts.

The next day, less than twenty-four hours after arriving, I was on the ice and feeling that my excitement about moving to Kenora and playing with the Thistles might have been misplaced. Within minutes, one of the other players, a huge guy, had skated up behind me and speared me in the leg.

"What are you doing here, ya stinkin' Indian?" he said.

I answered by spearing him back. Then we both dropped our gloves and let the punches fly.

The same sort of thing happened the next day. And the next. And the next. Racial slurs, followed by spearing, tripping and dirty hits. They just kept coming. I'd occasionally heard bigoted insults from opponents in the Soo rec leagues, but never from my own teammates and never accompanied by physical attacks.

Terry and the rest of my brothers had taught me how to defend myself and keep myself safe. They told us younger boys to always sit or stand with our backs to a wall, to watch what was going on around us, to get out of wherever we were if we had even the slightest feeling that it might be unsafe. But I'd never imagined these were lessons I'd have to follow during practices with my own teammates. It felt as if I was spending more time fighting than I was playing hockey.

Only one person in the team management addressed what was going on. One day, halfway through the training camp, the team trainer took me aside. He and I had already had a number of interactions. When I arrived at the club, I'd been given new skates. It was the first time I ever had skates that actually fit me. But then shortly after that, the trainer handed me a brand new hockey stick. I shook my head and hung on to the stick I'd brought with me. My father had always told me not to take anything you hadn't worked for, and I'd already broken that rule by accepting the skates. Besides, I'd always been able to make do, making sure I didn't shoot too hard or smash my sticks on the ice or boards, repairing any stick I had until it wouldn't stay together any longer and then fishing a replacement out of the garbage bins at the Soo arena.

A day later, the trainer tried again to give me a stick. When I waved it away, he frowned.

"Why don't you want it?"

"Just cuz I'm poor doesn't mean I take handouts," I told him.

"What are you talking about?" he said. "Every player on the team gets a new stick."

Maybe our exchange made him notice me, because now he was asking me where I learned to fight. I explained about Terry and my cousins, who were also boxers. The trainer told me he was a boxer too, but fighting on the ice wasn't the same as fighting in the ring.

"You've got to grab the other guy's sweater and hang on," he said. "It gives you more balance."

I put that piece of advice to use almost immediately. During the first exhibition game, guys on the other side came after me again and again, almost always with a few cutting words that made it clear why they were singling me out.

But knowing how to throw a punch on the ice didn't help me with the other attacks. Those came from the spectators.

As the game started, I began to hear calls from the stands.

"Go home, you stinking wahoo!"

"Back to the welfare line, ya drunk!"

And one I had never heard before.

"Ya f——ing prairie n——ger!"

The people shouting these things were grown men and women—many likely parents or grandparents. People from the community. I found it terrifying.

I wasn't the only magnet for this abuse. Another First Nations player was also trying out—a local fellow named Frazer Greene. After one of the exhibition games, he came up to me on the bus.

"I'm out of here."

"Why?" I said. "We're going to make the team."

"I don't care. It's just not worth it."

I couldn't really blame him. The racism in that place—I'd never experienced anything like it. It hit you right upside the head, and it hit you hard.

True to his word, Frazer was gone by the next practice. We hadn't really had time to get to know each other, but I was crushed by his departure. Now I was truly on my own.

I'd never felt so scared and alone. And the fact that I was staying by myself in a strange hotel didn't help. One night, when I came back to my room after a practice, an older woman dressed in fancy business clothes was unlocking the door to her room. She glanced over at me with an odd expression on her face. We exchanged a few words—the usual greetings between strangers—and then she surprised me.

"I'll come by and knock on your door a little later," she said.

My stomach clenched, and my heart began to pound as I disappeared into my room. Yet, confused and conflicted as I was, when she showed up a short time later, I opened the door and let her in. When she finally left, I spent a sleepless night, trying desperately to put out of my mind what had just happened. The next evening, when I returned to the hotel, I slipped into my room as quietly as possible. Still, there was a knock on my door a few minutes later. Shaking with fear, I crouched behind one of the chairs in the room, as if she could see through the shut door. I knew that what had happened could put me in big trouble, danger even, although I was only a teenager and she a grown woman.

◆

I was a seventeen-year-old First Nations kid. I knew about racism. But to this point, it had bruised my life—not battered it.

Back home, the white and First Nations populations kept to their own lanes—even in the schoolyard, we knew that mixing was taboo. And there were times I was made aware that white people thought we First Nations people were inferior. I'd wager that barber wouldn't have stuck a bowl on the head of a white kid. And I bet the white kids weren't given dog biscuits at school or followed around in convenience stores by the clerks like my siblings and I were when we went to buy chips on our afternoons in the Caswell parking lot. But those kinds of experiences, along with the occasional shoving match or name-calling at school or the hockey rink, were infrequent. I could go weeks or months without feeling the sting of bigotry.

But here, racism seemed to colour everything. The bars filled up on Thursday nights, most people's payday, I guess, and white folks drank until they staggered out at closing. But it was only the First Nations men and women who were "f——ing drunks." (I would discover this kind of double standard didn't exist only in Kenora. The following year, I took my mother, one of my cousins and his girlfriend to a Greyhounds team party in the Soo. As a white girl lurched and giggled on the dance floor, my mother said, "See that? When it's a white girl, everyone thinks it's cute. When it's us, they call us whores and tramps.")

In Kenora, it seemed that our very existence enraged people. Staying in our lane didn't help when some people's idea of a good time was to go to the "Indian side of town" to beat the crap out of us.

I had listened to Alex Akewense and the other AIM members with interest, but now I realized I had never fully grasped how important their work was and why it was so necessary to convert anger and outrage into action. And all of those times that my father, my mother and my older siblings told me to be proud of who I was and to be proud of our people, they had been telling me to prepare me for this moment. They had been trying to build up my defences for just this kind of assault on my dignity.

♦

After about a week, just like Frazer Greene, I'd had enough. I was tired and scared and demoralized. My enthusiasm for playing junior hockey had evaporated. I didn't want to quit like Frazer, but I wanted to be sent home.

The coach must have noticed. He came up to me at the end of one practice.

"I can see you aren't trying anymore, Ted," he said. "But I'm not going to send you home. I want you on this team."

He didn't ask why I'd lost my drive or comment in any way about what I was going through. But that little bit of encouragement was all I needed to start trying again. It was just enough to make me want to prove to him and to all the players that I deserved this shot.

I became more determined than ever to show everyone what I could do. Recently, I found an article that appeared in *The Sault Star* about five weeks after the coach had that talk with me. In it, he discussed the three Sault Ste. Marie players who had recently joined the Thistles. About me, he said, "Ted's been a real surprise. When he came to us, we had some reservations about his ability, but no more. He's improved constantly since arriving and has played real well lately. He scored two goals over the weekend." So my renewed effort, as well as the training regimen, must have produced results. Certainly, all the practices helped. In this level of hockey, we practised almost every day—intense workouts that focused both on skills and strategy. The practices I'd had in recreational hockey had been largely a version of shinny hockey or skating endurance. The only real drills I'd done in my life were the ones I did on my own in my backyard.

A few days after the coach pulled me aside, I found out I'd made the team. And I would be staying with the family of another player on the team, Rob Thomson.

Rob, a smart kid and great student, was pleasant, but we never seemed to click. The rest of the Thomsons—mom, dad, a daughter—were nice enough, but I was shy, and they didn't seem particularly interested in getting to know me. Probably because of our hockey schedule, I didn't eat meals with the family, and there didn't seem to be any house rules to follow or chores to do. Most often, after school or practice, I would retreat to my room—or to the shower. The best thing about the place, as far as I was concerned, was the indoor plumbing and abundant hot water. But all that quiet time made me ache for home and the companionship it provided. I longed for the hours-long chats I used to have with my sisters, all of us crowded around the kitchen table, drinking endless mugs of tea with powdered milk, talking about everything and nothing as the afternoons or evenings slipped by. Or the less chatty but just as companionable times I spent with my brothers, fishing, playing sports or hanging around a campfire.

♦

High school in Kenora, I soon discovered, wasn't going to be any more welcoming than my teammates had been. On the very first day, I was jumped from behind in the parking lot. After that, I was extra cautious whenever I was on the school grounds or in the corridors. But it didn't help. It seemed as if an attack was waiting for me around every corner. I had to fight to protect myself on the rink—I didn't want to do it here too. Besides, my brothers told me to leave a place if I began to feel unsafe. I most definitely felt unsafe at school. One day, not so many weeks after I started, I walked out of the school and never returned.

Looking back on it, I can't quite believe no one seemed to notice I'd quit. For one thing, the coach worked at the school. How it was that no one drew his attention to the absence of one of his newly arrived hockey players is beyond me. And I don't remember anyone from the management or my billet family noticing either. If they did, they certainly didn't talk to me about it.

I'm not sure if I could have lasted in Kenora if I hadn't escaped high school or if the mood hadn't shifted slightly at the rink. But fortunately it did. While the fans never let up shouting racial slurs, as the season got under way, the opposing players seemed to realize they would get as good as they gave if they took me on, so the targeted physical assaults eased up. My teammates were no longer trying to fight me on the ice, of course, but they were still pretty chilly. Until, that is, one of them needed my help.

Dan wasn't the biggest guy on the team, but he was a scrappy player, which is perhaps why, in an early-season game, one of the opposing players laid into him. When I looked over and saw what was happening, part of me was glad. Dan was one of the players who had let me know he didn't like me. And I sure didn't like him. But he was a teammate, and a teammate in trouble. I skated over and helped him end the fight. On the bus on the way back to Kenora, Dan approached me. He wanted to apologize for the way he'd treated me earlier. We sat together for the rest of the trip home.

After this, Dan became downright friendly, and the rest of the guys started including me more often in social events and locker room conversations. I worked hard at fitting in. When I first joined the team, I'd gone straight back to the hotel or to the Thomsons' immediately after coming off the ice. I couldn't bring myself to join the crowd of naked strangers in the shower room, so I cleaned up at home. But now that the guys were talking to me, they asked about that, and I realized I'd have to overcome my shyness if I wanted to be one of them. I started showering at the arena like everyone else. When the team was on the road or dining out, I ate what the other guys ate, even if I didn't like it. And I tried to restrain myself from responding to looks and comments when I was with my teammates. I wasn't always successful. It seemed like any time their local friends joined us, one of the friends would make a few nasty remarks to let me know he didn't want me around. At one party, one of the friends shouted out, "Hey, let's all go downtown tonight and beat up some Indians!"

I was stunned. No one else in the room said a thing, so I jumped up.

"Why wait?" I said, blood pounding in my ears. "You got one right here."

The fellow went silent, and the rest of the guys started talking again as if nothing had happened.

That incident made one thing pretty clear to me. My teammates had finally accepted me, as a contributing member of the team and as one of the guys, and they thought that their acceptance of me should be enough. Sure, I'd worked hard for that, yet I was also trying to show folks that First Nations people were good people, with the same strengths and weaknesses, joys and disappointments, as every-one else. But I could see that my teammates were willing to believe this only about me. They were treating me as one of them now but were ignoring the fact that I was still who I'd always been, just as they would ignore bigoted remarks about my people. I hadn't really convinced them to reject the stereotypes and the racism.

Since I found it so trying to let remarks about my people pass without response, I decided to join my teammates on evenings out only when it was players only. But of course, in a place like Kenora in the mid-seventies, that was no guarantee of safety for a First Nations kid.

One evening, a bunch of us snuck into the bar at a hotel overlooking the lake. After a while, I went outside by myself to have a cigarette. I'd walked over to a spot by the water and was leaning against the railing when I noticed a couple sitting in a pickup truck in the parking lot.

When I turned back to the water, I heard a car door open and someone shouting, "What are you looking at, you f——ing wahoo?"

The next thing I knew, the man's hands were slamming against my back, pushing my torso right over the railing. I grabbed on to the metal as tightly as I could, staring at the rock-filled water ten feet below me. The man continued to push and pull, trying to rip my hands off the railing and get my feet off the ground. I'm not sure if my teammates heard the commotion or just had decided to take a smoke break themselves, but the ordeal ended when a number of them appeared and pulled the guy off me just as I was about to go over.

I was overwhelmingly grateful to those teammates. I still am. Their reaction assured me that there were people out there who would do the right thing, that there was good in the world. But I can't honestly say I felt closer to any of them because they'd rescued me. I'd been labouring for their acceptance, yet I could still feel the distance between us. And the fear the attack ignited in me overshadowed everything. Next time, there might be no one to help, and I would just become another missing Indian kid, as far as most people were concerned. I never would be safe in this city. In the coming months, anytime I was on the "white side" of town or crossed paths with white guys on the street, I felt as if I had a sign around my neck. Even when I wasn't physically confronted, I was exhausted by the need to stay on my toes and by the effort it took to fit in.

Luckily, a number of folks from the local Ojibway community had been coming to our games. Sometimes, they would wait around after and introduce themselves to me. Since I wasn't going to school, I could accept their invitations to go fishing or hang out on the reserve or join them for a party. After a few months, most of my social life was with these fellows. It was a comfort to be able to spend a little time with people who accepted and understood me.

Still, my homesickness and the constant threat of racist attacks wore me down. I couldn't help thinking that all of this would be easier if my dad had been alive and I could hear one of his inspiring pep talks.

Since I couldn't talk to anyone (our Garden River house still didn't have a phone), I wrote letters to my mother, telling her how miserable I was. And I lay in bed at night, holding the medicine bundle she had given me before I left home, rubbing my fingers across the soft suede as tears rolled down my face. I wanted nothing more than to be with my family.

And then in early December, I had a great surprise. Leaving the arena after practice one evening, I noticed two familiar faces grinning at me—Steve and my older brother Tom were waiting for me in the lobby. They had decided they wanted to see me play, so on the spur of the moment they'd jumped in Tom's beat-up Vauxhall Viva Firenza and driven the twelve hundred kilometres to Kenora, straight through.

After a few hugs and much backslapping, they told me they had a problem. Despite the fact that Tom was an adult—twenty-nine, in fact—the clerk at the first motel they stopped at had refused to rent him a room. They went to another motel, with the same result. And then another. Having exhausted the motel possibilities in the little town, they were getting desperate. The only thing I could think of was to ask the coach if he could help. Luckily for us, the coach seemed to know everyone. He contacted a motel owner and got Tom and Steve a room. It was a blessing but also a blow. Standing at the front desk, Steve heard the coach on the other end of the phone, reassuring the clerk, "No, no, they're good Indians. They'll pay."

For my brothers, it was, perhaps, a good introduction to the challenges of being First Nations in Kenora.

Their education continued when they attended their first Thistles game. As soon as the Thistles skated on the ice, they heard the racist slurs that had greeted me at every game I played. It's not like they hadn't heard these words before, although, like me, they were new to "prairie n——ger," but the loudness and the relentlessness of the shouting shocked them. These were the kinds of things they'd heard quietly muttered from time to time by white kids in the Soo. They'd never witnessed this sort of open hostility from people of all ages.

When I met them after the game, they were both agitated.

"Why are you putting up with this shit?" Steve said.

"Yeah, to hell with this place," said Tom. "You don't need this. Come home with us."

I told them I was going to see out the year, so they dropped the subject and we headed back to their room to get some food and catch up.

We had a great weekend together. Tom and Steve stayed for a second game, and then they were ready to head back, but not before trying once again to convince me to leave with them.

In the years to come, Steve would always say he thought Tom had made a spontaneous decision to drive to Kenora to see me play. Yet now I wonder about that. Smart and generous, Tom was always the gentle soul of our family. When I think of his insistence that I wasn't safe in Kenora and his paternal look of worry and protectiveness, I think my mother must have shared the contents of my letters with him and he'd driven across half the country to bring me back to her.

Despite Steve and Tom's pleas, I refused to get in the car. "If I quit this, the next time I'm facing some difficult thing, I might quit again." Quitting might become a habit, I told them. I didn't want that. I didn't say it, but I also didn't want anyone on the team or in the city thinking, *There goes another lazy Indian.*

In the end, Steve and Tom left reluctantly without me. As I watched their car pull out of the motel parking lot and lifted my hand and waved, I thought about running after them, telling them I'd changed my mind. But my feet didn't move, and the car turned a corner and disappeared from sight.

I would later hear that their journey back turned into a bit of an adventure. The Firenza lived up to its reputation as an infamous lemon, its heater giving up just a short way into the drive. Steve and Tom travelled for more than twelve hours through the Ontario north with the temperature in the car well below freezing the whole way. Steve spent most of the journey scraping off the inside of the windshield as it frosted up.

Once they were gone, I thought again about my decision to stick it out in Kenora. My resistance to leaving was about more than my own future. Over the years, back in Garden River, I'd seen many people move away to search for opportunities and a better life. So often, they would be back after a few months or years, looking and sounding defeated. Sometimes, I heard bits and pieces about their experiences— around that kitchen table, at the parties I went to, at the baseball diamond or the ice rink. These folks felt unwanted. They felt that hurdles were thrown up in front of them everywhere they went. They felt that no matter what they did, they would never belong. My two uncles never talked much about their pasts, but I wondered if they had gone through the same sorts of things, and if it had driven them to despair and drink. Staying on in Kenora, refusing to quit even if I wasn't wanted, that was an act of defiance and a chance to show that we could succeed in the outside world, even if things were stacked against us. I'd come here looking to have some fun, but now, I realized, I would stay because I had something important to prove—to myself and others.

♦

The team had a break over Christmas, so the out-of-town players were able to go home for a short while. I managed to get a ride with a couple of teammates who lived in Wawa. One of my brothers was going to pick me up there. About halfway along the narrow two-lane highway that curves around Lake Superior, the car hit a patch of black ice, spun around and slammed into a rock cut. I ended up in a local hospital for a night with a torn up shoulder.

When I finally walked through the door of our house, my mother rushed to me and wrapped her arms around my back. It was all I could do not to burst into tears. And then the house began to fill with friends and family and the celebrations started.

It was a Christmas full of joy and sadness. The whole family chipped in to buy me a really warm winter coat. (Joe had given me his old leather jacket before I left for Kenora, but Tom and Steve must have seen how cold I was in that when they visited.) I avoided talking about Kenora. I didn't want my family concerned about me over the holidays—they had other things to worry about. A huge, heartbreaking absence shadowed every meal, gift exchange and kitchen table conversation. My father was gone. It was our first Christmas without him.

When it was finally time to leave, I put on a brave face. I pretended I was looking forward to going back, that I was eager to start playing with the Thistles again. But that was pure fiction. I was going back to finish something I had started.

♦

During my early months in Kenora, as I crawled under the covers each night, consumed with dread and homesickness, I found myself wishing away the time. In a sense, that wish came true. I remember hardly anything of the rest of my year in Kenora. Most of it is just a dark blur, with a few small breaks. I know I got a part-time job doing deliveries for a lumber company. I remember that a nice young woman asked me out: my first date with a white girl. She suggested that we meet in the theatre where we'd decided to see a movie. When she asked that we walk out separately as well, I decided there would be no second date. My time in Kenora had taught me why she was afraid to be seen with a First Nations boy, but I wasn't interested in the charade. I also recall sneaking out of the house after the Thomsons were asleep so I could watch the fights outside the bars on Thursday nights. I remember hanging out with my First Nations friends in hotel rooms they rented for the weekend, getting myself so drunk and so stoned that I didn't feel anything anymore. And I played with the same fellows in a First Nations hockey tournament at the end of the season.

As for Thistles hockey, I know I continued to improve, even as my love of the game was fading. But I don't remember a single game or anything much about the team's performance. I did, however, check the records recently. I scored 56 points in 51 games, the fourth highest on the team, and won rookie of the year. The team racked up 32 losses, 16 wins, and 4 ties. We didn't make the playoffs. I was probably relieved, and excited to be going home sooner rather than later.

Finally, finally, my time in Kenora came to a close. As I packed my few belongings for the long bus ride home, I was happy to be putting a truly awful time behind me. As I'd find out in the years to come, however, it wasn't going to be that easy.

4

—

THE GREYHOUNDS

A SIGN STRETCHES ACROSS THE GARDEN RIVER as it courses through our reserve. It's spray-painted on an iron railroad bridge, and it reads THIS IS INDIAN LAND.

That proud, defiant graffiti was executed by my brother Rick and his friends. One evening, around the time I was in Kenora, they walked out on the bridge, secured themselves to the edge by their belts and leaned over, spray paint in hand. Apparently, a few days later, some railway or government employee scrubbed the words off the iron. Rick and his buddies returned and wrote their message again. The scrubbing and rewriting happened over and over, until the authorities gave up and left the words there for all to read.

Every time it fades, the sign has been refreshed, becoming an iconic symbol over the years. It's been made into postcards and T-shirts. And in every dressing room stall or office I've ever had, I've put up a small poster with that image.

I don't know what inspired Rick and his friends to paint the original sign. But I do know why it's been so important to me. My time in Kenora fine-tuned my pride in the beauty and strength of my heritage, the pride my parents had instilled in me. And my troubles in Northwestern Ontario reinforced what I had learned from Alex Akewense and others: it was okay to be angry and outraged by injustice and to speak the truth without being afraid to ruffle feathers or upset those who benefited from those injustices. "This is Indian land" struck me then as both a necessary claim and a warning: don't try to take this from us too. Returning from Kenora, I knew in a way I never had before that Garden River was the place where I belonged and the place that belonged to me. Stepping through the door of my home in the spring of 1976, I wanted to stay there for the rest of my life.

But as it turned out, hockey was going to draw me away again.

◆

Shortly after I returned from Kenora, Bill LeClair reconnected with me. Ever generous and helpful, he used his contacts as the manager at a local cement company to get me a job with a construction business. I was grateful. The construction work paid good wages, giving me not only spending money but enough left over to help my family buy groceries and pay bills.

Bill also told me to get prepared for the Greyhounds tryouts that would be held in early September. It seemed they were interested in me.

My performance with the Thistles had caught some people's attention. While I was still in Kenora, I'd been approached by the Brandon Wheat Kings of the Western Canada Hockey League. Just a few days before that, however, I'd seen an article in the paper about a huge on-ice brawl the team had been involved in. I was having to fight more than I wanted to in Kenora, so the idea of moving to a league where slugging it out might be even more common didn't appeal to me at all. I had decided to stay put. Now that I was back home, I sure didn't want to return to the Thistles, but I have to admit that I might have, despite everything, if I'd been asked. What I really hoped for, though, was another chance to prove myself in junior, this time at home.

Bill told me I was going to get a formal invitation to the tryouts, but I wasn't a shoo-in. I should be conditioning all summer, he said. I didn't really know what that meant, but I figured that working construction and playing fastball with the Garden River men's team would do the trick.

At the end of the summer, our Garden River Braves travelled to the Canadian Native Fastball Championships in Saskatoon. We were scheduled to return the day before the Greyhounds training camp started. With the confidence of an eighteen-year-old kid, I wasn't worried about the tight schedule. But I didn't factor in the time change or the possibility of travel delays. As it turned out, it was four in the morning on the first day of tryouts by the time I crawled into bed at home. I slept for two hours, dug my equipment out of the shed and made it to the arena in time for the morning skate.

That first day on the ice was meant to be a test of endurance, pushing us to our limits. I reached mine in about five minutes. Fighting back the urge to puke, I was bent over, trying to pull myself together before I hauled my sorry ass off the ice, when I heard another player approach me from behind. As he skated past, he said, "Don't give up. We're almost done. Keep going." Then he skated away.

I never saw his face or figured out who he was, but if it wasn't for his pep talk and the distraction he provided, that would have been the end of training camp for me—and maybe the end of my hockey career. But two weeks later, I was standing in the coach's office being told I had made the team. I was also informed that I would have to cut my shoulder-length hair and move to the Soo. A billet was being arranged for me. I didn't want the haircut, but, happy to be on the team, I took myself to a barber straight away.

The second condition was a bit harder to accept. It hadn't occurred to me that I wouldn't be able to live at home if I played for the Greyhounds. I'd been looking forward to spending time with Janice, Steve and my mom. And our place was more comfortable than it had ever been. My mom had plumbing installed the year I was away, and we now had an indoor bathroom with a shower. An oil furnace with radiators against the walls had been added a few years before that.

The more I thought about it, however, the more I could see that getting back and forth to the Soo every day for hockey practices and games, as well as high school, would be both time-consuming and potentially problematic. I had a car now, but my 1958 Dodge Monaco might have not been up to the task. I'd bought it for all of $150. For that price, a working muffler wasn't included (there was a huge gaping hole in the one it had). My brothers helped me fashion a new one out of an old Libby's bean can and some clamps. It made for a slightly quieter ride, but it wasn't pretty. And I sure didn't have the cash for any expensive repairs and maintenance.

While I quickly came to terms with the requirements for joining the team, my oldest sister, Katie, wasn't so easily convinced. A few days after I made the team, she came by the house for a visit. When she saw my hair and heard about my living arrangements, she stormed out the door and into her car. *Oh, boy*, I thought. *Someone's in for it.*

Arlene and Katie, along with my mom, had always been loving presences in my life. Arlene was quiet, gentle and nurturing, just like Mom. Katie resembled Mom in her sheer energy. She was so constantly busy, we used to call her the Roadrunner, because of the way she tore down Highway 17, driving back and forth from Garden River to the Soo and points beyond on a string of errands. And just like my mom, and all my sisters, actually, she was a strong woman— and fiercely protective. As I expected, she'd driven straight to the Greyhounds office and torn a strip off of whoever was there.

In the end, nothing changed, but I understood her reaction and why she felt she needed to speak out. Forced hair cutting and relocation, two elements of residential school and reserve system horror stories, have painful associations for my people. But my hair was already cut, and I could see the sense of moving to town.

As it turned out, being billeted was not going to be the lonely, alienating affair of my Kenora year, largely because of my Greyhounds roommate, Don Roach. Don was also Ojibway, from the Couchiching First Nation, outside of Fort Frances, Ontario.

Our common culture and interests, however, did lead to one small catastrophe. Our first billet was a couple who put us up in the basement bedroom of their home. One morning, not long after Don and I moved in, we looked out the window of our room to see two fat partridges strutting slowly across the backyard. Without saying a word, we both moved to the closet and grabbed our pellet guns. Then we quietly went upstairs.

"You take the one on the right. I've got the one on the left," said Don.

When we fired, both birds dropped before us. As soon the guns went off, however, we heard screaming. Our landlady was in the dining room window, her camera in her hands. She was, apparently, an avid birder.

She said a lot of things, but the words I remember most clearly were the ones she uttered right after she told us to get out of her house immediately: "I wouldn't feed you two shit with sugar on it!"

I drove straight home to Garden River. "I've got good news and bad news," I told my mom. "The bad news is I got kicked out of the billet. The good news is I brought supper."

The team arranged another home for Don and me, and we refrained from any more backyard hunting.

◆

My first year with the Greyhounds was a good one. I was catching up on high school and catching up with my Garden River friends. When I first got back, I could tell some of them were a little suspicious that my time in the white world had changed me. I answered that by going to every party they went to and staying until the last person left. I also joined the reserve's bowling team and played in town at the Churchill Plaza Lanes. I spent many long afternoons at the pool hall with my Garden River buddies, and at the Indian Friendship Centre in the Soo, where I met folks from other First Nations communities in the area. That last activity was important to me, as I'd stopped going on the Pow Wow circuit with my mom when I hit my teens. Work and hockey took up too much time, and I couldn't afford the regalia needed to dance competitively. The Friendship Centre gave me back some of the broader connection to my First Nations community I'd had before.

I also discovered that hockey had brought a new mentor into my life. Jim McAuley, the team president who had allowed me to try out for the Greyhounds before my Kenora stint, came to my aid in a few surprising ways.

When I discovered I would need to wear a suit and tie to every game (once you hit Junior A, this pro hockey tradition usually kicks in), he explained that it was a pre-game "uniform" that turned your mind to hockey as soon as you put it on. Then he whisked me to a men's shop and bought me a suit.

No doubt realizing the straitened circumstances I'd been brought up in, he also gave me some financial advice. In the Ontario Hockey League (OHL), each player got a small monthly stipend so that he had a little spending money. Jim took me aside one day to talk about that.

"I have something for you," he said, handing me a copy of *The Wealthy Barber*, by David Chilton. "I'm not sure how much money you are going to make in your life, Ted, but saving even just a little of your pay every month can make a big difference."

Bill LeClair had talked about my future, and now Jim McAuley was doing it too. I was moved by that.

In this new, supportive hockey environment, it was easy to start really concentrating on my skills. In the rec leagues, I'd never had to push myself. I was always one of the better players on those teams and never felt any incentive to improve. (The Elks might have been slightly more demanding than house league, but whenever we played the Soo team, we got our asses kicked.) In Kenora, I guess I upped my game, but as I've said, I don't really remember the effort. The Greyhounds, however, was a Tier 1 junior team, a higher level of hockey, and I had to work to keep up.

That first year I was with the Greyhounds, I couldn't have weighed more than 175 pounds. At six feet, I was a skinny guy, with no bulk or muscle tone to speak of. The young men I was meeting on the ice were big and strong. I listened to them talk about what they did outside of hockey to get that way, and I finally understood what Bill LeClair had been referring to when he talked about "conditioning."

When that first season was over, I decided to start my own regimen. I knew a fellow from the reserve who was a body builder, and I asked him if I could work out with the equipment at his place. He helped me learn to do weight training properly. Sometimes, I went to the boxing gym in town and worked out there as well. And then I ran. My favourite drill was to sprint the railway tracks that ran through the reserve. For two miles, I would hit every tie so that my strides were small but my steps were quick. Then I'd walk back along the rail itself to work on my balance. Other times, I'd run up and down hills. Usually, I'd carry a heavy axe while I ran so I could stop at a certain point and cut down a tree to strengthen my arms. I ran in the bush during the day and on the highway at night. I never ran on the highway when the sun was up, because invariably one of my friends would drive past and ask what the hell I was doing. I'd tell them I was trying to become a better hockey player, but I knew from the look on their faces, they thought that was a pointless goal. Where was that going to take me?

By the time my second year with the Greyhounds rolled around, I was bigger and stronger than I'd ever been. I felt pretty good about how I might perform at training camp. At least, I thought, I'd do better than the skinny little blond guy I spotted getting dressed on the first morning.

The kid, who I assumed was some local, maybe a walk-on, like I had been two years before, was about five foot eight and even lankier than I had been. He probably weighed only about 155 or 160 pounds. A real string bean of a guy. *Oh, boy*, I thought, *he's going to get killed.*

And then he stepped out on the ice.

In our very first exhibition game, Wayne Gretzky, a sixteen-year-old rookie, led our team to an 8–3 victory over the Sudbury Wolves.

He set up five goals, including one from me, and put one in the net himself. Craig Hartsburg, who would go on to have a ten-year career with the Minnesota North Stars, had been the points leader of our team the previous year with 93 points, but Wayne would end the 1977–78 season with nearly double that number.

Of course, by that first exhibition game, the buzz about the team's number one draft choice had finally reached my ears. In fact, when time came for all the rookie players to go through their unofficial initiation to the team, Wayne's outsize celebrity would prove a problem. In the late seventies, "streaking" (running naked through a public place) was a popular prank and publicity stunt. When I joined the team, the Greyhounds already had an established ritual of making the rookie players streak across the field at the local high school football tournament. (When I'd heard about this in my rookie year, I'd flat out refused. To their credit, no one on the team forced the issue.) But we could hardly expect a player whose every move was being reported in the sports media to participate in such a public display. So it was decided that a bunch of us would bring Wayne to a local park. He'd be dropped off on one edge of the park, and then we'd wait on the other side to be the sole witnesses to his naked run. When head coach Muzz MacPherson heard of our plan, however, he had a better idea.

Someone dropped Wayne off, and the rest of us waited on the far side of the park, just like we said we would. But so did a police cruiser and van. As soon as the cops spotted the shimmer of white skin emerging from the shadows, they blasted the cruiser siren and turned on their flashing lights. Then they hustled a shaken Wayne and us, his waiting teammates, into the back of the police van and drove off. In the van, Wayne scrambled to come up with a plausible explanation for why he would be naked in a park. The rest of us played along, suggesting ridiculous scenario after ridiculous scenario, until the van stopped and we were all hustled into the police station to be "booked." Seconds later, Muzz walked through the doors, and we all burst out laughing. Wayne, always a good sport, joined in immediately.

I certainly didn't need the sports reporters or the sold-out arenas to tell me Wayne Gretzky was a player to watch. I couldn't keep my eyes off him—the way he turned so quickly, the way he practised his shots from every possible angle. At one practice, he called out to me, "Watch this one, Chief," and then he moved in front of the goalie, setting himself up for a backhand shot. The goalie dropped down in anticipation, and in a blink of an eye Wayne flipped to a forehanded shot and put the puck in the net.

But Wayne showed me something far more important than shooting manoeuvres. My dad had always emphasized the importance of working hard and making do with what you had. Living in the circumstances we did, it was easy to link those two—we had to work hard because that was the best way to address scarcity. Yet here was a young guy with an abundance of talent, and he was working harder than any of us. When it came to practices, Wayne was on the ice first and was always the last off. Sometimes, Muzz would have to insist Wayne head to the dressing room. Wayne's extraordinary effort made me realize what makes truly great athletes, and that work, *hard* work, was the single most important element in performance.

◆

Muzz MacPherson wasn't a bad coach. He liked a rough-and-tumble approach to the game, and he seemed to respect my style of play and the fact that I could take care of myself on the ice when I had to. But I can't, in all honesty, say I learned much from him—either about my own playing or about the game itself. And the team didn't exactly flourish under his leadership. We didn't make it past round two of the playoffs in 1976–77, and by the time the second half of the 1977–78 season rolled around, the management evidently thought it was time for a change.

In February 1978, Muzz was fired and Paul Theriault brought in to finish the season. As a result, I played for Paul for only a few short months. Yet Theriault managed to give me a whole new kind of hockey education.

He seemed to think I was a better player than I'd been given credit for, so put me on a higher line. The added ice time and a few instructions (one was how to get the puck off the boards better) certainly helped me improve. But everyone benefited from his great knowledge of the game. He explained strategies, like the value of having one of the forwards fall back during an offensive play so that if the puck was sent back out, he could help the defencemen. And when he dove into these kinds of explanations, he always spoke with a calm clarity that all the guys could understand. His lessons were accompanied by plenty of encouragement. If he ever corrected us, it was never with bluster and threats. I was impressed by the way he worked at developing a good rapport with individuals while always keeping his focus squarely on the team.

MacPherson had sometimes hauled Wayne off the ice during practices if he thought he'd been on too long, but with Muzz as coach, Wayne was the show, on the ice for forty-five minutes of each game, doing most of the heavy lifting for the club. When Paul arrived, he started rebalancing the team. As a result, the rest of us started performing a little better. As a player, I appreciated the chance to play more, but I could also see the wisdom of Paul's decision. Wayne would likely be gone the next year, but many of the other players would continue with the Greyhounds. Paul wanted to build a team, not just a support system for a star. That was a lesson I wouldn't forget.

Even under the new coach, our team was again knocked out of the playoffs that year by round two. Despite that, I felt pretty good about my performance. I almost doubled my points over the previous season, earning 44 compared to 24 the year before. (Wayne racked up 182, but who was going to compare himself to a player like that?) I won the Sault Star Trophy, also called the Unsung Hero Award, for the second year in row—a nice acknowledgment that my efforts on the ice made a difference. And unlike during my time with the Thistles, I never once felt hostility from my own teammates, or on the city streets for that matter. Every once in a while, I heard racist remarks from opposing players or fans, but even in our travels across the province, that was infrequent. Yet there is no doubt that my experience in Kenora stuck with me, and a couple of incidents contributed to that lingering cloud.

In the first half of my second season with the Hounds, my nose was broken in an on-ice fight. To protect my healing face, I was supposed to wear a face shield, but I found it difficult to see through. A month later, I decided to abandon the shield partway through a game against a team from Niagara Falls. As soon as the Niagara goaltender noticed I was maskless, he took a swing at my face with his blocker, breaking my nose again. I returned his swing with a lunge of my own. In seconds, five players from the goalie's team were beating the daylights out of me. The linesmen pulled my attackers off. Not one of my teammates was in sight.

In the dressing room after the game, Jim McAuley gave the team hell for not coming to the aid of one of their own. Some of the guys looked sheepish, but no one approached me to apologize. It was unsettling.

And then there were the times I was left standing at the side of a road.

During my first year with the Greyhounds, I was seeing a girl from Kettle Point. She drove to London, Ontario, for one of our games. After the game, I went out into the lobby to say hi. I hadn't been there for more than a minute when I noticed the team bus pull away from the building. Another player, Brian Gualazzi, was also in the lobby— he had stopped to get himself something to eat. We both tore into the parking lot, waving our arms, yelling and screaming, but the bus continued to barrel out of the exit and down the road. Luckily, Brian's dad was a man of means. He got us bus tickets to Toronto and put us up at the Royal York for the night. Then he booked us flights back to the Soo the next day.

That wasn't my only experience of being left behind. Another time, the team was on its way to Sudbury when we stopped at a roadside diner for snacks. I was standing in line at the till with one other player, waiting to pay, when we heard the bus start up. Once again, the driver pulled onto the highway without a second look. The other guy and I paid for our food and then raced out to the road. My teammate stuck out his thumb in the direction of home. I went to the other side of the highway to hitch a ride to Sudbury. I actually ended up at the rink before the team did.

In each of these busing mishaps, another boy was with me—but why was I the common denominator? In the two years I played for the Hounds, there were no other incidents in which players were left behind. I found it hard to think that these two events involving me were pure coincidence. And frankly, I still do.

Despite my positive experiences playing with the Greyhounds, I couldn't shrug off the persistent suspicion that I was still a bit of an outsider, always seen by some as a little less.

♦

Improving as a player, hanging with my family and old friends, finishing my high school diploma—all good things about my two years with the Greyhounds. But the most important thing was something I didn't fully appreciate at the time.

In the late fall of my second year in the Soo, I was standing around outside the bowling alley in the Churchill Plaza with a few friends when I spotted a girl a little further along the walkway. She was with a bunch of white girls, but I thought she might be First Nations. And I thought she was beautiful. One of the guys noticed who I was looking at.

"I know her sister," he said. "I'll give you their phone number."

A week or two later, I gave her a call and we went out to a movie. We hit it off immediately. Her name was Sandra Howe.

It turned out I was half right about Sandra's heritage.

Her mother, Shirley, is Wolastoqey from St. Mary's First Nation, near Fredericton, New Brunswick. Her father, Morley, is white, from Saint John, New Brunswick. Together, they raised seven daughters and lived in town in what seemed to me a pretty luxurious house, although it was actually a very modest bungalow. Unlike my family's fridge, theirs was always full, but that didn't mean there was a lot of extra money to go around. In December, I asked Sandra to go to the Greyhounds' Christmas party with me, but she said she was babysitting. It was only later that I found out she'd lied. She turned me down because she didn't have a dress to wear or any money to get one.

I thought Sandra was wonderful and within weeks brought her out to meet my family. Despite having grown up in a quiet household, Sandra accepted my loud, talkative, chaotic family with warmth and good humour—and didn't seem unnerved by mother and sisters' slight coolness. They had wanted to see me with a Garden River girl, and it would take them a long time to trust this "city" woman. Yet Sandra embraced my family—and our dating relationship—with a patience I still marvel at.

Looking back, all I can say is, boy, was I a lousy boyfriend. More than once, I told Sandra I'd pick her up after her shift at the movie theatre and then completely forgot and went out with my friends instead. I might spend an evening with her talking about deeply personal things, like how many children I hoped I'd have one day, and then I wouldn't call her for days and days. When the hockey season was done, I joined my brothers and friends in ball tournaments in other cities, never telling Sandra when I'd be leaving or when I'd be back. When I did return, I might let her know right away—or not.

Part of this was teenage self-absorption. No doubt. But I'm sure another part of it was a kind of self-protection. As soon as I met Sandra, I recognized something in her that I was deeply drawn to. I could sense her kindness and compassion, and I felt instantly at ease with her. But I'd never met anyone who shared feelings so readily. My family, especially my sisters and I, loved to talk, but when we talked, we told stories. When it came to emotions, we were people of few words. Sandra talked about how she felt, and she wanted me to do the same. I wasn't interested in that kind of closeness. My father's death had made me realize how much it hurt to lose someone you loved. I wasn't keen to add another potential source of pain to my life. It was safer to be single, I thought. Yet I kept seeing Sandra. And remarkably, she kept seeing me.

◆

One afternoon in June, just as spring was changing into summer, Sandra and I were at the kitchen table, playing cribbage with Mom, when the local news came on the radio.

"Ted Nolan, Soo Greyhounds left winger and resident of Garden River, has been selected in the fifth round of the NHL draft by the Detroit Red Wings."

I nearly dropped my cards on the floor. I had no idea I was being considered by the NHL.

I know it will seem incredible to many people when I say I really had no clue there even was such a thing as a professional draft. How someone became an NHL player, or even that anyone other than a big star was paid a salary to play hockey—that such a thing as a minor league pro career existed—was nowhere on my radar. I suppose Bill LeClair and Jim McAuley had never sat me down and walked me through the process because they assumed I already understood it. But they obviously didn't fully get how isolated the world I lived in was. Of course, I had played junior in Kenora and for two years with the Greyhounds. Sure, I'd gone to a few parties with teammates in Kenora, and I'd done some bar-hopping with my Greyhounds team-mates, but we hadn't hung around talking about our hopes and dreams. We hadn't sat together and dissected our chances of making the pros or speculated on what lay before us. Well, I'm sure some of the team did this—but not with me. I spent most of my time with my family and friends on the reserve. No one in my circle knew anything about pro hockey. And certainly there wasn't a single hockey parent in Garden River who was carefully grooming their kid for a shot at the NHL. To us, that would have been unimaginable.

Recently, someone showed me an article in which my brother Steve reminisced about him pretending to be a Canadien and me a Black Hawk. And he mentioned that I told my sister Arlene that when I grew up I would buy her a house. The article makes it sound as if these two things were related in my mind, but they weren't. When I made that promise, my sister was going through a rough patch in her marriage. I heard the talk, and I saw the pain in her kind face, and I desperately wanted to help her the way she'd always helped me. And so I told her I would buy her a big house that would keep her safe and warm. But that, just like the idea of playing in the NHL, was a little kid fantasy. It wasn't me thinking about a career trajectory.

What made the idea of playing pro an even greater shock was that while I'd always dreamed of travelling and seeing the world, I had never considered living anyplace other than Garden River. In fact, when I was about sixteen or seventeen, my mother had asked me where I wanted to settle when I grew up. I thought she meant where I wanted to live on the reserve. On Indian reserves you can't really "own" land the way you can elsewhere, but you can claim lots to live on, farm or use in some way. I gather that when my parents were young, this was a fairly informal process. And my great-uncle Jack had, over the years, acquired the rights to a sizable number of plots of Garden River land. By the time I was a young man, however, the band office issued "certificates of possession" for these parcels. Jack had the habit, especially after a few drinks had fuelled his generosity, of offering to transfer some of these certificates to friends and relatives. I knew this, so when my mother asked, I said I wanted to live down by the river, by Uncle Jack. When I got back from Kenora, my mom suggested we pay Jack a visit. When we got there, she told him I wanted a piece of land close to the river. Jack was happy to oblige—but he wanted one hundred dollars. My mother was annoyed, as she knew he'd given away many other lots for nothing, but I had that job in construction at the time and had managed to save a little money. I was happy to hand over the hundred dollars for my future home. (It was indeed the best hundred dollars I've ever spent.) I was still thinking about applying to be a police officer. When I started earning a good salary, I would build my house.

When I heard on the radio that I was a draft pick for Detroit, I was surprised to realize there might be a few fun diversions in store for me before I settled for good in Garden River.

I was about to say something to my mother about that, but I stopped, looked over at Sandra, and shook my head. My mother had clearly not understood what the radio announcer was saying. She knew nothing about sports at any level. And the last few years had been so tough on her. It didn't seem right to make a fuss about my success or talk with excitement in my voice about going away. So we finished our cribbage game and I excused myself from the table. Sandra and I went outside, got in my car and drove a few kilometres to a dirt road that led deeper into the forest on the reserve. I pulled my car into the trees, got out and climbed onto the hood. I stood there, with my arms raised above my head, and hooted and hollered with joy until my lungs were sore. Then I got back in the car and went home to calmly share the news.

5

THE MINORS

WHILE I WAS JUMPING FOR JOY ON THE HOOD OF MY CAR, I had forgotten one key thing: playing pro meant moving from home. Before the night was out, I was beginning to feel uneasy about that.

I had mixed feelings about the Motor City. My earliest associations with the place were happy. When my parents didn't have the radio tuned to a country music station, I always turned the dial to a station in Detroit known for their great Motown playlists. And when I was really young, my sister Rita had moved to Detroit with her husband. My family and I visited them and their kids often, sometimes stopping in Flint, Michigan, to see my sister Barb, who was living there. From the time I was about eight until I was about twelve, Steve and I spent several weeks a summer with Rita and her family. Unfortunately, by then my cousins had become a really wild bunch, often dragging me along with them on their nights out. Sometimes, I would wake up in strange houses, not exactly sure how I'd got there. Far worse was the time they brought me to a party where a woman was "entertaining" one fellow after another in one of the bedrooms. I was not even in my teens yet, but my cousins and their friends threw me through the open door, telling the woman to make a man out of me. To this day, I don't remember what happened in that room or how I got out, but for years, anytime I was reminded of that evening, I felt ashamed and sick to my stomach.

Detroit, therefore, held both good and bad memories for me.

There was a lot to like about the Red Wings franchise, however. I was an admirer of general manager Ted Lindsay. To be honest, since I didn't follow the NHL that closely, I wasn't very knowledgeable about current players or coaches—I only knew who the stars were. I was aware of some of the greats of the past as well. Ted Lindsay was one of those, a small scrappy player with a huge passion for the game. I also knew he had been a trailblazer organizer of the first players' union. I liked the idea of being part of his team.

About a week after I heard that radio announcement, a letter from the Red Wings organization arrived. It detailed the fitness expectations for those showing up at their training camp, being held in Kalamazoo, Michigan, in September. You had to be able to run so far in so many minutes, lift so much weight and so on. I returned to the boxing gym and began to run the rails again. I also began to talk with Sandra more seriously about the future. I didn't propose to her, but I made it clear that I saw us together—wherever I might end up.

Shortly before I was set to leave for training camp, Rod and I were at the kitchen table, chatting about what lay ahead for me.

"You know," he said, "Dad always thought you were a good player. Thought you had what it took to make the pros."

With Rod's words, a mix of emotions came at me. I felt an immediate pang of longing for my father's presence. Pleasure that he'd thought I was talented. Pride that I had lived up to his prediction. Sorrow that he wasn't there to witness it. And, finally, wonder that he, such an avid sportsman, felt this about one of his own sons but had never once put pressure on me or voiced any sort of expectation about my future. "Did you have fun?" It was all he ever said to me about hockey.

♦

As the summer days disappeared, I cycled between excitement and uncertainty. The shadow of Kenora hung over me, and as I lay in bed at night, I sometimes found myself nervous about leaving home again. But when it was time to board the bus for Kalamazoo, I got on.

At training camp, I soon discovered that my homegrown fitness regimen had not been quite up to the task. The testing was more clinical than anything I'd imagined. We were hooked up to a VO_2 max machine to measure our oxygen consumption and then told to pedal a stationary bike as hard as we could. Once the oxygen mask was clamped to my face, I became claustrophobic and leaped off the bike before the test was even finished. Then, lying on a weight bench during the strength tests, I lowered a two-hundred-pound barbell onto my chest and discovered I couldn't lift it back off. Instead, I had to roll it down my body to escape— to a chorus of laughter from the other players in the room.

"Dumbbells don't hit back—I do," I muttered, when I finally got off the bench.

It was no better on the ice. Flying around me were some of the best athletes in the world, players like Rogie Vachon and Pete Mahovlich. I was still struggling to do crossovers smoothly—like some little kid playing with grown men.

After two days, every bit of confidence I'd been able to muster had gone. Without a word to anyone, I packed up my equipment and caught a bus home.

♦

Whenever I walked through the door of our house when my mother was there, she would rush over and give me a hug. This time, however, she stood where she was and gave me a look of concern. She stared for probably only a few seconds, but despite the love and caring I saw in her eyes, those seconds were long, long hours to me.

Finally, she spoke. "What are you doing back?" When I didn't answer, she said, "Ted, someone called and left his number. You should call him back." And then she came and enveloped me in her arms.

I gave myself a few hours to get my nerve up, and then I rang Ted Lindsay. (We now had that party-line phone in the house.) I hadn't connected with him at camp, or even seen him, so this was our very first exchange.

"Hey, Ted," he said, "why'd you leave?"

I am struck now by the memory of his warm and open voice. If he had asked in a way that expressed disappointment or anger, I never would have answered honestly. But his tone set me at ease. I explained how overwhelmed I'd been by the calibre of play at training camp.

"The other guys are too strong, too fast," I said. "They're too good. I can't keep up."

Lindsay didn't try to talk me out of those feelings, but he was reassuring.

"We're going to teach you all that," he said. "We'll show you how to become stronger and faster."

He began to ask me questions about myself. Where did I live? What had I been doing all summer? Next, he patiently explained to me how the farm system worked and what I could expect in the coming year. He laid out what it might take to be called up to the NHL. He told me that he'd like me to spend some time with the Kalamazoo Wings in the International Hockey League. I'd heard a bit about this league during my short time at training camp. It was reportedly long on fighting and short on hockey playing. It wasn't where the best minor professionals went.

"I'm not interested in fighting," I told Lindsay. "I think I'd rather stay home and become a police officer."

Lindsay was quiet for a minute. Then he came back. "How about our Kansas City franchise? The Central Hockey League?"

I was encouraged by his flexibility, reassured by his honesty and caring. By the end of the call, I had agreed to fly down to Kansas City and join the Red Wings operation. It wasn't until years later that I would realize how truly rare that kind of outreach was in the pros, never mind coming from a hockey legend to a fifth-round draft pick.

◆

Lindsay had convinced me to give Kansas City a try, but I knew I couldn't do it without Sandra. I drove into town and brought her back to Garden River. Then, sitting at our kitchen table, I asked her to come with me. She said she would.

In January, Sandra had finished high school, but she wouldn't turn eighteen until mid-November. Her parents were understandably dead set against her following an inattentive boyfriend fifteen hundred kilometres into another country. But Sandra, quiet and soft-spoken, showed her determination by packing her bags anyway.

I went ahead by myself. I wasn't too sure Ted wouldn't change his mind and insist I play in Kalamazoo instead. I told Sandra to wait until I was certain I would be staying in Kansas City. After about a week or two, my spot seemed safe enough, and I called Sandra and asked her to book a ticket down.

To this day, I'm overwhelmingly grateful that Sandra came with me. I just wouldn't have made it without her. I had no idea how to live on my own. Barely eighteen, Sandra was the one who opened a bank account for me, found us an apartment, rented furniture and housewares. Sandra was the one who helped me buy a used Ford Mustang (the Monaco couldn't make the trip down). Sandra was the one who drove me to every game and practice—even navigating around the sizable city was beyond me. And it was Sandra who shored me up each time my confidence began to slump.

Once I started playing with the Kansas City team, I could see that Ted was right: playing in the minors was a good opportunity for me to grow, both on the personal front and with my game. For one thing, there were significant differences on the ice. The rink surfaces were no larger than those I'd played on in junior (and most teams didn't come close to drawing the crowds the way young Gretzky had for our junior games), but the players themselves were a whole lot bigger. Most of the guys were mature adults, not boys like me, with huge chests, deep voices and even beards. Their sheer size intimated me. But their dedication made an even bigger impression. The effort and focus they brought to their games showed me that you didn't just walk into the NHL—you had to earn your way. That said, the calibre of play, while certainly better than what we'd faced in junior, was not so much better that I felt beyond my depth or was relegated to the bench for any period of time. So in the end, I held my own, and by the end of the season felt confident that I had earned my keep.

But it was not an easy year. Far from home, uncertain of my place in this new world, I staved off homesickness and nerves by throwing myself into the team camaraderie, accepting every social invitation that came my way. There were a lot of late nights out, drinking and partying. Yet, these were not the relaxed times I liked to spend with my brothers and old friends. They were long hours of distraction, and rarely ones spent with Sandra. She had made friends with the wives and girlfriends of a few of the players, but she was not a party girl, preferring quiet nights in our poky apartment to raucous evenings in a crowded bar.

◆

The Kansas City Red Wings lost in the first round of the playoffs, ending my first pro season in early April. Sandra and I returned home so we could both find summer jobs.

This was my pattern during my early pro career: hockey all fall and winter and then various jobs in the summer to pay our bills. I worked as a night security guard at Ojibway Park and helped construct homes in Garden River. One summer, when I was a delivery helper for Coca-Cola, I showed up at a customer's wearing a shirt with "Property of Detroit Red Wings" on it. The fellow receiving the order gestured to the lettering on my chest.

"Too bad that's not true, eh?" he said.

"Yup," I replied.

As training camp approached that year, I realized I no longer thought of playing pro as a great adventure. In fact, I wasn't entirely sure I wanted to return, yet I couldn't throw away the opportunity. No matter what happened there, at least I wouldn't be returning to Kansas City. The Red Wings franchise had decided that it wasn't the best location for a minor league club. Kansas City was more than twelve hundred kilometres away from Detroit, but more importantly, it wasn't much of a hockey town, and filling the stands had been a struggle. The club had decided to move the team to the American Hockey League (AHL) and give it a home in Glens Falls, New York, a few hundred kilometres closer to Detroit (and to Canada). They renamed the club the Adirondack Red Wings.

This time, I got through the entire training camp, and once it was over, Sandra and I made our way to Glens Falls. I happily settled back into team life, which was a sea of familiar faces, with some great new players added to the mix. Greg Joly, who'd been a number one draft pick for both the NHL and the WHA, joined us, as well as Bill Hogaboam, who had nine years of playing on various NHL teams. There was Jody Gage, who'd just played a year with the Kalamazoo Wings, George Lyle, who had played three years in the WHA, and Rick Shinske, who'd moved from the St. Louis Blues franchise. Many of these new teammates became good friends as the year unfolded.

But one thing became pretty obvious once we'd moved. I was the most poorly paid player on the team. When I originally signed my contract with the Red Wings, I'd accepted what they offered: a $17,000 salary with a $6,000 signing bonus. I was thrilled to be getting paid to play, and given that it was about the same as I could have made as an OPP officer back home, it never occurred to me to ask for more. One evening, however, when I was out with my teammates in Kansas City, someone had asked what I was getting. In short order, I learned that most players were getting paid multiples of my salary. I suppose my naïveté contributed to the lowball offer, but even if I'd been a bit more savvy, I was a relatively low draft pick, so my negotiating position hadn't exactly been strong. My "cheapness" probably made me an attractive addition to a minor league team that had limited resources and plenty of higher-paid players they had to work into their budget (and I didn't need a green card because of my First Nations status). My second-year contract bumped me up to about $20,000 and whatever was the minimum salary for the NHL if I was sent to Detroit, but that still put me at the bottom of the pay scale.

When we first got to Glens Falls, we were put up at a hotel by the team. During that time, Sandra searched for apartments we might be able to afford. She noticed an ad for an "office apartment" at the Tall Pines Motel and called the manager so we could go see it. The place was really little more than a housekeeping unit, and had certainly seen better days, but Sandra and I happily looked past the mousetraps and the peeling linoleum and moved in. For the rest of the year, the guys on the team would tease us about our new home.

"Hey, let's go to Ted's for the evening," they'd say. "He's got a pop machine in his front room."

◆

Despite the fact that Glens Falls was my second year with the Red Wings franchise, it was the year I truly became a pro player. Bill Hogaboam took an interest in me when he first arrived in Glens Falls. He provided me with wise advice about life, but also valuable and much needed tips about my game. My skating had improved by then—I'd learned to really bend my knees and do smooth crossovers, and I was no longer dulling my blades against the wooden benches so I could revert to my old skating habits, the way I had with the Greyhounds. In Kansas City, Terry Harper, a teammate and former Canadien, had shown me a few tricks to build up my endurance. In Glens Falls, coach Tommy Webster helped me work on my shot. And my observations of the other players had taught me a few other tricks of the trade as well, like how to "spot pass," sending a puck into the path of a skating player instead of aiming it directly to him. But despite all that, I still had plenty to learn. Even though I was a left winger, Bill taught me how to take a faceoff, in case I ever had to. He showed me ways to keep my head down but still watch everything around me. He demonstrated how you could cut off a puck carrier's angles so that his shooting options were limited.

Rick Shinske also taught me a lot, including how to position the puck. Jody Gage, another new arrival, showed me how to improve my stickhandling and my shot. One of the smartest hockey players I have ever met, Jody shared lots of hockey wisdom, including the fine art of pacing yourself.

My approach to every moment of a game was full-out effort. I was a mucker, a grinder—the kind of player who went into every corner, never stopped digging, got in everyone's way. That made me a solid penalty killer, and Jody wasn't about to suggest I play in a less gritty, physical style. He just wanted me to be a little more efficient.

"Ted," he said, "you've got to stop working so hard during your shifts. Rest when you come back to our end or you won't have anything left." (He also advised me to consume more salt to prevent the muscle cramps I was getting.)

Those are just a few of the things I learned from Bill, Rick and Jody, and there were many other lessons provided by Greg Joly and others. In truth, my teammates were the hockey school I never had. And they taught me more than any coach ever did.

♦

Despite still battling homesickness and the loneliness that being apart from my family always brought on, I was growing more comfortable and confident, both professionally and personally, as the year in Glens Falls unfolded. My game was improving, and by the end of that second season I was fourth in points. And I loved living in the little city. There was only one road from my motel home to the rink, so it was pretty much impossible for me to get lost, even if I tried. Having made good friends on the team, my social life was more relaxing too, if still lively. The guys would often meet to play pool or darts at a local bar. I was always careful not to get staggering drunk, but I was happy to have a few beers and stay out until the last guy in the group wanted to head home.

But our time in Glens Falls wasn't as easy for Sandra. She had struggled through our year together in Kansas City, but now that she was faced with another season of spending evening after evening sitting alone, this time in a motel room, she decided she'd finally had enough. One evening, in the late autumn, she told me she wanted me home a bit more, and when I did go out, she'd appreciate it if I didn't return with the sun.

I'd never had a curfew in my life. In fact, when I began dating Sandra, I was confused when she said she had to be home at a certain hour. I couldn't figure out why anyone would care what time she walked through the door. And here I was, a twenty-one-year-old man, with a good job, earning his own way, and now I had to follow someone else's rules? I told her that if she didn't like the way I was living, she could go home.

And she did.

It only took two or three days for me to figure out what an ass I'd been. I called Sandra up and we set a date to get married that summer.

◆

The Adirondacks made it to the playoffs that first year but were knocked out in the first round, so by mid-April I was packing my belongings into the trunk of the car, eager to get back to Garden River and everything that awaited me there.

On June 7, 1980, Sandra and I got married in St. John's Anglican Church in the Soo and then had a reception in the Garden River Community Hall followed by a dance at the Rankin arena. Sandra and her sister did all the cooking. It was a great day, but as it began, I took one more turn at being a lousy boyfriend.

Standing in the church next to Sandra, as the minister read the vows, I was suddenly overcome with panic and sadness. At the words "until death do you part," I thought immediately of the loss of my father. The idea that death might take Sandra from me too, or that my own death might be in her future, made my mind go blank. The next thing I knew, I was standing alone outside the church, trembling.

While my faith in God had been shaken when my father passed away, I'd never lost it. Yet in all the days leading up to the marriage ceremony, I hadn't really thought about the fact that my wedding vows were about making a commitment to both Sandra *and God*. Now, I was being asked to make a promise to the Creator I had been so angry with during my first days of grief.

A few seconds later, my brother Tom was by my side. Steve showed up right behind him. As Sandra stood alone at the altar, in front of the bewildered minister and her family and friends, my brothers talked me down.

It didn't take long. I knew that marrying Sandra was what I wanted to do, that it had been in my mind from our very first date. When Tom, Steve and I got back in the church, Sandra was waiting at the altar, her flowers in her hands and a patient smile on her face.

If I didn't fully understand it before, I certainly did at that moment: I was one of the luckiest men in the world.

◆

My second season with the Adirondack Red Wings, my third year in the pros, started out promisingly. Sandra and I were happily settled in an upgraded housekeeping unit in a beautiful resort nestled on the edge of Lake George. My friends Rick, Bill and Jody were back, and some great new players had joined the team. Tom Bladon had come to us after eleven years in the NHL and two Stanley Cup wins. Dennis Polonich had clocked seven seasons in the NHL with Detroit. And Pete Mahovlich was winding up his career after sixteen years of playing in the NHL. Of course, I was well aware of the Mahovlich brothers and their extraordinary records. Pete had been a scoring star in nine seasons with the Canadiens, winning four Stanley Cups with them. It was a thrill to be on the ice with a player of that calibre and accomplishment.

Two other new players would become particularly important to me that year: Brian Johnson, a powerful right winger who had come from the Quebec junior leagues; and a Hollywood star, Dave Hanson.

The movie *Slap Shot* had come out in 1977 and was a huge hit with hockey fans—and hockey players. All my Soo Greyhounds teammates had flocked to the theatres to see it. Dave Hanson had inspired a character in the movie dubbed Dave "Killer" Carlson. Dave was cast in the film as well, although he didn't play himself. A number of other real-life hockey players also played major roles. I suppose it's worth mentioning that the movie starred Paul Newman, but what we young hockey players were excited about was seeing the real pros on the screen.

So I was intrigued to see what Dave Hanson was all about on the ice. Dave was a wonderful, caring man and certainly was a tough winger unafraid to rack up the penalty minutes. That first year with the Adirondack team, he tallied 267 minutes in the regular season, eclipsing the runners-up by 74 minutes. But what I remember most clearly is his skill on the ice. He was a talented player, certainly not a "goon" like the character he played in the movie and the character who was based on him. (In 2016, Dave and I would both get inducted into the Adirondack Sports Hall of Fame in Glens Falls.) That said, Dave's willingness to fight when necessary saved me on more than one occasion.

When I had moved from Kansas City and the Central Hockey League to Glens Falls, I had gone knowing that the AHL was a more aggressive league. I was ready for increased roughness. What I hadn't expected was more overt racism as well. Even on my own team.

During an early-season practice during that first year, I was playing miserably, missing passes, letting the puck bounce over my stick. At the end of the session, one of the coaches grabbed a stick and started raising it up and down, doing a tomahawk chop.

"This is the way Ted stickhandles," he laughed.

The next thing I knew, I was flying across the ice with my fist swinging. After landing a blow, I skated off the ice, got dressed and went home. When I walked through the door, the first thing I said to Sandra was, "That's it. We're out of here."

Later that day, I got a call from Detroit. The management was suggesting that the coach and I talk it out, which we did, at a local pub over a few beers. We were both happy to put the matter behind us.

Another time, during a pre-game talk, the coaches warned us about blindly chucking the puck out from behind the net. One of the players on my line did just that, and the other team scored. When we got back to the bench, somewhat frustrated, I reminded him what the coach had said.

"What did you say, you f——ing wahoo?" he fired back.

I didn't say another word during the game, but in the dressing room later, I answered him with my fist.

While those were the only two incidents from my own team, remarks from other teams were a constant feature during games. Some opponents would skate by me while I was on the bench and make war cries. Or they'd throw out "welfare bum," "drunk" or "wagon burner" as we moved past each other on the ice.

Ever since I'd played in Kenora, I had taken care of myself on the ice—and that included responding to each and every racist provocation that came my way. As my years in the pros continued, however, I'd learned to see the differences in the taunts. Sometimes, I looked over at the player who'd just called me a wahoo and notice a sheepish look cross his face or his gaze fall in embarrassment. Sometimes, especially with the really young players, I'd get the sense they were just parroting someone else, that they didn't even know the meaning of what they were saying. If I thought the slurs were just a misguided form of the chirping we all did to rattle our opponents (usually along the lines of "You call that a pass?" or "Nice play, asshole"), I wouldn't retaliate. But other times, I'd see the loathing and viciousness in my opponent's eyes and know the words were a message: I wasn't welcome in this world. And when that happened, I'd go after the guy. A lot of the penalties I drew over the years were big ones—five-minute majors for fighting. Many of those were provoked by hateful words.

In those early days in the minor leagues, especially in Glens Falls, many teammates, particularly my pal Jody, came to my defence whenever they could. But during my second year with the Adirondacks, coaches Tommy Webster and Jean-Paul LeBlanc decided to try to stop some of altercations before they happened by putting Dave Hanson and Brian Johnson on a line with me. Brian was one of the few Black players in the league. He was receiving abuse too—I once saw another player pretend to peel a banana in front him—but his sheer size appeared to be a natural deterrent to some of the trash talk. Certainly, his intimidating physical presence combined with Dave's seemed to reduce the racial slurs that came my way. And when someone did say something ugly to me, Dave or Brian would be after him in a flash. Suddenly, I didn't have to fight all the time. It was an enormous relief.

A year or two after this, during a game against the Fredericton Express, an ugly brawl broke out on the ice. During the fight, one of the Fredericton players started to do a war cry on the ice. It was so loud and obvious that it drew the attention of everyone in the arena. I even heard some in the crowd laughing. After the game, I got a message from the Fredericton coach, Jacques Demers: he wanted to see me outside our dressing room. Demers had come to apologize.

"What that player did was wrong," he said. "It was disrespectful. And it will never happen again."

I don't suppose Demers ever realized how much that meant to me, and I never saw him again to thank him, but that moment was one of my best memories of my whole playing career.

I should make clear, here, that the name-calling was usually limited to the players. Not once in Glens Falls did I ever hear it from the stands, nor did I hear it much from the crowds in other places.

The casual racism that seeped into the game made my connections with other First Nations players even more meaningful than they might have been ordinarily. During my very first year with the Kansas City Red Wings, our team got into a huge on-ice brawl with the Tulsa Oilers. I looked up to see Mike Penasse making a beeline towards me. Mike is Ojibway, from the Nipissing First Nation, not so far from Garden River. When Mike got to me, he grabbed me roughly and whispered in my ear, "Let's pretend we're fighting over here and watch all the white guys beat each other up." Years later, I faced Stan Jonathan on the ice. As soon as we got close to each other, Stan made eye contact, giving me a little nod. He was far too tough for me to fight, so I was pretty relieved about the unspoken rule that we First Nations guys weren't going to mix it up with each other if we could help it.

Perhaps the apology from Demers had such a profound effect on me because even at the best of times, and there were plenty of those, the reminders that I was different came from all sides—including from my friends. The most consistent was the nickname I was given automatically by every white player: Chief. It wore on me that no one, not even the most kind, empathetic guys, understood why it was a loaded term. Finally, when we were out one night, I asked Jody to stop calling me that.

"But why, Ted?" he said. "Aren't Chiefs like great men or something?"

"That's the point," I said.

I explained that within a First Nations community, a Chief was a position of great honour. Chiefs are leaders of our people, men and women who work long and hard to be role models, impart wisdom and help their nations navigate the world. I was none of those things—literally or figuratively. To call me Chief was an act of disrespect to the individuals who really held these positions. And while I knew that most people meant it in a friendly way, all it did was remind me of how little non-Indigenous people knew or cared about my community.

Jody never called me that again. But I could hardly have this conversation with everyone who called me Chief, so the name continued to follow me.

♦

The racism was wearing, without a doubt. But my great teammates and the friendships we had helped enormously. And during that second year, we really gelled as a team on the ice as well. As the second half of the season began, we were playing better with every passing month and racking up wins. Our games were sold out night after night. It looked as if the Adirondack Red Wings were heading for a great year.

And then *my* year shattered.

On February 14, 1981, the team was on the road. As I was getting settled into my hotel room, the phone rang. Coach Webster wanted me to come down to his room. When I got there, he told me my mother had died. Then he put me on the phone with my brother Joe.

I could tell Joe had been drinking. He was blunt. He, my mother and a few others had been driving into the Soo when a white drunk driver hit them. My mother was killed instantly.

"Shit happens," he said. I wanted to jump through the telephone line and strangle him.

I stood in the coach's hotel room in a stupor of shock and disbelief. I phoned Sandra. She tells me I got a flight to Albany, New York, where she met me. She tells me we flew to the Soo from there. I guess we did.

By the time I was home in Garden River, sitting in our kitchen, Mom's casket against the wall, that brain fog had given way to grief and anger. I could barely look at Joe. He had struggled with addiction for a number of years. And during that time, he'd caused plenty of worry and anguish for my parents. Before my father passed away, Dad had bought himself a car—the only car he ever owned, I think. Joe had stolen it, totalling the thing within days. There were so many blows like that. I was furious at him for those. And furious at him for telling me about our mother's death in the unfeeling way he did. I suspected that Joe's experiences out in the world had been far more traumatic than mine and that, like so many people, he was numbing his emotions with alcohol and drugs, but I still couldn't manage any empathy or forgiveness for him. My mom was everything to me. My father's death had made me feel as if part of me had been extinguished, but my mother's death—that was a blow like no other. It was as if the whole world had darkened and withered away. As if it had slipped out of my grasp, leaving me completely alone. I felt numb yet in ceaseless agony at the same time. I couldn't have put any of that in words. Words, thoughts and other feelings were gone. There was only pain left.

Sandra and I were home for four days—just long enough to attend my mother's wake and burial. What happened in those four days is lost to me, but my family's trauma is still crystal clear in my mind. My mother had died on my youngest sister's birthday. That complete transformation of what should have been a time of celebration seemed an appropriate symbol of what was happening to our family. Mom was the glue that had held us all together. Even in those early days after her death, it was clear that, without her, our family was beginning to fall apart. After my father's passing, she'd shown us how to go on, how to continue to be a family. It was a role no one else seemed able to fill.

Over the coming months and years, every one of Rose's children had their lives upended by the tragedy of her death. Hurting, we would go our separate ways to try to cope. A few of my siblings were already struggling with alcohol and drug use. Soon, more than half of us would be dealing with our pain that way. Every one of us was suffering greatly. Our family became truly broken, and it would take years and years for us to heal enough to come together again, although even to this day our bond is not quite the same.

Most of my siblings had of course moved out of the family home, and Janice, just eighteen, and Steve, twenty-one, would now be there by themselves. I just couldn't imagine that. So Sandra and I invited them to come down and stay with us in the States for as long as they needed to. Steve had a girlfriend, Colleen, who he'd eventually marry, so he remained in Garden River. But Janice agreed to fly down in about a week to join us in Glens Falls.

When it came time for Sandra and me to leave, I wasn't ready. I had no choice, however. The team expected me back. During my first game after returning, I went out on the ice thinking, *Score a goal for Mom*. When the puck flew into the net, there were tears running down my face.

The Adirondack Red Wings had a great second half of the year. Despite trailing the Hershey Bears in the regular season by 28 points, we bested them in the Southern Division finals to make the AHL's Calder Cup finals. There, we faced the Maine Mariners, a famously tough team that had racked up 22 more points than we had in the regular season. And we trounced them too, winning the cup four games to two. I scored six goals and had ten assists. The playoffs were the stuff of memory for everyone—except for me.

In all of my playing days, I'd worked hard for a reason: I wanted to win. That's what it was all about. And finally, we had. We won the Calder Cup. Yet I remember none of it.

Just like my year in Kenora, the pain I was experiencing put me in a trance. When I finally began to feel alive again, I could recall not one moment of time that had passed.

6

—

THE NHL

THE SUMMER THAT FOLLOWED, the first without my mother and my father both, was disorienting and difficult. As training camp approached, I began to feel the usual queasiness about leaving Garden River. Returning to Glens Falls, however, was easier than heading anywhere else—it felt as close to a home away from home as I could imagine. And I wasn't unhappy about the prospect of another year with the Adirondack Red Wings. Still, a kind of greyness had settled on me that muted my reaction to what should have been one of the biggest highlights of my life.

Three months into my third season with the Adirondack Red Wings, I got the call from Detroit: I was to join the Red Wings in Chicago on Sunday, January 3, for a game against the Black Hawks.

As I put down the receiver and went to tell Sandra, I thought of Mom and Dad. I thought of my brothers and sisters. I thought of Jim McAuley. And I thought of Bill LeClair. All those years ago, when he told me about the Greyhounds tryouts, Bill said that something could happen for me in five years. It was now a little more than six years later, January 1982, and I was going to be playing in the NHL.

I arrived in Chicago before the rest of the team and checked into the Drake hotel, where we would all be staying. It was, without a doubt, the fanciest place I'd ever been. I'm not sure, then, why I was surprised when the bill came for the cup of coffee I'd ordered in the hotel restaurant. The number that stared back at me was so astronomical, I wondered if they'd charged me for champagne. *You're in a different world now, Ted*, I thought.

That impression stayed with me when I arrived with the rest of the team at the old Chicago Stadium—a massive building steeped in sporting history. It wasn't quite what the Forum or Maple Leaf Gardens was to a Canadian kid, but its size and grandeur were still awe-inspiring.

As the team members began to go in, I lingered for a few moments outside. The building was surrounded by concrete sidewalks and busy city streets, but I found a patch of dirt around a small tree. I pulled a cigarette from my pocket, broke it open, and laid the tobacco on the damp earth. I was making an offering to the Creator and to my mom and dad. And I was remembering my people's history—the broken treaties, residential schools, all the things we had suffered. I wanted to honour my family and all of those who had gone before me and whose sacrifices had allowed me to get to this point in life. Then I stood up and followed the last of my teammates inside.

The dressing room, tucked in the basement, under the rink, was far less impressive than the rest of the stadium—but that didn't take the shine off seeing a red-and-white jersey with my name emblazoned on the back hanging in one of the stalls. Goosebumps rose on my skin.

And then, before I knew it, I was following my teammates up the stairs and into a pulsing wall of sound—the arena's famously giant organ was pounding out its music against a background of thousands of excited voices. Tears filled my eyes.

As I got closer to the rink, my mind turned to the many First Nations kids who weren't able to pursue their dreams. I knew there were thousands of them, many as good as me, many more who were no doubt better, who would never have the chance to do what I was doing. Too many obstacles, too many closed doors. *This is for all of you*, I thought, as I skated out onto the ice.

I don't remember a lot about the game. What sticks in my mind is the thundering organ music, the number of people in the stands and the way the crowd erupted in cheers, a raucous, overwhelming wave of noise that seemed to roll through the arena over and over again as the game went on. The whole atmosphere was electric—and nerve-racking. I have now learned, however, that we narrowly lost the game, and I got an assist, earning my first NHL point.

Our next game was in Buffalo, and then, on January 7, I had my first game on my new home ice: Detroit's Joe Louis Arena. Thirteen minutes into the second period, I intercepted a pass, flew down the ice and scored an unassisted short-handed goal. It broke a tie and helped us secure a 5–4 win over the Pittsburgh Penguins. But that wasn't the most thrilling part of the evening. Not by a long shot.

In the stands that night were two busloads of my family and friends from Garden River. All game long, I was aware that some of the voices I could hear cheering and chanting were doing so specifically for me, that my people were up in the stands, watching one of their own play in the NHL.

In fact, I was so excited about the Garden River crowd that as soon as I got to the dressing room after the game, I pulled the skates off my feet, shoved on my shoes, then raced back out and into the stands. My family were sitting in the first balcony, and I wanted to get to them before they started leaving. I have a photograph taken moments after I made it to them—me, sweaty, fully dressed in my game-soaked uniform, grinning broadly as my happy family, as well as Chief John Duke Corbiere from the Rankin Reserve and my cousin Chief Arnold Solomon from Garden River, pose around me.

I have to laugh when I think of the excitement that led to that moment. Despite all the NHL games I've attended in my life, I don't think I've ever seen another player do that. And it's not like I wasn't going to see my family that evening. I'd invited them to join me in the Olympia Room, the reception area where season-ticket holders, players, Red Wings staff and their family and friends could have a drink together after the games. (A few members of my family hadn't realized there would be a dress code and had to borrow jackets from the wait staff. We teased my brother Joe, in particular, about that for years.)

The pride my family felt to be there with me in the Olympia Room was so obvious it was almost overwhelming. I felt it so strongly in the first few minutes that I had a sort of out-of-body experience. It was as if I could see myself standing in the room surrounded by all those people. Just before I came back to reality, a thought flashed through my mind: *It would be great to be in that group, celebrating that guy. Our people have so few of these moments.*

Of course, there were other highlights. In the forty-one games I played with Detroit that season, I earned seventeen points, which I didn't think was a bad record for a guy not known for his scoring. And I had the opportunity to face some of the greatest players in the league. After three years, I was on the ice again with Wayne Gretzky—this time as his opponent. (Wayne said hi, asked me how Sandra was doing and welcomed me to the league.) Playing the Canadiens in the Forum felt a little like walking into the glorious history of the Canadiens' past—and an encounter with Guy Lafleur was like crossing an important threshold. During one game, Lafleur skated past me and slashed me across the shins. I didn't try to hit him back—I was too busy savouring the pain, savouring the moment. *I was just slashed by a legend!* I couldn't wait to go home and tell my friends and family. (I didn't have to tell Steve. He called me right after the game. "I can't believe you were slashed by *Guy Lafleur*.") That cheap shot got me over many of my doubts—the fact that Guy Lafleur wanted to slow me down, take me out of the action for even just a second, made me feel like I deserved to share the ice with a player like him.

I'd always found playing against other First Nations players particularly exciting, and now with Detroit I got to face Reggie Leach and Gary Sargent. But for me the real thrill was playing in a league with such history, where the legends of the Original Six era of my childhood had worked their magic—and where Jim Neilson, and of course George Armstrong, had once blazed trails for my people.

One of my regrets about that season, however, was that I missed playing for Ted Lindsay. Just the year before, he had been replaced as the GM. And while I was excited about playing in the majors, it wasn't a particularly easy transition. For one thing, I was acutely aware of how hard I needed to work just to keep up with the calibre of play. I gave it everything I had every game, and felt good about that. I never doubted my ability, yet the pressure was immense. My new world was also a bit lonely and disorienting. So much about it seemed strange and foreign to me—the luxury cars, the fur coats, the expensive hotels, the high-powered agents, the sponsorship deals. And there didn't seem to be as much socializing between the players as there was in minors. At least, if there was, I wasn't a part of it. I hadn't, in a long time, felt like a little boy from the reserve, out of place and far from home, but life in the majors brought some of that back.

That feeling wasn't helped by one incident in the Olympia Room a few weeks after I came up. I had been mingling for only a few minutes when one of the bigwigs in the room approached me. After a short chat, he said, "Hey, Ted, you know how to Indian leg wrestle, don't you?"

I couldn't imagine why he was asking.

"Uh, yeah, I guess," I said.

"Well, come on, then," he said with a laugh. "Let's see what you've got."

Everyone was now looking at the two of us. There seemed to be no way of getting out of it without making a scene. So a few seconds later, there I was, in my expensive new suit, lying down on the floor beside the man, my leg raised in the air. *How many other new players have to submit themselves to this sort of public spectacle?* I wondered. We hooked legs, and I let him flip me over. I wanted to get it over with as soon as possible.

After the first few weeks or so, I confessed to Sandra that I wanted nothing more than to return to Glens Falls and all my friends there. But then, near the end of January, Jody, who'd played the first half of the 1980–81 season in Detroit, was recalled to the majors, as was Greg Joly, who'd been back and forth between Detroit and Glens Falls in the previous few years. It was great to have some old friends in the dressing room, although I quickly noticed we didn't go out after the games the way we did in Glens Falls—or if we did, we didn't stay out as long. Everyone was too focused on their performance to allow for the relaxed dressing room rapport and after-hours socializing we'd had in the minors. It was as if we were all sitting on the edge of a narrow ledge, making sure nothing we did pushed us off.

♦

Playing a half year at NHL wages meant that once the hockey season was over, I didn't have to take a job over the summer to make ends meet. Indeed, my first NHL paycheque had been a huge shock—the amount was six times my AHL salary. One of the first things I did with the windfall was trade in my old car for a Cutlass Supreme (which was stolen in the summer when I went back down to Detroit to watch a Tigers game). That car, however, was my only real indulgence. I wasn't interested in buying things or changing the way Sandra and I lived. Other than not working in the summer, what the money meant to me was security—the comfort of knowing I could keep my fridge full and help my family when necessary.

Playing in the NHL also brought me a measure of local celebrity I hadn't really had before. That spring, I was invited to speak at the Sault Ste. Marie recreational hockey league end-of-season banquet.

During my time in the minors, I'd been asked questions by reporters once in a while, and I'd done a few longer interviews with local Sault Ste. Marie journalists, but I'd never given a speech in my life. I figured it would be best to keep it brief. I planned to introduce myself, explain a little about where I grew up and give a brief summary of my hockey career to that point. When I finished writing all that out, I thought I had a pretty good little speech.

Before I was called on stage, the MC announced that Ted Nolan would be next up. He explained a little about where I grew up and gave a brief summary of my hockey career to that point.

I sat stiff with horror. He'd covered everything I'd planned to say. But then he was waving me to the podium, and there was nothing to do but walk up there. I stood behind the microphone, cleared my throat and began.

"Hi, my name is Ted Nolan."

I scanned through my notes. The only thing on the paper that the MC hadn't already said was "Does anyone have any questions?" So that's what I came out with next.

Thankfully, a kind man in one of the front rows jumped right in to ask me something.

The next day, when I saw Steve, he immediately started laughing.

"I heard about your little talk last night," he said. "Don't think you'll be going out on a speaking tour!"

I decided right then that I was going to need some serious public speaking help. That summer, I enrolled in a Dale Carnegie course.

In the following summers, I would continue to volunteer to speak anywhere I could get experience. I also took other courses to help me with my communication skills, including one offered by Harvard University on negotiating. (When I first moved to Glens Falls, general manager Ned Harkness had negotiated with a car dealer for me. He got me a good car at a good price. The only problem was the car was a standard. I had no idea how to drive a standard. It seemed like learning to negotiate for myself in the future might be a good idea.)

While that last course no doubt helped me financially, it was the speaker training that was most important to me. After playing with Detroit, the invitations to speak, especially to Indigenous youth and First Nations communities, continued to come in.

In fact, in 1984, a couple of years after that disastrous rec hockey league speech, I would be asked to join the National Native Role Model Program, along with actress Joy Keeper, Olympic gold medal kayaker Alwyn Morris, and fellow hockey player John Chabot. The program was started by Health Canada to encourage Métis, Inuit and First Nations youth to strive to meet their goals. For several years, each spring and summer, I travelled to reserves across the country to talk with children and young adults, sometimes also helping out at hockey clinics and camps. Each time I did one of those trips, I was reminded how hard it so often is for our young people to believe in themselves—to believe that they and their futures matter. One visit to a northern Cree community has always stuck with me.

The other speakers and I had finished our presentations and workshops and were at the airport, about to walk across the tarmac to where the small plane was waiting to take us back south. I noticed a boy peering through the chain-link fence. When I got closer to him, I recognized him from the activities earlier in the day.

"See you later," I said to him.

He looked straight at me.

"No you won't."

"What?" I said.

"No one ever comes back," he replied, matter-of-factly.

"What do you mean?"

"Do you know how many teachers we've had here?" he said. "In eight years, we've had eight teachers. They come for a year or two and then they leave."

I'd seen a little of that in Garden River too—non-Indigenous folks coming to teach or run programs and then disappearing after a few months, their departure often shuttering the programs they'd led.

"I'm going to come back," I promised. "I will."

I recognized the look on his face. He was trying with all his might to believe me.

Right then, I made a vow that I would return to that community, no matter what it took, and that I would accept every invitation that came my way from a First Nations community. I would come back to remind the kids that they weren't forgotten. I would try to give them some reason to hope. Part of that hope, I understood, would come from seeing someone like them succeed. I had to succeed for them.

In the summer of 1982, I was still years away from that particular encounter, but I knew that the feeling I'd had walking up those arena stairs in Chicago the previous winter wasn't misguided. My career and my achievements were not just about my own satisfaction—they could be important to many more people. And I needed to learn to communicate those messages.

◆

I started out the 1982–83 season in Detroit again, but it was destined to be a short run. During one of the early exhibition games, I played terribly. Every puck that came my way bounced over my stick—a series of missed passes so embarrassingly obvious and consistent that I knew my fate the moment I skated off the ice.

"Oh, boy," I said to Sandra as soon as I saw her. "They're going to send me back down."

"Yup," she said with a chuckle.

Sure enough, the very next day, GM Jim Skinner called to say I would be suiting up for the Adirondack team.

When I got off the phone, it felt just like Christmas morning. I couldn't wait to put our stuff in the car and drive to Glens Falls and the life I loved there.

It may sound strange when I say I wasn't disappointed—was even relieved—to be sent to the minors, especially as I was increasingly aware I was becoming a role model for young First Nations kids. And I did want to succeed for my community, no doubt. But I didn't think of this as the end of my NHL chances—I was confident in my ability to move back up. Unlike those couple of days at the Kenora training camp, I wasn't unconsciously sabotaging myself. I was doing my best, and this move was beyond my control. It helped that I knew my family and friends were proud of what I'd done during the last season, and that wouldn't be diminished even if I never played another game in the majors.

I also didn't care about the reduction in salary. All that mattered to me was that I had a roof over my head, a happy marriage and good friends. And I had all that in Glens Falls.

♦

The following season was a good hockey year for me. But it was an even better year on the personal front.

On July 18, 1983, our son Brandon was born. It was an occasion of sheer delight and good fortune and one that moved me completely out of my sometimes undisciplined youth and into the adult world.

During the first few years we were together, Sandra would often ask why I couldn't have just one beer when I went out. Since her departure and return during our first year in Glens Falls, I had learned to do that, cutting back on my late nights, spending more time with Sandra and the other couples we knew. I continued to go out with the guys too, but I'd realized I could have a different sort of life than the one I'd been leading. Sandra and I grew closer after that shift. I still found talking about my feelings difficult, but I was opening up more. That new approach got reinforced when I became a parent.

I have nothing but love and admiration for my own parents. They made all of us kids feel cherished and deeply supported. And they provided for us as best they could. But when it came to physical comforts, I wanted a little more for my own children. I wanted my kids to be able to take for granted some of the things I didn't have growing up—a full stomach, warm clothes and a ride to school when they needed it. (To this day, when I open the fridge and see the shelves loaded with food, I get a little thrill.) But there was something even more important, I wanted to give them—a sense of safety.

Sure, I had always felt loved. But I have to admit, I hadn't always felt safe.

Those afternoons that my brothers and sisters and I spent playing in the parking lot of the Caswell Hotel while my parents drank with their friends were often tinged with unease. I didn't like the looks people gave us as they drove by, or the smirks we got from people walking into the hotel. And I was always nervous on the drive home. As soon as we all piled into the car, the smell of alcohol was thick, even on the breath of the driver.

During all of the hours spent waiting outside hockey arenas for our rides home, Steve and I knew someone would be coming. Eventually. But watching each car as it drove towards the arena and sped straight on past us was unnerving. And then there were those parties we eagerly attended as we entered our teen years. It was exciting to join the older kids as they smoked and drank. It made us feel pretty grown up to sip a beer, listen to the conversation and laughter, copy the behaviour we saw around us and pretend like we knew exactly what was going on. But every once in a while things got frightening. Sometimes, fights broke out and bodies would go flying around the room, knocking over furniture and partygoers. Sometimes, people drank too much and started to behave in ways that reminded me of my uncles—the throwing up, the passing out. Sometimes, things got confusing. I remember once being called from across the room by one of the women at the party. From my current vantage point, she was likely a very young woman, but to my twelve- or thirteen-year-old self, she was a full-blown grown-up.

She was sitting with a bunch of other young women. They were all clearly tipsy. "Teddy, come here," the woman called again. When I got close to her, she reached out and pulled me into her lap. She wrapped her arms around me, hugging my head to her chest. "You're such a cutie, Teddy." Embarrassed and frightened, I managed to wriggle out of the embrace.

And then, of course, there were those frightening parties with my cousins in Detroit.

Now, I thought how easy it had been to find myself in those sorts of uncomfortable, sometimes terrifying, situations. If my parents had made it difficult for me to go to those parties when I was really young, if they had set curfews and demanded to know my whereabouts, if they had reacted if they smelled beer or cigarettes on my breath, well, I would have been pissed off, but I think, underneath my complaining, I would also have been a bit relieved. It would mean I didn't have to keep myself safe all on my own.

One of my best childhood memories is one filled with a sense of comfort and protection. My family was visiting my sister Barb in Flint, Michigan, one New Year's Eve when I was about twelve. All the adults were going out on the town. We kids were pretty excited about the evening ahead of us—Barb had a colour TV, which seemed like an unbelievable luxury, and Flint offered more than the one grainy station we got in Garden River. Barb had provided us with some snacks. It was going to be as good as going to the movies. But Dad wasn't feeling well. At the last minute, he decided to stay home with us. Rather than spoiling our evening, however, his presence made everything feel more special, including going to bed. Knowing that he would be there if we woke up in the night, knowing that he would be up in the morning with us, made me feel wonderfully warm and secure. I loved every minute of it.

I knew that's what I wanted to do for my kids. Not one night like that, but every night. I wanted to be truly present for them. I wanted to make my children feel both loved *and* safe. I knew Sandra would do this for our children without even thinking. She would provide structure and security for them, as well as affection. I realized that I wanted to do it too. I wanted us to do this together.

Sadly, part of that would involve protecting our children from the instability and unpredictability of others. Of course, I'd over-indulged myself a few times, but by the time Brandon came along, I was pretty much just a moderate social drinker. And since Sandra was never one to have more than one drink while we were with friends, we never had much, if any, alcohol in the house. When my brothers had come to visit in the past, they'd brought their own. One day, when Brandon was a toddler, Terry showed up at our place with a bag of bottles and a look in his eye that told me he had already had a few. Brandon was at the age when children are curious about everything. I didn't want him to see Terry, or anyone, drinking or drunk. I told Terry he could no longer come to the house carting alcohol, and he couldn't visit my son if he'd been drinking. But the summer Brandon was born, those kinds of tough conversations were still in the future.

♦

The training camp in September 1983 went well, and by the end of it I knew I was going to be starting back with Detroit in the fall. Head coach Nick Polano was quoted in the press about his concerns that the Wings weren't physical enough, fighting hard enough along the boards or in the corners, and that Brian Johnson and I were getting another shot on the team because of that. I was happy to take it.

Sandra and Brandon joined me, Brandon sleeping in a dresser drawer in the hotel room until Sandra and I could find an apartment.

Unfortunately, my second year in Detroit was a short one. For the first nine games, I was only doing spot duty, but I guess Polano liked what he saw enough to tell me he planned to give me more ice time. Then, in the first shift of the first game after that conversation, a match against the Rangers in mid-November, I was checked by defenceman Willie Huber. At six foot five and 240 pounds, Willie could knock me off course at the best of times, but unfortunately, for this hit, Willie was knocked off-balance too. When I fell, he came down right on top of me. The ligament in my left knee was so badly torn, the team doctor told me I'd need surgery and would likely be out of commission for the rest of the season.

To my relief, my recovery post-surgery went much faster than anyone expected, allowing me to rejoin the team near the end of December. On New Year's Eve, in a game against the Black Hawks, I scored the winning goal with less than seven minutes remaining. But it just wasn't enough. By February, I was back in Glens Falls.

As you might expect, I slipped back into my Glens Falls life smoothly enough. At the end of the season, the new Adirondacks coach, Bill Dineen, came to talk with me.

"Do you want to come back?" he asked.

When I said I did, he wanted to know for how long. Would I rather a two- or three-year contract?

"A three-year deal," I said. "Without a doubt."

I left the office feeling pretty good about my future. Just a few hours later, however, the new Detroit Red Wings GM, Jim Devellano, called.

He told me the franchise was "going in a different direction," which was hockey-speak for cutting me loose—completely. I wasn't going to be a Red Wing in either Detroit or Glens Falls.

I called Bill Dineen right away to tell him.

"Well, Bill," I said, laughing, "I guess that's the last time I'll use you as my agent."

For the first time in six years, I was going back to Garden River without a home in professional hockey, and with a future that was as clear as mud.

7

THE END OF HOCKEY

DURING THE SUMMER OF 1984, hockey slid into my rear-view mirror. After being let go by Devellano, I'd chatted with my old Detroit teammate Walt McKechnie, who recommended I get an agent. I understood that I needed all the help I could get in finding another hockey home, so I gladly signed on with the fellow Walt recommended. But as August approached, it was becoming pretty clear that the agent wasn't having any luck. Everyone seemed to have full rosters—I wasn't invited to a single training camp. After a while, I'd given up on my off-season training, focusing on softball instead. I began to think about going back to school.

Finally, in late September, while I was playing in a softball tournament, Sandra, always my biggest champion and never one to give up easily, decided to call Jim Schoenfeld. I'd played with Jim in Detroit, but he was now the coach for the Rochester Americans, the Buffalo Sabres' AHL franchise. When Jim heard I hadn't landed anywhere, he sounded genuinely shocked and immediately invited me to join the team. I jumped at the chance, leaving for Rochester before Jim had a chance to change his mind.

By the time I joined the Amerks, however, training camp was long gone, and the team was playing their third or fourth pre-season exhibition game. When Jim and I had chatted after his call with Sandra, he'd asked if I had been keeping in shape, and I'd brazenly lied about the intensity of my non-existent regimen. Sitting in the hotel room the night before my first game, I realized I was terrified. I hadn't had a pair of skates on my feet for over five months. *What am I doing here?* I thought.

I was right to be scared. When I got on the ice, I knew I had to do something to get through the game. I figured a five-minute major would be just the rest I needed. For the next few exhibition games, I made sure to get myself in the penalty box for five-minute breaks at least twice each game. I suspect Jim and the rest of the team thought I was trying to prove something by being super aggressive, but frankly I just needed to sit down.

I hit the gym every day during those first weeks with the Americans, and luckily I was able to get back in form fairly quickly. After two weeks, I was offered an AHL contract with Rochester. The agent and I had parted ways, so I negotiated the terms myself, ending up with a much better deal than I'd had with the Adirondack Red Wings.

Rochester, New York, turned out to be a great fit for me and Sandra. It was, of course, bigger than Glens Falls, but not so big that I felt claustrophobic, as I so often did in large cities. I liked the larger crowds at the games, and I liked the team, which seemed to offer a new role for me.

I was now twenty-six, a real veteran in the eyes of some of the younger players. Realizing this reminded me of how much Bill, Jody and Rick had helped me when I was new to the league. I began to give the younger players as much advice and as many playing tips as I could, and I tried to be as encouraging and supportive as my old Adirondack teammates had been to me. John Van Boxmeer, who'd taken over as coach from Jim, noticed the relationship I was developing with the younger players and in mid-January made me captain of the team.

I was also voted the team's player rep in the Professional Hockey Players' Association (PHPA), a group representing minor league players in the American Hockey League, the Central Hockey League and the International Hockey League. I appreciated the faith my teammates had put in me, but the best thing about the position was the chance to speak for those players who felt voiceless in the face of the management. The PHPA was working for better terms for its membership, including better medical coverage. But there were other, seemingly minor issues that I knew had a big impact on the players. For example, clubs loved to book team buses to depart for away games immediately after lunch or supper so they wouldn't have to provide meal money. It meant a lot of late-night bus trips, which always put unnecessary strain on teams, who had to be up early the next day for pre-game practices.

At the end of the season, the PHPA and the NHL general managers met at a hotel in the Bahamas to negotiate. During one of the social events, I got talking with Eddie Johnston, the GM of the Pittsburgh Penguins. Eddie asked me what I was doing the next season.

The truth was, I wasn't sure. I was pretty confident the Amerks were going to invite me back—I'd scored twenty-eight goals with them, the most of my pro career. But I hadn't heard anything definitive.

Eddie then offered me a two-tiered contract—with a salary for NHL play and a salary for playing in the minors, just like the one I had with Detroit before they cut me loose.

While the pay scale he offered for the minors represented a considerable increase over my Amerks pay, I'm not sure how tempting the move would have been if Eddie hadn't made me an even bigger promise.

"Don't worry about the two-way contract," he assured me. "I'm going to keep you in Pittsburgh for the whole season."

◆

Things didn't unfold quite the way Eddie promised. The next September, before the Penguins training camp for the 1985–86 season even finished, I was told I'd be on my way to the minor league team in Baltimore. To add insult to injury, it wasn't even a close call—I'd been one of the guys in the very first cut.

I was crushed. After hearing the news, I retreated to my hotel room. But I didn't pack my bags. Instead, I sat on the bed for hours, trying to figure out what had happened.

Eddie had given his word. I'd grown up with people who'd gone by their word—verbal agreements, not contracts. Words mattered. I could hear my mother: "Never trust the joganosh, Teddy." I hadn't wanted to believe her, but here I was, nursing a deep suspicion that this had been a bait-and-switch scheme, that Eddie had always wanted me for the Baltimore Skipjacks, and the Penguins offer was just a way to get me there.

I stayed in that hotel room, by myself, for several days. During that time, I called Steve Bartlett, the agent who was now representing me, to see if I could get back to Rochester. NHL contracts weren't that easy to get out of, apparently. Next, I considered whether I should walk away, go back to Garden River, start some sort of college program. Just get on with the rest of my life. But then, near the end of the week, Eddie Johnston called me.

"I know what I said to you, Ted," he said. "But things didn't go as planned. Go to Baltimore. Get a few games under your belt. We'll call you back."

I'd been loafing around the hotel room for days. If there was any chance for me to return to the Penguins, I needed to get back in shape. I said I would go.

I flew to Baltimore, and Sandra drove our car down from Garden River with the baby.

The coach of the Skipjacks was Gene Ubriaco, an ex-NHL fellow left winger who also happened to be from Sault Ste. Marie. He was eager to help Sandra and me settle in. Shortly after we arrived, he called me into the office with a great lead on a house for lease.

"That's a pretty expensive place for a two-week stay," I said.

Gene, clearly unaware of Eddie's promise, was under the impression that I was in Baltimore for good. True to his word, however, two weeks later, Eddie called me and said I should return to Pittsburgh.

I started back as a Penguin in the third week of November. On December 2, in a game against the New York Rangers, I scored my first goal for them. But it appeared I wasn't going to get much of a chance at a repeat performance. I was scratched more often than I made it onto the ice. Eddie might have been a fan, but clearly the coach, Bob Berry, wasn't.

It was pretty obvious what was going on. At that time, if you had a two-way contract like I did, once you had played ten games in the majors, they had to put you on waivers if they wanted to move you down. I realized that the decision-makers were keeping me from that tenth game because they were getting ready to send me packing. A number of my teammates figured that out too and decided to help. During a late-December game, as one of the wingers came off the ice, he looked at me and shouted, "You're up." A few guys on the bench echoed him. "Chief, Chief, you're up." I leaped over the boards and onto the ice.

When I got back after my shift, Bob Berry was fuming.

"Who told you to go out there?"

"I thought I was up," I replied.

That move may have prevented me from getting sent down right away, but it didn't get me more ice time. In fact, as the new year started out, I watched night after night from the stands. And then, after sitting out nine straight games, on January 25, 1986, I was put into a match in Calgary, against the Flames.

As soon as I hit the ice, I could tell I was rusty. My timing was off. As I skated up centre ice, I let my head drop. One of the Calgary defence-men must have noticed. The next thing I knew, I was flying ass over tea kettle and landing hard on the ice. When I tried to pull myself up, pain shot up my back and my body didn't move.

In the dressing room, the trainer gave me some aspirin and cycled through heat packs and ice packs until I could shimmy myself off the treatment table and head back to the hotel. I hobbled into my room, rang the front desk for a wake-up call and went straight to bed.

The next morning when the phone rang, I went to reach for it and realized I couldn't move. After a few minutes of struggling, I managed to get a pillow off the bed and throw it at the phone to make it stop. I spent the next excruciating minutes inching my way out from under the covers and over to the phone to call the trainer for help.

The team flew me back to Pittsburgh, where I had X-rays of my back. The team doctor said my injury wasn't serious and prescribed a bit of physical therapy. I would heal, he assured me.

For the rest of the season, I continued with the therapy and tried to regain my mobility. But there were days when I couldn't feel my legs, and even when the sensation returned, I couldn't summon an ounce of power in my lower body. I didn't play another game.

♦

My back didn't get better even once I was back in Garden River. I couldn't work at all in the summer or do much of anything.

As the fall approached, I began to feel a bit desperate. Neither the Penguins nor the Amerks were going to renew a contract for an injured player. Until I could play hockey again, I needed a little income. One of my friends suggested I apply for worker's compensation since I'd been hurt on the job. But when I got my health records from the Penguins, the team doctor's report stated that there was nothing wrong with my back. Finally, I decided that even if I couldn't manage playing NHL-calibre hockey, maybe I could at least have another season in the minors. I called the general manager of the Adirondack Red Wings and asked if I could try out.

At training camp, one skate around the rink and my screaming back made things loud and clear: there was no way I could play hockey.

Just like that, our future was up in the air again.

We had plenty of reasons to stay in Glens Falls. A local businessman and old friend named Gary Bowman had invited us to live in his father's vacant house. He offered me a job with his company. Sandra had a job as ticket taker at the Civic Center. We had a great life and great memories in the area.

After a few months, we were just about ready to settle down there. Gary suggested we buy a house in a gorgeous subdivision he was building at the base of a nearby ski hill. But the evening Sandra and

I sat down with the paperwork, we both paused with the pens in our hands and looked at each other. Neither of us wanted to sign the offer.

We loved Glens Falls, but it wasn't really home. We were missing our families, missing the places where we grew up, missing our roots. Despite the fact that we had no jobs to go to, no opportunities that we knew of, we thanked Gary and headed back to Garden River and the Soo for good.

♦

In the autumn of 1987, I enrolled in a business administration course, at Lake Superior State University, in Sault Ste. Marie, Michigan—an easy commute from Garden River. I convinced Sandra to enrol as well, so I could have a study partner.

Sandra and I hadn't been in school long when the coach of their NCAA hockey team, Frank Anzalone, asked me if I was interested in giving him a hand at some of the practices. I was happy to share what I had learned in the pros—happy for the opportunity to help some young players.

One day, after a game, the team doctor, Richard Ganzhorn, asked why I wasn't still playing pro.

I told him about my back injury and explained that while the team doctors were hopeful for a full recovery, the healing just hadn't happened and I was still in a lot of pain. Dr. Ganzhorn offered to give me an exam to see what was going on. I went to his office a few days later for X-rays and a full checkup. When Dr. Ganzhorn was finished, he looked grim.

"Ted, you've got two badly ruptured discs," he said. "To be honest, I don't know why anyone would suggest you'd ever play again. That's a career-ending injury."

Then he advised me that since my initial diagnosis had been so inaccurate, I might be able to get compensation for lost wages.

As I left the office, I was overcome with a sense of lightness. And I realized it wasn't because I might recover some of my lost salary. It was because of the other message Dr. Ganzhorn had relayed: I would never play hockey again. Those words were repeating in my mind— and to my surprise, I was overjoyed to hear them. I was finally free from hockey.

When I thought about that reaction in the weeks to come, I came to acknowledge the unexpected truth that lay behind it: I no longer loved hockey. And there were many things that had chipped away at that love.

The last year with the Penguins had been full of disappointment and frustration. But my disillusionment had started long before that.

There was the racism, of course. In the NHL, it was more subtle, but the name-calling had continued in the minors for the entire time I'd played in the pros, and I knew that wouldn't change anytime soon. Frankly, I was exhausted by it.

No doubt another thing that took the shine off pro hockey was the pressure to fight. The seventies and eighties were an era of tough, aggressive play. Coaches wanted players who could physically intimidate opponents on the ice. I got that. I liked a rough, scrappy sort of play—tight checking, intense fighting for the puck, going hard into corners. I had always been the kind of player who got into an opponent's face and tried to throw him off his position. In short, I was a fan of body contact. I always remembered Terry's advice about boxing: the best way to defeat your opponent was to wear him down, give him no chance to rest, let fatigue force him into mistakes. Of course, I had no issue with defending myself, coming to the aid of a teammate or retaliating if I'd received a dirty hit. And when I'd been on the receiving end of a racial slur, I'd been grateful that the acceptance of fighting in hockey allowed me to respond with my fists and receive nothing more as punishment than a short stay in the penalty box. I was well aware that off the rink, such a response likely would have put a First Nations man in a prison cell. Yes, I'd certainly collected penalty minutes and got slapped with ejections. But I had long ago decided I was never going to be a goon.

Back when I had been playing with the Greyhounds, Muzz MacPherson had sent me out to "get" another player. Behn Wilson, who would later go on to play with the Philadelphia Flyers and the Chicago Blackhawks, was an enormous guy, six foot three, 210 pounds (three inches taller than me and thirty-five pounds heavier), and built like a mountain of solid muscle. As soon as I came at him, I was flat on the ice. He let me get up, and I went after him again. He sent me crashing back down. Like some kind of masochist, I got up a third time, and we repeated the scene. Finally, I had the sense to give up. The guy had just destroyed me—it wasn't even close.

When I got off the ice, I swore that was the last time I was going to fight someone for the sake of fighting them. It wasn't that I lost to Behn, and it wasn't that I was afraid of getting hurt. But at heart, I was a gentle kid who'd only fought because I felt I needed to defend myself. I never liked it. Never. If I had, I would have gone into boxing.

But when you are on a pro team, it's not always that easy. You're supposed to follow orders. Once, during a game with the Rochester Amerks, I was told to get on the ice and take out a particular player.

"Fuck you," I snapped. "You get him."

It will surprise no one to hear that I spent the rest of the game on the bench.

Besides the fighting and the racism, the sheer mechanics of playing in the pros were wearing for a homebody like me. In the eight years since Sandra and I had lit out for Kansas City, we had moved from Kansas City to Glens Falls to Detroit to Glens Falls to Rochester to Pittsburgh to Baltimore to Pittsburgh and finally back to Glens Falls.

With every move, there were weeks in hotels, some less pleasant than others. (In the first Baltimore hotel Sandra and I were in, someone tried to break into our room one evening. I had to slam his fingers in the door. The very next day, there was a shooting in the lobby.) Then there were the repeated challenges of finding an apartment to rent. And with each move, I had to get to know my new teammates.

Of course, the list of moves doesn't include the relocations to the Soo and Garden River each summer. Even those visits home could be challenging. I always felt I was living in two separate worlds: the white hockey world and my First Nations one. When I'd first returned to Garden River after my year in Kenora, it took a while for my friends to warm up to me again. They seemed to feel I'd abandoned them. By the time I'd entered the pros, however, my friends knew I was never going to turn my back on them or on my First Nations identity. But a few of my Garden River neighbours weren't so sure of my loyalty. Sometimes, they'd comment on the way I now talked, or they would glare at my fancy jeans or my nice car. When that happened, they might call me an "apple" (red on the outside; white on the inside), or worse. Sometimes, their words led to fist fights. (I had my last such fight at twenty-six—too old to be scrapping over hurt feelings.) I was tired of all of that.

During my final pro years, I felt I'd lost the Glens Falls camaraderie and social life that had made living away from Garden River and my family agreeable. But it was more than that. The moment I moved up to play in the NHL, hockey changed from being a game to a job. When I'd played with the Adirondack Red Wings, I'd given each game everything I had. And so had my teammates. We were all hoping to move up. But once in Detroit, as I've said, the NHL brought a new focus and intensity.

I know that to my old friends, the new intensity was worth it. Playing in the NHL had been their dream. But once I got there, I had to admit it hadn't really been mine. It wasn't like playing hockey was a miserable grind or anything. On a purely selfish level, getting paid for playing a game had always seemed like a pretty good gig. Yet even those fun years in Glens Falls weren't ones I hungered for. Each summer when I went home, it was as if I'd been holding my breath for the whole hockey season and my lungs were finally filling with air. In Glens Falls, in Detroit, in Rochester, I'd been relieved to go out to bars with my teammates. I welcomed that sort of release. But back home in the summers, I rarely drank. And every September, I would lie in bed, dreading the trip back down south. In fact, it wasn't until I was in my mid-twenties that the nights before I left for training camp weren't marked by tears. Sandra talked me through it each and every time.

That was really it. Hockey was a job, and it wasn't a job I loved that much. The magic I'd felt all those years ago in my backyard, under the stars, was just a memory. A distant memory. I had never been able to recapture it in the pros, even if I was skating in the Forum or the Gardens—or facing some of the greatest players about to go down in hockey history.

Truth was, I'd felt trapped for a long time, unable to leave the sport. But the thought of quitting hadn't sat well with me. I not only had a wife but also a young son to support. I knew how hard it was to find well-paid work around Garden River. But even if a good job had been waiting for me back home, I wouldn't have quit. I had a responsibility to my family, my friends and my larger First Nations community to take the great and rare opportunity I'd been given and show our young people that we could succeed and compete with the best. I didn't feel I had the privilege to walk away from that.

Now that the opportunity was gone, I was finally free to find another way to contribute to my community.

When I left the doctor's office that day in Soo, Michigan, I stopped at the top of the steps to the front door. The sun was on my face, and the air was clear and crisp. I was smiling as I began to descend the steps. A sharp twinge of pain shot up my back, but I didn't stop smiling. My life in hockey was finally over.

8

THE MAKING OF A COACH

BY THE TIME COACH FRANK ANZALONE ASKED ME TO help out with the Lake Superior State Lakers, I'd pretty much washed my hands of hockey and was looking forward to a change.

I was a twenty-eight-year-old father, thinking about a new career. I'd given up the idea of becoming a police officer a few years earlier. Steve had served as an OPP officer for a while and found the work didn't suit him. I suspected the same would be true for me. Returning to the building industry was also out. If I learned one thing during my time as a construction worker, it was that I wasn't a handy guy. I'd enrolled in college thinking the business program might set me up for some sort of office job. My father had been the administrator for Garden River, as had my brother Tom. I wondered if I might follow in their footsteps.

It's not like I wasn't interested in volunteer work—I just didn't think it would be with hockey. But Frank held out a carrot: he suggested he could really use my help with the younger players. I'd gravitated to that role when I was with the Rochester Americans, and I liked the idea of continuing to be a kind of mentor. I couldn't say no.

And I found I loved it.

Hockey wasn't about me anymore—and I didn't have to prove myself. My own experience as a journeyman player meant I could put the struggles of some of the young players into context for them. I could help them improve and at the same time assure them they didn't have to be perfect to contribute to the team. It was okay not to be a star. It was even okay not to be okay.

I'd been working with the Superior State team for only a month or two when I got a call at home one night from Phil Esposito. Phil and his brother Tony grew up in the Soo, and Phil still had strong connections to the city, including an ownership stake in the Greyhounds.

"What are you doing, helping Superior?" Phil asked. "Why aren't you helping us?"

"Well," I said, "no one asked."

By the time I got off the phone, I'd agreed to become a part-time assistant coach, along with Terry Tait, of the Greyhounds, helping head coach Don Boyd. The position came with a "salary" of about $6,000 a year. Thanks to Dr. Ganzhorn's diagnosis, I was now likely to get a medical settlement from the Penguins, which might be enough to live on while I went to school, but the extra cash would be welcome.

Being back in the world of Major Junior A hockey, now standing behind the bench instead of sitting on it, felt a bit surreal. But it didn't take me long to realize that, just like with the Superior State team, the enjoyment I got working with the players made the world of hockey bright again. And Boyd, a knowledgeable coach, was someone I liked working with.

The 1987–88 season wasn't exactly an easy one for the Greyhounds or for Don. The team was not performing well, and fans and journalists spent a lot of time calling for Don's head. But I was only part-time and thoroughly focused on the players, so I had a good time despite all that. In fact, working with the team had me wondering if my future really was in some office job. When the season finished, I knew I wanted to come back as an assistant. When the owners offered me a full-time assistant position that summer, with a proper, if modest, salary, I was happy to shelve my studies and accept the job.

Unfortunately, the following season, nothing improved for either the team or Don. By mid-November, rumours were floating around that Don was going to be let go. But I was still surprised when Phil called me with an offer.

"We'd like you to take over," he said.

I didn't feel I was ready.

"I haven't coached a day in my life," I said to Phil. I'd subbed in for Don during a few games the previous year, but that didn't count, as far as I was concerned. "It would be an injustice to the team."

But Phil wore me down, and by the end of the call I'd agreed to try to fill Don's shoes.

I hadn't been wrong. I had no idea what I was doing. And to complicate matters, the Greyhounds had no GM. Don had done both jobs. I tried to learn as much as I could from the front office staff about my managerial duties, but I was on my own in the coaching corner. Suddenly in charge of running the practices, I realized I hadn't been studying what Don was up to the previous year. Being part-time hadn't helped. And while I'd had hundreds and hundreds of practices as a player, I'd never paid much attention to how my own coaches had structured them, or how the drills were designed. I'd just done what I was told to do for as long as I was told to do it.

Bill Dineen had always had us doing the same things over and over again, so a few of those routines were still with me. And I did remember a couple of the things Don had done. When I ran out of those, I tried to craft some exercises of my own, only to find that I'd moved into dangerous waters. In one drill I came up with, I had the players divided into two groups and they were skating as hard as they could towards each other. As soon as I saw them all tearing down the ice, I realized the chance of them colliding and taking each other out was about 100 percent. When they miraculously finished without killing each other, I breathed a sigh of relief and scratched that drill off my list.

And it wasn't just during the practices that my coaching inexperience was obvious. I didn't know how to put together lines, design on-ice strategies or do any sort of seasonal planning.

The only thing I was sure of during my first season as head coach was that I wanted to build a strong relationship with the team—as a group and as individuals. And much of that certainty came from my experience with Bill Dineen.

By the time Bill arrived in Glens Falls in 1983, I'd had many, many coaches. While most were talented and knowledgeable, no one had such a profound effect on me as Bill. A former Detroit Red Wing and Chicago Black Hawk, he'd coached for six years with the Houston Aeros of the WHA, where he had Gordie Howe on the roster for four seasons. For a few years before Glens Falls, he'd been scouting for the Whalers.

But it wasn't Bill's knowledge of the game (or his incredibly predictable practices) that made him such a memorable, inspiring, effective coach. It was his empathy and ability to connect.

Unlike so many other coaches, Bill never yelled or screamed, even in the heat of the game, even when the stakes were high or things were going badly. There was absolutely no bluster. Instead, much like Paul Theriault, Bill talked with the team, making us all feel part of every coaching decision, every play. And perhaps even more importantly, he talked to us one-on-one. I remember after one game, he took me aside to talk privately about the way I was playing. I had made a subtle change, a slight modification of my offensive style, and he'd picked up on it immediately.

"Ted, this fancy stuff isn't you," he said. "Always remember who you are."

He could have called me out when I'd returned to the bench after a play, but he hadn't. And his comments seemed just as much motivated by his interest in my well-being and success as a player as they were by the need to maximize our scoring chances. Bill's concern for his players was always evident. If you had to leave during a game, he wouldn't simply let the trainer take care of you, like most coaches did. Instead, he'd make sure to get to the dressing room as soon as possible to see how you were. Bill regarded each player as a person. He talked with you. And his attention made a difference. I would have skated through a wall for Bill.

I'd always thought that Bill had a powerfully positive effect on my attitude as a player, but now I was seeing that he had given me something much more life-changing: an insight into the power of personal connection and open communication. A model for the way I wanted to coach a team.

So with the Greyhounds, I helped the guys with their skills, sharing with them all the things I'd learned from my teammates over the years, but I also tried to get to know them as people. One thing I'd discovered during my playing days: no one has a bad game for no reason. Yet it was so easy for a coach to make assumptions or jump to the wrong conclusions about what was going on. It struck me that few of my coaches had ever asked me much about myself. So how could they have understood why I was having trouble, what motivated me or what I needed in order to improve as a player? And if they didn't understand their players as individuals, how could they really have insight into how we might best play together as a team?

I thought about how I'd felt when I was a junior player myself—in Kenora, far from my family for the first time, with nobody checking in on me, no protector at the rink or at home. Maybe if the coach had talked to me about why I'd stopped trying in training camp, he might have helped me personally *and* on the ice. And if he'd talked with the other players individually as well, he might have helped us develop sorely needed camaraderie and team spirit. Even if the young men on the Greyhounds were in different circumstances than I had been, I knew you couldn't have too many supportive, attentive adults in your life when you were starting off on your own. I wanted to be one of those adults, always around to provide encouragement, safety and a sympathetic ear.

I started having regular one-on-one meetings with the players—not about their performance but simply to get to know them. Sometimes, I'd set them little challenges to see what their character was like. I might bench someone for something minor, or for no reason at all, and then watch his reaction. If he lost his temper or acted out, I'd wait to see if he apologized. And then we might talk about how to handle frustration and anger.

I tried to find ways to help them build bonds with each other too. I figured for that to happen quickly, teams needed to spend time outside of the rink as well as on the ice. In the early fall, when the salmon began to run, I took the guys out to Garden River. I divided them into teams, took each one to a different part of the riverbank, and told them they were now competing to see which team could snag the most fish. The fellows loved it.

The talks I had with individuals could sometimes be a little difficult. More than once, the opposing players made war cries or shot imaginary arrows in my direction. I knew my players and the young people in the stands were watching me, the way children always watch their elders, so I never reacted, other than to raise my eyebrows or sigh. But I had to respond when my own players acted out. A couple of times, angry that I'd made a comment about his play or behaviour on the ice, a player would call me a "f——ing wahoo" or something similar. I was more understanding when young guys used slurs than I was with adults. After all, I had no idea how they'd been raised, and I understood that they probably didn't know the impact of their words. I also knew that when I was their age, I'd lost my temper many times. But I couldn't let it pass. When something like that happened, I'd take the player aside after the game and explain not only how inappropriate his actions were but also what would happen if he did the same thing in the pros or in his adult working life. "No one will put up with it," I said. "If the scouts find out about this, they won't touch you." I knew from my own pro hockey days that might not be exactly true, but I figured it was a point worth making.

As the 1988–89 season unfolded, it became clear that the players themselves were feeling a strong connection to the team and each other. In fact, just before the trade deadline was about to pass, we got several inquiries about one of our best players: Wayne Muir. I called Wayne into my office and explained about the offers—offers from much better teams than ours. I told him that we didn't want to lose him but this was a great opportunity for him. It had occurred to me that no one in my junior days had ever asked me what I wanted, but they should have. I told Wayne that I wasn't going to try to convince him of anything. I just needed to know what he wanted. Wayne didn't hesitate. He said he wanted to stay.

Though the players had responded well to the connections we were making on the team, I can't say that made up for my other coaching deficiencies or that our playing improved. The guys were all working as hard as they could, but it simply wasn't a very strong roster. And I wasn't a very strong coach. The fans reminded us of that often, booing energetically—although those boos were mostly aimed at me.

When the season finished, we'd won just 21 games, lost 43, and were dead last in the league.

♦

The season had been a bit tough, but the spring of 1989 was magical for me despite that. On June 23, Sandra and I welcomed our second son, Jordan, into the world. Brandon wasn't quite as thrilled as we were, suggesting that we bring the baby back to wherever he came from, but within a few days he was as much in love with his little brother as we were.

The spring and summer of 1989 were bumpy times for the Hounds, however. The owners, including Phil Esposito, were thinking of selling the franchise to Compuware, an American corporation that was planning to take the club south of the border. Some local Soo business interests, including Jim McAuley, were trying to put together a competing offer that would keep the team in town. Sherwood Bassin, who had just resigned after twelve extremely successful years as the general manager of the Oshawa Generals, had been brought in to advise on the deal.

By mid-July, with a loan guarantee by the city, the local group was able to purchase the team. One of the first things the new ownership did was convince Bassin to stay on as governor and director of operations of the club, although he would remain in Oshawa and work long-distance.

I don't think I've ever met a smarter guy than Sherry Bassin. He had a PhD in pharmacy, a master's degree in hospital administration and a law degree. At the time, he was working at the Oshawa General Hospital, but he also taught at Durham College. And on the side, he devoted himself to junior hockey. By the time he came to the Greyhounds, he had established an impressive record with the Generals. More impressive still, in the early eighties, while with the Generals, he'd been instrumental in convincing the Canadian Hockey League, the group that oversaw the three Junior A leagues in Canada, to put together a team of the very best hockey players from across the country to compete at the World Junior Championship. (Before this, the team that won the Memorial Cup to become the CHL champions would be sent.) He then served as assistant coach and assistant GM of the Team Canada Juniors for four years, during which time they won not one but two gold medals at the World Juniors. But you didn't need to know any of that to see he had an exceptional mind and a huge range of talents. And there sure wasn't much he didn't know about hockey.

As the director of operations, he was going to decide who would be the coach for the Greyhounds in the future, and he set up an interview with me. I wasn't looking forward to it.

I was embarrassed by the job I'd done. I felt bad for both the players and the fans. No one could have blamed Bassin for showing me the door without so much as an interview, so I was glad he was at least giving me the opportunity to meet him. I wanted to convince him to give me another shot to prove myself. Because by the end of the season, I'd discovered something a little surprising: I really loved coaching.

In fact, I loved it more than I had ever loved playing.

Our interview started out more smoothly than I had any right to expect. Then Bassin said something that really surprised me.

"In school, if you think the way the teacher thinks, you're likely to get an A. And if you half agree with what the teacher says, you'll probably get a B. But if you don't think what the teacher thinks, you're going to fail. Right?"

I couldn't argue with that.

"But that kind of thing doesn't matter here. I'm not going to tell you what to do. I want you to think for yourself, Ted. I want you to be yourself. Can you do that?"

I nodded. Sherry's instructions weren't what I expected, but they were what I needed to hear. More than ever, I wanted to coach the team again.

Then Sherry offered me a two-year contract.

◆

One of the things the new management and coaching team had to tackle right away was the problem with one of our draft picks. The good thing about being in the cellar the previous year was that we had the number one pick in the junior draft at the end of May. The previous ownership had chosen a young player named Eric Lindros.

Right from the start, the Lindros family made it known that Eric wasn't interested in joining the Greyhounds. We'd always known it would be a hard sell—not only were we not the strongest franchise, but being located in Northern Ontario, our team had to spend more time on the road than many others. Players regularly missed days and days of school. And for parents, getting to and from the Soo to attend games and paying for their kids' trips home could be costly. Before the

OHL draft, Sherry, Phil Esposito and I decided to visit the Lindros family at their home in Toronto.

When we walked in the door, we were greeted by stone-cold faces. And when we started to make our pitch, the f-bombs began to fly.

"We won't report," Eric's dad, Carl, snapped.

And that was that. Sherry and Phil were both disappointed and frustrated that we didn't even get a proper hearing, but despite the unpleasantness, I was impressed by the way the Lindros family stood up for Eric. I couldn't help think about all the people in my family and in my community who'd had to leave home against their will. I was glad that Eric had a say in his future and could, supported by his parents, make choices for himself. And I suppose making a choice to stick close to home had some meaning for me.

On top of that, I couldn't get too worked up about not having Eric suit up for the Greyhounds. He was already such a big star, it was unlikely he would have played for us for more than a year before he was gone—just like Gretzky. And indeed, we were able to build a much stronger roster that lasted for years by trading Lindros to the Oshawa Generals for three players: goalie Mike Lenarduzzi (who would be drafted by the Hartford Whalers) and right wingers Mike DeCoff and Jason Denomme. We also received future draft picks (the next year we'd pick up Joe Busillo and Drew Bannister) and $80,000 from the Generals.

♦

While Sherry's instruction to do things my way was a huge boost, it also underlined the fact that I hadn't done a heck of a lot of thinking when it came to coaching. I was reminded of this early, at a presentation to prospective players before training camp. Speaking to the group,

Sherry said, "I can't stand people who say practice makes perfect. Practice doesn't make perfect. Perfect practice makes perfect."

He was talking about the effort and discipline he expected from everyone on the team. But it had a ring of truth for me. The practices I ran were definitely not perfect. I needed to get more serious about what I was doing.

One of the first things I did after signing my contract was hire Mike Zuke to be my assistant coach. Mike was a local minor hockey coach whose son played for the St. Louis Blues. He was also a devout hockey enthusiast—his backyard rink was the best in the city. Everyone went there to skate. And he had a wealth of knowledge about the sport, in particular about the European style of play, which emphasized puck possession and teamwork over a dump-and-chase approach and a focus on star players. From Mike I learned that the Europeans were taught never to give up the puck. If they didn't see an opportunity to make a pass or take a clear shot at the net, they wouldn't fire it into the offensive zone and then follow, hoping the defencemen didn't get to it first. Instead, they circled back and looked for another opportunity. He emphasized getting to the puck first and knowing exactly what you were going to do if you didn't manage it, if you arrived at the same time as or after the opposition. And like the Europeans, Mike believed in making use of the whole team, playing all four lines, rather than relying heavily on only the strongest players.

While Mike helped me improve our practices and skills development, Sherry helped me create a more disciplined team environment. One of the things Sherry and I agreed on early was that the players needed to pay attention to their schooling. We decided that if they weren't in school on time each day and we found out, we'd move the next day's practice to 5 A.M. We dubbed it the "stupid practice," their reward for being stupid about getting to school. And if they missed school, I would make them miss the next game.

Of course, attending practice itself was important too. If a player was late or absent for no valid reason, that was another 5 A.M. practice, and usually a "wally" skate—non-stop back-and-forth dashes across the ice. The players hated it.

And I benched players for other reasons. If players talked back or made a nasty remark to a teammate or opposing player, or if they couldn't control their tempers, I'd correct them and then make them sit out. Even our stars. I knew that in the long run, learning to manage their emotions on the ice would help their careers more than another shift would.

Sherry was a big fan of these kinds of predictable consequences for young players. And they struck a note with me. The family environment that Sandra and I had created for Brandon, which would now support Jordan too, provided structure and predictability that I hadn't had as a kid. I'd learned the value of that, and I wanted to provide it for the young players as well. To be honest, I didn't really care if any of them made the pros, but I wanted them all to have a bright future— and that meant not neglecting their schooling, and learning to be disciplined, responsible adults.

◆

Over the course of the year, I could see that the new routines were improving player attitudes, and the team culture was becoming more positive and forward looking. When the regular season ended, the Greyhounds were no longer at the rock bottom of the league—but we didn't make the playoffs either.

There was no doubt about it—Sherry's influence had helped to transform the team, bringing an observable measure of improvement.

Sherry, Mike and our whole coaching staff had helped me to focus on bettering my skills as well. But the truth was I still wasn't a very good coach. As I left the Greyhounds office for the last time that season, I remembered what the spring and summer months had been like for me as a junior and a pro. I'd learned back then the importance of using the off-season to condition—to build strength and endurance that would improve my skill on the ice the following year. *I should be doing that for my coaching fitness as well*, I thought.

All summer long, I pored over every book on coaching I could get my hands on. I also phoned the coaches I had played for and admired in the past: Bill Dineen, Tommy Webster, John Van Boxmeer. I picked their brains about drills, putting lines together and recognizing players with potential. I remembered how impressed I'd been as a teenager with the Philadelphia Flyers' Stanley Cup wins. Their coach, Fred Shero, had been running coaching clinics after he retired from the NHL. I'd met his son Ray during my hockey playing days, so I decided to give him a call to see if he had any of his dad's coaching materials that he would be willing to share with me.

When I got the package of Fred's notes in the mail, there was one that stopped me in my tracks. "You have to learn to win with what you've got, or you won't win at all," it said. An echo of my father's own advice: "Make do with what you have." My head almost exploded.

In all my previous conversations with my past coaches, I'd been peppering them with questions about planning and schedules and talent. I was focusing on logistics, sure, but I was really thinking most often of that last one: talent. If I could find better goalies and better scorers, I thought, I'd start winning.

I'd spent my entire childhood unconsciously following my dad's advice. My belly might be empty, but I was loved. I might be cold, but I had a cozy bed to share with my brother. My skates were three sizes too big, but I could shoot a puck on my very own outdoor rink. I didn't spend any time wishing for something I didn't have. And life was good. Here I was, an adult, and all I could do was focus on what was missing: the brilliant goal scorers, the hulking defencemen, the lightning quick goalie.

Reading Fred's note, I knew my thinking had been dead wrong. It wasn't the players who'd been falling short. It'd been me. I'd been letting my players down.

Fred had told me I had the players I needed to win.

Sherry told me to think for myself.

What I needed to do now was figure out what *I* actually thought was the best way to do the job I'd been given.

Bringing a little of my own culture to the practices and games, I soon concluded, could be part of that.

One opportunity to do this happened before an early-season away game against the Windsor Spitfires. As the trip drew near, I realized that the team was anxious. Many of them were aware that the Greyhounds had a long, seemingly unshakable record of losing to the Spitfires in Windsor. It had apparently been something like eight years since the Soo had won a victory there.

I wondered if some of our First Nations' ceremonies could be helpful to others. The game in Windsor seemed like the perfect opportunity to find out, to bring my two worlds together, and to maybe let the players get to know me a little better. In the dressing room before the pre-game practice skate, I said to the team, "We have everything we need to win here. The only reason we lose in Windsor is bad vibes." And then I explained that the practice of smudging was the First Nations way of ridding ourselves of negative thoughts and embracing positive energy. I told them I had brought a bowl and some sweetgrass to the arena, and they could give it a try before the game if they liked.

So, once on the rink, I gathered everyone at centre ice and got them to put their gloves and sticks down. Then I lit the sweetgrass and invited each player to come up and guide some of the smoke over their heads and shoulders. After everyone who was interested had smudged, I told them to skate once around the rink and head back to the dressing room.

Interestingly, the players began the game no longer worried about where they were or who they were playing. They won handily.

I also continued to let other personal convictions shape how I did my job. When the players came off the ice after a practice, I often found myself thinking of my father's post-game greeting: "Did you have fun?" It was an excellent question. After all, we weren't soldiers trying to capture enemy territory. We were playing a game. It was supposed to be enjoyable.

The previous year, I'd discovered that Mike Zuke was of the same mind. And he was great at coming up with ways to make our practices original and fun. He suggested we put small wooden boxes at centre ice for the players to hit and that we get players to practise their flip passes, which were a bit of a novelty at the time. He also got us all to bend down low so that we could see the net from almost ice level. That was how goal scorers saw the net, he explained: from the puck's vantage point. Another time, he came up with a relay race to push the players to their skating limits. And he suggested that I keep a pen and paper by my bed to jot down any ideas that came to me. At the time, I couldn't imagine that I'd be thinking of drills as I drifted off to sleep or that I might wake remembering a "dream drill." But by my second season with Mike, I was.

So I started introducing more of my own drills. In one, I put the players into five different colours of sweater. Then I outlined a pattern of play: one colour would pass to another. Only the fifth colour, the last to receive the puck, could take a shot. The point of the drill was to get them to see the whole ice at once, to be aware of everyone and where they were. We also spent some time practising in the dark so that the players had to further sharpen their powers of observation.

And in another drill, I'd tell the guys to go out and do shooting and passing drills without any puck at all. I explained to the players that we were working on our imaginations, because if you could imagine the various ways the action might go on the ice, you could better anticipate and better prepare for whatever came your way. Hockey is a game of mistakes. If you could imagine the possibilities, you could avoid mistakes, and the team that made the fewest mistakes was likely to win the game.

"If you're using your imaginations, you can make it a perfect practice. *Your* perfect practice."

In no time, the players would be flying back and forth on the ice, having the time of their lives. It was amazing to watch how well they shared a vision—how they accepted that one of them had made a great pass or another had scored a goal. One time, however, the goalie shouted out excitedly that he'd blocked a shot. "F— you," said the shooter. "That went in!" Yet usually, the practice went smoothly. In fact, after one of these imaginary drills, a scout came down from the stands to tell me it had taken him five minutes to realize there was no puck on the ice.

Sometimes, we'd have a standard practice but I'd play loud music the entire time, so the players had to sharpen their focus on what they were doing to tune out the sound.

When I first started coaching, I'd made up drills because I didn't know enough of them to fill the time. Now, Mike and I did it to create an atmosphere where the players could not only enjoy themselves but were also distracted enough that they lost themselves in the action.

I could see it lessened their anxiety about their performance and allowed them to actually play better.

I turned my attention to how I wanted to play the lines I was putting together as well. One of the things I'd always hated about hockey was the way the very best players, the first- and second-line guys, got stronger and stronger and racked up the points because they got so much ice time, while players who were talented but not first-line players never got to improve or score many points because they spent so much time on the bench. Listening to Mike explain how the Europeans focused on making every player a strong link in the chain, I immediately recognized the wisdom of allowing the weaker players the ice time they required to improve. That way, when they were needed, they could really contribute. After all, these were the guys who would have to move up when the first- and second-line guys got injured. Letting them get rusty or so unpractised that they couldn't pull a double shift when they had to was just short-sighted. And having everyone playing as well as they could helped prevent the team from losing confidence or panicking if one or more of our best players was missing. Championships are won by teams, not by a line or two.

Of course, I wasn't going to give everyone equal ice time, but I played my third and fourth lines as often as I could. And I treated the third- and fourth-line players just the way I did the first-line guys. In my pro days, if a player on the first lines messed up, he'd still be sent right back out for the next shift. But if a fourth-line player turned over a puck (or refused to fight), he'd warm the bench for the rest of the game. I wanted everyone to be able to make mistakes and learn from them without being punished.

That included the coaches.

During one game, I decided to ask the team to play whatever

position they wanted. I thought the novelty might give them some energy and also insight. Maybe it did, but we sure didn't play any better. The final score was 8–1. Speaking to the team later, I admitted it had been a stupid experiment. What I didn't tell them was that it had been an important one too—a chance to show them I was learning from my mistakes, just like them. So it wasn't as if we lost games because of them and won them because of me. It was always a combined effort.

With everybody getting plenty of shifts, many different kids began scoring goals, not just our very best offensive players. At the beginning, however, some of those star players pushed back. They wanted to see their tallies rise.

"When geese fly in formation," I told them, "it's not always the same ones in the front. The lead geese will fall back when they get tired, and other geese will take their spots up front."

"Besides," I added, "the scouts aren't looking to see you score your eighth or ninth goal. They're looking to see you score the *winning* goal."

I tried to explain that if the team won, they all won. Because if the club was strong, the scouts were going to want to know why it was doing so well and look at the individual players more closely. No one got that kind of attention as the best player on a losing team.

I would also throw in a different kind of realism. Not everyone was going to make the pros. But as a team, they could make sure that *some* of them did. (Sure enough, in the 1992 NHL entry draft, the Greyhounds would see eight of our twenty players picked up.)

"If you want to go somewhere fast," I told them, "go alone. If you want to go somewhere far, go together."

Eventually, most of the players came around. Some of the veterans would even wink at me and gesture to the younger, weaker players when they thought I should send them out.

That's what I wanted the players to understand. Not everyone was going to get exactly the same time on the ice. But even in just one or two shifts, a player could make a difference to the outcome of the game. Everyone had something to contribute, and everyone was valued.

♦

While my coaching evolved during the 1990–91 season, I got a huge help from another source. Mike was a great assistant, but he had a full-time job, so he couldn't travel with the team or be there for every practice. Before the season started, Sherry told me that Danny Flynn was now available and would make a terrific full-time assistant coach. I'd actually interviewed with Danny when he was head coach of the Belleville Bulls and I was an assistant coach and unsure if the Greyhounds were going to keep me on. I hadn't taken the job but had been impressed with Danny. I knew he was a great technical coach, with a head for strategy and the Xs and Os of the game. That had never been my strength and I suspected never would be. But together, Danny, Mike, and I made a great coaching team.

That season, with the combination of a roster strengthened by Sherry and his scouting team and our new coaching approach, the tide turned for us. We started to win. And win big. We marched through the regular season, into the OHL playoffs, and by the time we hit the finals against the league's top-rated team, the Oshawa Generals, we were coming off nineteen straight wins.

No one was more pumped about those finals than the Sault St. Marie fans. People were camping out overnight for tickets, and every game was sold out in hours.

The press was keen to know how we were going to stop Eric Lindros, and we did have a plan. We would have our speedy centre

Ralph Intranuovo and left winger Joe Busillo on him in the neutral zone and leave him to our all-star defenceman, Adam Foote, in our end. But I wasn't going to put two defensive players on him, as some teams had tried earlier in the series. That had led to goals by his wingers.

The first game against the Generals was in Oshawa, and we shocked the crowd by dominating the ice, outshooting the home team 48 to 23 and winning the game 4–2. Adam was on Eric every second. Bob Boughner and Denny Lambert, two players who'd been on our team when Eric refused to report, also made sure they were in Eric's way all game, keeping him goalless. One of the papers would say we'd used Eric "as a human trampoline." And it was hard not to take a little satisfaction from the fact that one of our four goals was scored by a player we got in exchange for Lindros: winger Joe Busillo.

The next game in Oshawa was an intense battle. Eric would tell reporters that the two teams were "in a war." This time, Eric scored two goals and we lost 4–5, despite outshooting the Generals again. That only seemed to raise everyone's fighting spirit as we headed back to the Soo for the next two games.

But as excited as we were, we were no match for the enthusiasm of our hometown hockey fans. While I hadn't been upset that Eric Lindros had tossed over the Greyhounds in favour of the Generals, the same couldn't be said of folks in the Soo. The chance to see their home team take on the guy who had jilted them had fans completely revved up. In fact, as we came out to the jammed-packed arena for game three, we could spot people in the stands sending pointed messages to Eric. Many were holding up posters. A few grown men and women were dressed in baby bonnets and diapers. But other than a few boos whenever Eric got near the puck, the crowd was civil and spent the bulk of their energy cheering us on.

It was another hard-fought game. At one point, we were down 5–1. But we rallied, scoring the next five goals, the last one in overtime. Jason Denomme, another ex-General, made that one. And we did even better the next night, with an 8–5 victory, leaving us one game away from taking the series.

When we got to game five in Oshawa, however, we had a setback. Eric Lindros was hard on our forwards, although he never seemed to get called for his spearing and slashing until he broke his stick over Ralph Intranuovo. But the 2–4 loss just meant that we had another chance, this time on home turf.

That proved a little problematic for me. Since I was in town, my brother Joe called me at three in morning the night before the game, looking for money for his next drink. I didn't have any cash on me and told him so.

"Well, don't be surprised if I'm not here in the morning," he said.

His threat had me tossing and turning until the sun rose. I called Joe first thing to make sure he was still alive and then set my mind on the coming day.

Despite my sleepless state, the energy in the dressing room before the game erased my fatigue. The game was tight. Tied in the first period, scoreless in the second, but in the third period our team did what they knew they could do, outshooting the Generals again and scoring two goals to win 4–2 and claim the title.

When the final buzzer sounded, the arena exploded in cheers. People were on their feet, hugging and dancing in the aisles. They continued their celebrations outside in the parking lot and out onto the roads. We could hear the car horns honking for close to an hour as we celebrated in the champagne-soaked locker room.

The press called us a Cinderella story, since we'd come from the bottom of the league the previous year to win it all. And it was hard to argue with that. So many on our team played their hearts out (among the others already mentioned, Colin Miller, Tony Iob and goalie Kevin Hodson come to mind), but they had also played with confidence. They'd gone into the series as underdogs, but they always knew they had what it took to win.

The OHL finals were certainly a high, but when I think back on that season, my warmest memory is of a brief moment on the ice during the third round of the playoffs.

Denny Lambert was a left winger from the Batchewana First Nation, east of the Soo. He had joined the Greyhounds the same year I became head coach, and I'd noticed immediately that he was a fierce competitor, a player who just never stopped operating in high gear. But he was also a guy who earned the disapproval of management for being undisciplined. They complained that he didn't have control of his temper, took too many penalties and was often late. They wanted to cut him loose. I ignored their advice. I kept him on, but I was tough on him—probably tougher than I was on any other player. In practices, I would skate him hard. When he took a bruising shot at our goalie in practice, despite being told repeatedly that he shouldn't do this, I benched him for the next game. I knew Denny had not had a lot of structure growing up, and I wanted him to learn the value of listening to good advice. I'd tried to encourage him to tamp down on his outbursts and avoid unnecessary penalties so his talent could take centre stage. He'd been making strides with all of it, but controlling his temper was still a challenge.

We were playing the Niagara Falls Thunder in the third round of the playoffs. In the very first match, we were up 3–1 late in the second period, but the other team had a power play and were pressing hard. With twenty-one seconds left to go in the period, a Thunder player met up with Denny at centre ice. The two exchanged words, and the Thunder player dropped his gloves. Denny made a motion to do the same. Then, to everyone's amazement, he stopped himself. The next thing we all witnessed was Denny receiving a punch to the head—and then Denny continuing to stand there, his hands at his sides. The Niagara fans were so astounded by Denny's restraint, they got to their feet and cheered him. And it got even better. The Niagara Falls player was sent to the penalty box, cancelling their power play. Eight seconds later, Ralph Intranuovo scored a goal to cement our lead and eventually our win.

Having learned the value of control, Denny continued to improve as a player. He would go on to have a twelve-year career in the pros, playing for such teams as the Anaheim Mighty Ducks, the Ottawa Senators, the Nashville Predators and the Atlanta Thrashers. After retiring, he coached the Greyhounds for eight seasons, three as head coach, and eventually became a First Nations police officer with the Anishinabek Police Service.

♦

The OHL championship took us to the Memorial Cup, the competition between the victors of the Ontario Hockey League, the Western Hockey League (WHL) and the Quebec Major Junior Hockey League (QMJHL). While we didn't make it to the final, it was the farthest the Greyhounds had gone since 1985.

I was hugely proud of that year. Proud of the players and, to be honest, proud of myself. In just about everything I'd ever done, I'd felt I had to prove myself. Now, from leading a team to a championship to helping players overcome their bad habits and shine on the ice, I'd shown that coaching was something I could be good at. I felt I'd discovered my place in the world. More important still, coaching had given me a way to make a difference in people's lives. Since I'd started, I'd thought over and over again, *I'm going to give these players everything I didn't get.*

That feeling of purpose and contentment was truly life-changing. One night, several months before the season ended, my mother appeared to me in a dream. Since her death, I'd always felt her presence, and I knew immediately why she'd come.

"You don't have to look out for me anymore, Mom," I said. "I'm okay now. You can watch your other kids."

Coaching had brought me a sense of peace. It got me up every morning, eager to start the day. It brought me home at night, happy and ready to enjoy my family. And watching the team come together on the ice, it gave me moments in which I felt the way I had skating on a backyard rink in the moonlight.

It was magic.

I can't tell my story without honouring my parents and my family.
These are the people who showed me how to live.

Whatever you do in life, it's a lot harder doing it on your own. My family and the people around me taught me that knowing who you are and drawing on the strength of our culture would see me through.

I learned a lot about the world playing junior hockey. My time in
Kenora playing for the Thistles opened my eyes to the wider world
of hockey. It showed me that while my people might not always be
welcome in the game, we could make it there. My sons proved me
right. Here I am on Garden River's famous bridge with my two sons,
celebrating Jordan's Stanley Cup victory.

I was lucky to find Sandra, and even luckier that she stuck with me.
From the very beginning, she has been the one who has seen me clearly.

TED   LEFT WING
NOLAN

When I started out in minor hockey, I was sharing equipment with my brother—even though he was on the same team. Somehow, I made it to the NHL. I consider that a victory in itself. But I had more to give.

I never set out to be a hockey coach, but when the job found me, I discovered I loved it. It took me from my hometown to the Winter Olympics in Russia. Along the way, I got to share the bench with my son in Buffalo, and with Islanders legend Al Arbour.

© Janet Schultz

© Daniel St Louis

I am very proud to have won the Jack Adams Award for NHL coach of the year. But coaching is just as much about the players as it is about Xs and Os. I'm very proud of the way all of my teams have played, even when they weren't rewarded in the standings. They always played with their hearts and came through for each other. And that goes especially for the young men on those championship teams in Sault Ste. Marie and Moncton.

I grew up knowing that the people around me had my back, and my whole family is committed to being there for our community. Sandra and I loved being there for Brandon and Jordan. They thrived, and now all of us are finding our ways to help others along the same path. At the top, that's Sandra and me at First Nations University, and at the bottom, that's me at the Rose Nolan Foundation, which we set up to honour my mother and all she has done.

9

BRINGING HOME THE CUP

THERE'S NO DOUBT ABOUT IT—the 1990–91 season brought some incredible highs my way. But the year wasn't always easy. Sometimes, it was downright heartbreaking.

On September 22, 1990, my brother Rod passed away suddenly at fifty-one years old. His death was shocking to me and my family, a horrible echo of my mother and father's early and unexpected passings.

There was so much to miss about Rod, our eldest sibling, once he was gone. And so many wonderful memories that I hung on to tight. One of the more recent ones was the way in which Rod supported me and the entire Greyhounds team. He attended every game he could, sitting in the corner of the arena where my dad used to sit when I played. Every now and then, he would bring his hand drum with him, playing it as the Greyhounds skated onto the ice, punctuating every great play and every goal with a First Nations beat. And when we were heading out to away games, I'd often arrive at the bus station or airport to see him there, instrument in hand, ready to drum us onto the waiting bus or plane. I would feel Rod's presence during every coaching season to come.

◆

The team's strong performance drew attention I hadn't expected. In the late spring of 1991, I got a call from the Detroit Red Wings. They were wondering if I would be interested in taking the head coaching position for the Adirondack team in Glens Falls the following season. I didn't know what to say except that I would think about it.

I hadn't started coaching with any thought of the NHL or the minor professional leagues, just as I'd never thought about the pros when I was playing junior. But here it was again: an opportunity to join the big leagues, maybe eventually end up behind the bench of an NHL team. And I would have the chance to start in a town that Sandra and I knew and loved.

When I told Sandra about the offer, she said that we were a team—she'd move whenever and wherever I wanted to go. But I knew how much we'd both miss our Garden River home.

For the eight years I'd been playing professional hockey, we'd lived in apartments and rented houses. In that time, I'd got some more land from Uncle Jack, so my lot now extended to the beautiful river's edge, and with the help of a small subsidy from the reserve, I'd started to build a house on it as soon as I got my first NHL paycheque. By any standards, the home that resulted was a small place. The problem with housing on First Nations reserves was that the banks weren't willing to give mortgages or building loans, because if the loans weren't repaid, the land couldn't be repossessed. (This policy has changed only recently, but band offices still have to co-sign any loans.) Any construction or renovations, therefore, had to be paid up front by most folks. I'd never made much money as a pro. What I'd been able to put aside for my Garden River house had been modest—just enough for a living room, kitchen and two bedrooms. Brandon and Jordan's room was so tiny, I had to build a shortened version of bunkbeds against one wall, as regular ones wouldn't fit. More than once in the years since I'd finished the house, I'd bring a friend or co-worker home and notice the shock on his face when he saw the place. A few even put their surprise into words: "This is it? I thought hockey players made good money!" Their reaction never embarrassed me. I was happy with my life and proud of who I was.

By the time the Adirondack coaching offer came, Sandra and I had added a small family room to the place, and we loved it. We weren't eager to leave—even for Glens Falls.

And there was another thing that was niggling at me.

Getting as far as the Memorial Cup was a thrill, but I couldn't stop thinking about how wonderful it would be to go back, get into the finals and win the whole thing. And there was a part of me that wanted a repeat visit to the championship to show that the past year hadn't been a flash in the pan. I didn't want people to be able to dismiss the Greyhounds or put our accomplishments down to luck. I wanted to prove we really were good enough to win—and win again. Bringing home the Memorial Cup would seal it.

I became so preoccupied with this idea while working out my feelings about the Adirondack offer that I called Sherry.

"Do you think it's possible for us to get to the Memorial Cup again next year?" I asked him.

Sherry said he couldn't make any predictions, but we would still have a strong team next season. "There's a chance, Ted," was all he would say.

That evening, sleep eluded me. After tossing and turning for hours, I must have dozed off, because I woke sometime in the middle of the night to my mother's voice. All she said was "Hey, Teddy." And yet I was certain what that meant. *You are okay where you are.*

I knew that was the truth. I felt born to be where I was just then. At home, doing something I loved.

I called Detroit first thing in the morning and told them I was going to stay put.

♦

That summer, I asked the team to double down on their off-season conditioning. And we pulled out all the stops during the season, with better designed, better implemented practices. Many of our younger players, like Ralph Intranuovo, Perry Pappas, David Matsos and Tom MacDonald, had matured into stronger, more skilled players. And older players, like Tony Iob, Colin Miller and Jarret Reid, were really hitting their stride. While we'd lost defencemen Bob Boughner, Adam Foote and Brad Tiley, new defensive players, like Drew Bannister and Mark Matier, had stepped up. Plus, in November, we added a new formidable young player to our roster.

Sometime in the fall of 1991, Sherry told me about a player he had his eye on: Chris Simon. Chris, whose father was from the Wiikwemkoong First Nation, on Manitoulin Island, grew up in Wawa, just a few hours north of the Soo. A hulking kid at six foot three and 232 pounds, he was a bruising left winger with remarkable talent. He'd been playing for the OHL's Ottawa 67's for three seasons, starting out his fourth year as a Philadelphia Flyers draft pick.

But Chris was also a young man whose unresolved issues and traumas drove him to abuse alcohol and succumb to fits of anger, making him a problematic presence on the ice. In early October, he'd high-sticked an opposing player, knocking out seven of the kid's teeth and leaving a gash that needed twenty-one stitches. He received an eight-game suspension. He followed that up with a two-game suspension for talking back to a rep in another game.

After that, the management of the Ottawa 67's had decided they'd had enough. They wanted to trade Chris. Sherry wondered if the heritage Chris and I shared, as well as my own family's history with addiction, might make it possible for me to help him deal with his demons and become a more disciplined player. We agreed that bringing Chris onto the team would come with risks. We had a great bunch of players, and introducing a troubled young man into the fold might be costly. But we decided it would be worth it if we could help Chris salvage his career.

So, in mid-November, Chris joined us. Before I'd had any time to connect with him or figure out a way to help him, things went off the rails. From the moment he arrived, it was obvious he was spending his off-hours partying without restraint. No doubt because of the partying, he came late to several practices. By this time, the team was a disciplined unit. The previous year, I'd been forced to call a 5 A.M. practice only once, and this season we hadn't had any. I could see, however, that there wasn't any point in using the early-morning-practice rule to address Chris's tardiness. Peer pressure wasn't going to work. In fact, most of the players were giving Chris a wide berth, as he treated them no differently than he treated anyone on an opposing team. During practices, if someone checked him or lifted his stick to get the puck away from him, he was likely to respond by spinning around and slashing or punching his teammate. Within days of his joining our team, the other players were letting him carry the puck without interference and keeping out of his way on and off the ice.

Chris had only been with us for a month or two when I gathered the team captain and some of our older players to discuss the disruption. I could see that Chris's presence was not only affecting our practices but also our focus during games, as the players knew that at any moment, without warning, there might be mayhem on the ice. All of this was causing considerable stress for the other players.

Just like with Denny Lambert, there was talk about cutting Chris— an easy solution to the problem. The idea of dumping him struck a nerve with me. It was the way society seemed to handle all its problems— walking away from them or shunting troubled people off where no one could see them. I told the players I didn't want to do that.

I like to think I would have felt the same way even if Chris wasn't First Nations. But certainly our shared background helped me understand that he wasn't a "bad" guy, just a hurting one. I also understood how some of the love and support I'd had in my life had kept me from the kind of anger and self-destructive impulses that seemed to plague Chris. So I explained to the team that I thought we should work harder to help him.

I wasn't surprised by their warm response. So many of the older players had become mentors to their young teammates, leading by example and taking responsibility for the team when coaches weren't around. They said they were willing to try to do the same for Chris. They would reach out to him, invite him to spend time with them in the evenings and weekends. Give him something to do other than drink and somewhere to go other than to parties

But I knew I needed to work harder to help Chris too. The structure and team environment Sherry, Danny and I had built was just not going to be enough for Chris. So I went downtown to the bus station and bought a one-way ticket to Wawa. And then I called Chris into my office.

When Chris walked in and sat down, I pulled the ticket out of my pocket and put it on the desk between us.

"Chris, I have a new set of rules for you," I said. "And if you don't want to follow them, that's fine. You can go home."

And then I laid it out: Chris had a 9 P.M. curfew every night. He was not allowed to drink. When he wasn't at school, I wanted him at the arena, working and helping out, starting at 6 A.M. every day. And until I felt he was ready to rejoin the team, he was suspended. He had to attend practice, but he'd be running laps while the rest of the team skated.

Finally, I told him I knew things weren't easy for him. I understood he was struggling. I'd seen it many times with members of my own family, and I'd seen the way they'd received blame when what they needed was compassion. I assured him that I would always be there for him. Anytime he wanted to talk, anytime he thought he couldn't do it, anytime he was lonely, he could reach out. And it wasn't just up to him. I would check in with him daily.

Things didn't change immediately, but they did change. Within five months, Chris had stopped drinking completely. Long before that, the other players had discovered his huge heart and caring spirit. When a teammate made a great play, Chris would be the first one jumping up and cheering for him. If opponents ran at our smaller players, Chris would be sure to say something to the offender to discourage future aggression. Knowing that Chris was in their corner seemed to make players feel a little bigger, a little braver. Of course, he remained a nerve-racking presence for our opponents. In the years to come, a few would admit they developed the "Soo flu," before matches, sometimes vomiting or feeling so ill they didn't make it to our games. With Chris on our team, we often felt we won a game even before it started. But now that

Chris was playing in a supportive environment, his true talent could really shine. With his speed and incredible stickhandling, he was a perfect power forward, making great plays and well-placed hits. He became the player he was meant to be. And he made our team better.

At the end of the season, Chris was traded by Philadelphia, who had signed him two years earlier, to the Quebec Nordiques (as part of the package for Eric Lindros) and began an incredible eighteen-year run in the NHL, playing for the Calgary Flames, the Colorado Avalanche, the Washington Capitals, the Chicago Blackhawks, the New York Rangers, the New York Islanders and the Minnesota Wild. (Our paths would cross for two of those eighteen years.) He went to three Stanley Cup playoffs, including a win with the Colorado Avalanche in 1996. After coming off a season-ending shoulder surgery in December 1998, he had an NHL career high the next season by becoming the Washington Capitals' top scorer with 29 goals in 75 games. The stats, however, don't really capture Chris's formidable presence on the ice. For some, the flowing black hair he sported during his NHL days was an unnerving reminder of his fierceness. To me, however, it was a heartwarming sign of his renewed First Nations pride. But no question, he was an intimidating player, who received more than his fair share of penalties and suspensions. Yet he was also a highly skilled powerhouse who gave the game everything he had. I'm incredibly proud of what he accomplished. The credit goes to Chris, of course, but I have to admit, I consider the team's small part in his rise to the pros as one of our greatest accomplishments.

◆

Despite Chris's presence and our strong roster of other talented players, we were perhaps not as strong a team as we'd been the year previously, or would be the year after. That said, we performed well throughout the season, won our division and then advanced steadily through the OHL championship series, making it into the finals once again, this time to face the North Bay Centennials for the cup.

The Centennials were heavy favourites to win: we'd hardly won a match against them all season. They were a tough club, with strong scorers like John Spoltore, Jason Firth and Drake Berehowsky. On top of that, the Centennials management had insisted we play only one game in each city before switching, so every other game, the teams would be sitting on a bus for five hours to the Soo and then five hours back. We knew it was going to be the survival of the fittest.

Our first game gave us a decisive win on our home rink. But our next game, on enemy turf, was a bit unsettling—the Centennials scored three goals in the first thirteen minutes, and it took us over forty minutes to respond, which we did thanks largely to Chris Simon, who was able to muscle right through their defence and score two unassisted goals. We still lost that game 3–4, but back at home for the third we took it 4–2. Then, in game four, our top scorer, Ralph Intranuovo, was injured, and Chris received an indefinite suspension for spearing, taking out two-thirds of our second line. We lost that game, and the next.

By game six, the Centennials were leading us three games to two, and their management seemed pretty confident about the final outcome. As our team came into the North Bay arena, several of us noticed a few of the Centennial staff carrying cases of champagne and armfuls of party hats into their dressing room. I think their presumption ignited something in our players. Our goalie, Kevin Hodson, was particularly energized. He put in a spectacular game, stopping three breakaway shots and at least fifteen shots from point-blank range, keeping the Centennials to just one goal while we put two in the net.

We returned home for the championship game, and once again the Soo fans jammed the stands, as boisterous as they'd been the year before. When we came away with the win, the first back-to-back league titles since the Kitchener Rangers had done it in 1981 and 1982, the crowd erupted. Sherry was thrilled. In all his years in junior hockey, he'd never won twice in a row.

Once again, we had a run at the Memorial Cup, this time in Seattle, and this time we made it much further, winning our first three games in the round robin tournament to take us straight to the finals—the first time in the franchise's history that the Greyhounds had reached a Memorial Cup final.

We were feeling good, especially as we'd lost three straight at our previous Memorial Cup showing. But that final game against the Kamloops Blazers, who we'd beaten 6–3 in our first game in the tournament, was tight. The Blazers started off with a blast, scoring three goals in the first period. In the second, we were able to pull up alongside them, but then a puck bounced off one of our players' skates and went into our own net, pushing the Blazers ahead. We managed to tie it up, and that 4–4 score held for most of the third period. But then, with only 14.6 seconds on the clock, Zac Boyer from the Blazers took a pass from defenceman Scott Niedermayer and scored the winning goal.

The loss was heartbreaking, but it didn't take away from that year's accomplishments, including scoring more goals than any other team in the OHL and allowing the fewest goals in the league. (Kevin Hodson won the Dave Pinkney Trophy for that feat.) Our performance in the OHL championships and in Seattle proved we weren't a flash in the pan, but I think everyone on the team was now itching for one more chance to come home with the Memorial Cup.

♦

That summer, I hired Bill Hughes to be our goaltending coach. Bill's expertise would turn out to be a boon for our goalies, and his unofficial role as team psychologist would give the whole team a huge boost.

For the 1992–93 year, it was the OHL's turn to host the Memorial Cup, and the league announced that the hosting team would be determined in a "Super Series." It would be a great financial boon for whichever city hosted the cup, but it also guaranteed the home team a spot at the Memorial Cup, even if it didn't win its league title. In late March, we met the Peterborough Petes to decide the series. The Petes were the top team in the OHL that year, with impressive scorers like Jason Dawe and Mike Harding, as well as defenceman Brent Tully and arguably the best player in the whole league, defenceman Chris Pronger. And their confidence was clear. We heard that even before the series started, the city of Peterborough was doing prep work for its hosting duties.

Yet when we met the Petes on the ice, we surprised them. We blasted through four games straight to become the hosting city. In one of the games, Chris Pronger became so frustrated by how our players were sticking to him like burrs that he took a slapshot directly at me as I stood behind the bench. But when we met the Petes again in the OHL championships, our luck ran out. They beat us four games to one to secure the J. Ross Robertson Cup.

Some of the players were upset about that loss, but I reminded them that the previous year we'd waltzed right into the Memorial Cup playoffs only to lose in the finals. This year, our guaranteed berth meant that I'd been able to rotate our players a bit more—some of our best players were a little more rested than they had been the year before. And we had a strong roster: Jarret Reid, Ralph Intranuovo, Aaron Gavey, Dave Matsos, Rick Kowalsky, Drew Bannister, Mark Matier and newcomers Chad Penney and Steve Sullivan were playing well all season. What's more, the tournament would be held in the Soo. We would play every game at home, in our own Memorial Gardens, we'd eat in the restaurants we liked, and the club could provide some extras for the players, like a team psychologist and a masseuse. And perhaps most importantly, we'd have the enthusiastic Soo fans at our backs.

When the tournament got under way in mid-May, we won our first round robin game against the Laval Titan. But our energy was a little zapped in game two, which took place only fourteen and a half hours later, against the much-touted Swift Current Broncos. Like us, the Broncos were a well-balanced team with a lot of speed, and they bested us 5–3. A few nights later, however, our OHL rivals, the Peterborough Petes, trounced the Broncos and gave us a chance to get to the finals (if the Broncos had won, we would have advanced to the semis). The Petes, who the Soo fans had regarded as their arch rivals all season, were our opponents in our next game, and the fans in the "Soo Zoo," as it had been dubbed, were pumped, yelling and cheering before the puck even dropped and not letting up until the final buzzer.

Kevin Hodson was on top of his game in goal, the team's tenacity never wavered, and some truly great shots were made (including four goals during power plays). By the third period, we were comfortably up 6–2, so I decided to put on a player who had been spending a lot of time warming our bench. Jodi Murphy was a big guy—over six feet and maybe 240 pounds—who'd been playing in the Western Hockey League before joining us at the beginning of the season. He wasn't the most skilled player, but his toughness reminded me a bit of Chris Simon. The faceoff was in front of the Petes' bench, and before the puck was dropped, Peterborough's tough guy leaped over the boards and joined the game. The action had hardly started when Jodi and the other player were after each other. To the fans' shouts of "Murphy, Murphy, Murphy," Jodi came out on top.

I hadn't sent Jodi out to take anyone on, but the brawl seemed to give not just the Greyhounds fans but also the players another burst of energy. We finished the period 7–3.

That victory meant that we'd meet the Petes, who'd advanced by defeating the Titan, for our ninety-fifth game of the season: the Memorial Cup final.

The cheering in the standing-room-only arena began a full fifteen minutes before the game started on a wet Sunday afternoon, May 23. And, of course, it wasn't only the Soo fans who were desperately hoping for a win. Nine of our players had been to two previous Memorial Cups and come away empty-handed. Many of those were playing their last year in junior.

So I wasn't surprised to see those guys come out blazing. Ralph Intranuovo, Rick Kowalsky and Chad Penney, who were all in their last year with the club, scored in the first period. Steve Sullivan brought the tally up to 4–0 in the second. In the third period, the Petes rallied, with Dave Roche and Bill Weir putting two in the net. But it wasn't going to be enough.

Ninety seconds before the buzzer sounded, the arena exploded in cheers. And the roar grew louder, with horns, noisemakers and stamping feet adding to the chants of "We're number one!" At rink side, I found myself doing a little dance, spinning in circles. Drew Bannister and Sherry Bassin leaped into each other's arms. (It was Sherry's first Memorial Cup win. "Now I know what ecstasy is," he told a reporter.) Just like the night of our first OHL championship win, outside the arena, horns were honking and people were waving flags— this time in the pouring rain. Queen Street was clogged with cars. Two arena staff got the Zambonis out and drove them down the street in an impromptu parade, accompanied by fireworks. And while the celebration was every bit as intense inside the dressing room, Jarret

Reid and Perry Pappas couldn't be contained—they bolted out of the Gardens in their uniforms and stocking feet to join the crowds.

◆

There were a lot of great times during those three Memorial Cup runs with the Greyhounds. But maybe my favourite happened not during our eventual win but in our third game in Seattle the previous year, when a penalty-killing goal won the game for us. And not because it was the winning goal, but because of who scored it: Rick Kowalsky.

Rick, a right winger, had been a thirteenth- or fourteenth-round draft pick for the Hounds a few years earlier. He started out the first year on our farm team. The management wasn't convinced of his potential, but I just loved his attitude. He was a guy who played with passion and all-out effort. In his second year, we brought him up, and he got better and better, but he still wasn't our star player. In Rick's third year on the team, we were having a management meeting and I said I wanted to appoint him as team captain. Someone dropped a glass on the floor—everyone looked shocked. Finally, one of the scouts said what everyone was obviously thinking: Rick wasn't good enough. But the scout hadn't seen what I'd seen. He hadn't seen how Rick supported the rest of the players, how he went out of his way to help those who were struggling, how he had been there for Chris Simon, even in the toughest times. Rick was a player with heart. A player who understood that a team was a family, and when a family member gets in trouble, you're going to be there for them. In other words, Rick was the kind of guy who knew intuitively how to lead.

I made him captain.

To this day, Rick is one of the best team captains I've ever seen. And certainly during the 1991–92 season, he became an important member of the team. But in our 1992 Memorial Cup run, Rick finally had a moment to really shine. He scored the deciding goal in each of our first three wins, including a penalty-killing breakaway that gave us the by into the finals. When Rick scored that goal, I was screaming with joy for our team, but also for Rick. He got the glory he deserved.

Rick would spend just one more year in the OHL. The 1993–94 season would mark the beginning of an eleven-season stretch in the minors. As a player, he was never quite able to break into the NHL, but he ended up with a long and continuing coaching career in the minors and for three seasons with the New Jersey Devils.

Perhaps one of the reasons the memory of Rick's performance is so special to me is that as the years have unfolded, I have seen an interesting parallel in our careers. Rick might have started out as a player, but that seemed to be only a way station for him, the starting point on the route to his true calling. Coaching was what he was meant to do. Rick eventually found a real home behind the bench. And while Rick was at the beginning of his journey, my time in the Soo and my work with the Greyhounds had brought me to my destination, although it was one that would still hold many surprises.

10

—

THE WHITE BUFFALO

I PULLED UP AT THE US CUSTOMS BOOTH AT the Peace Bridge on warm mid-July day in 1995. The border guard looked at my ID and before handing it back said, "What are you going down for, coach?"

"Just visiting some friends," I said.

That wasn't exactly the truth. I was on my way to a press conference where Buffalo Sabres president Doug Moss was going to announce that I would be the club's head coach in the fall. Doug had asked me to keep my new position quiet until after this event. He even suggested that I drive instead of flying so the press wouldn't get wind of the trip.

"Do you mind popping the trunk for me?" the guard said.

I was a bit confused by the request, given how the guy seemed to know who I was, but I did as I was asked, and the guard disappeared around the back of the car. Watching him through my rear-view mirror, I noticed that he hardly glanced in the trunk before slamming it shut. Then he was at my window again.

"I just wanted to see if you had any blood and guts in there," he said with a laugh. "Because that's what we need on this hockey team."

The fellow knew what was up. I guess he'd heard speculation about candidates for the coaching job and put two and two together. As I drove off, I was feeling even more upbeat than I'd been before. It seemed as if at least some fans would be happy I was joining the franchise—just like I was.

◆

The two years that followed the Greyhounds' Memorial Cup win had been full of ups and downs. That spring and summer after we brought home the trophy should have been a time for all of us, players and coaches alike, to kick back and bask in our accomplishments. I hope the players were all able to do that. Unfortunately, my shiny off-season had been a little dented.

My contract had run out at the end of the season, and so I decided to approach the management to try to broker a slightly better deal for myself. (Sherry had just left the organization for the Quebec Nordiques and the Cornwall Aces.) It would be the first time I'd ever negotiated with the Greyhounds. Despite my contract experiences during my playing days, my desire to work with this particular team and to stay in Garden River were so strong, I'd always accepted whatever the management had offered. That said, I knew my salary was low, and in the summer of 1993 I decided to find out just how low. I discovered that most OHL coaches were making a lot more than what I was getting. I was near the bottom of the pay scale. Despite that, a modest raise was all I was looking for—not an increase that would bring me up to the league average, but just enough to help Sandra, the boys and me live a bit more comfortably. The management's response came as a shock. It was as if I was trying to rob a bank, as if I was using the team's success to strong-arm them. They eventually agreed to the small raise I'd requested, but my heart was broken by their reaction.

That unpleasant negotiation made me feel underappreciated, no doubt, but it was possible to chalk it up to a tight budget and the short-sightedness of a small-town club. But another episode helped sour that time, one that might have served as a cautionary note for what lay ahead in my coaching career.

After we'd won the Memorial Cup, Sherry asked me if I would be interested in coaching Canada's World Juniors team. But the team played over the Christmas break, and I couldn't see being away from the kids—Brandon was ten and Jordan just four—during the holidays. So Sherry suggested I consider the World Under-17 instead. Three Canadian teams were playing in a tournament being held in Japan in July. That got my attention—and my application.

As I walked into the interview with the Team Canada board a few months later, I was feeling pretty confident. Nine coaching positions were available, and as far as I could tell, I was the winningest candidate.

The interview seemed to be going pretty well until one of the interviewers asked me why I hadn't got my coaching certification. I'd started taking the courses offered by the National Coaching Certification Program when I was an assistant for the Greyhounds, but I'd found the lessons too basic to hold my interest. I'd given it one more stab a few years later, when I was trying to build my coaching know-how, but I found I was getting a lot more from my own study than I was from the expensive courses. So once again I'd stopped after a few sessions. I explained all that to the panel.

When I got back from the interview, Sherry asked me how it had gone. When he heard about my certification answer, his mouth fell open.

"Teddy, you dumb shit," he said with a chuckle. "Those are the guys who designed the program."

"Shoot," I said. "I didn't know that."

While I was embarrassed that I'd put my foot in my mouth, I couldn't imagine I'd hurt myself too much. Wouldn't the group be more concerned with my coaching record and the fact that I had taken the Greyhounds from the basement to three Memorial Cup appearances and a win? But Sherry, with his years of experience with Team Canada, and knowing just about everyone there was to know in that world, wasn't so confident.

Sure enough, I wasn't offered any of the nine positions. I didn't even get a phone call to tell me. Instead, I read about the Team Canada coaching appointments in the sports pages like everyone else.

Maybe there were other reasons they passed me over, but no doubt Sherry was right. I'd insulted the hockey power brokers by failing to follow the routine they had set out—and failing to pay for the courses they ran.

Yes, I'd gotten a glimpse of hockey politics and its old-boy clubbiness. Maybe it should have prepared me better for the future.

◆

The season following the Greyhounds' Memorial Cup win was a time of rebuilding, as we'd lost a good many of our older players. Perhaps not surprisingly, we narrowly missed making the 1994 OHL championships. When the season was over, I attended the OHL draft in late June, and there I bumped into Jimmy Rutherford.

Jimmy had been the general manager of the Detroit Junior Red Wings, the Detroit area junior team we had bested to play the Petes in the Super Series in 1993. During those matches, things had become heated between Jimmy and me, and I came away not too fond of the guy. The feeling had clearly been mutual. Nevertheless, I wanted to congratulate him on becoming part of the ownership group for the Hartford Whalers. We chatted a bit about the team's prospects. Then he asked me what I was doing the next year.

My contract talks the previous spring had left me feeling pretty uncertain about the Soo management team. I told Jimmy that I wasn't sure.

"What about coming to us?" Jimmy said.

I almost dropped my coffee at that.

The following January, I was standing behind the bench as one of Paul Holmgren's assistant coaches for the Hartford Whalers. My first season coaching in the NHL had gotten off to a strange start.

The previous year, the Players' Association had been without a collective bargaining agreement. The stalemate in negotiations continued through the early fall, and in early October the NHL owners locked the players out. The season hadn't started back up until mid-January.

It wasn't the easiest way to begin a new job, that's for sure. On top of that, I could tell that Holmgren wasn't my biggest fan. I got that. Coaches like to bring in their own assistants, and I'd just been thrust on him. I had the feeling I might not have that long with the Whalers, so I tried to learn as much as I could as fast as I could.

Even though I'd played in the NHL myself, watching the action from behind the bench made the pros seem like something altogether new. The pay had improved enough in the minors, apparently, that most players didn't take on jobs during the summer. Instead, intense year-round conditioning had become the norm—and I could see the results in the players who'd recently arrived from the minors. It was as if the playing bar had been raised. In a way, I felt I was learning hockey skills all over again just by watching the players.

My time with the Whalers also allowed me to weigh the differences between coaching junior hockey and coaching an NHL team. First, obviously, there was a difference in the maturity level of the players. While the essential principles of coaching are more or less the same at every level, the way you speak with the players changes. And some of the challenges are a bit different. You certainly didn't have to impose a 5 A.M. wally skate to get NHL players to show up on time. I was also reminded of another difference: in the pros, there was an intense hierarchy on the bench that didn't exist in the same way in the junior world. In the big leagues, there were the star players and then there was everyone else. When I was a player, what had struck me most about the top guns were the obvious differences in lifestyle (as well as their talent, of course). What I noticed now was the way in which they often drew a special sort of care from the coaching staff. Some were like high-strung stallions that needed a calm, patient, maybe even deferential touch. But it seemed as if all the stars got special treatment. I noticed that if one of them made a mistake, when he came off the ice, more often than not, he'd get a pat on the back and some words of reassurance or even a "well done." That never happened with the journeyman players. In fact, it appeared to me that when the stars weren't playing well, it was the third- and fourth-line guys who bore the brunt of the coaches' frustration about it. That made me uneasy. I remembered how my parents managed to treat all of their kids the same and how that lack of favouritism had given us comfort and confidence.

By the time the shortened season had wrapped up, I'd learned a lot from Holmgren, and I'd enjoyed my time working with him and the team. But I wasn't expecting a return gig with the Whalers.

♦

I wasn't wrong that my time in Hartford would be brief. The next spring, before I could start a second season with the Whalers, Doug Moss of the Sabres reached out. A short time after that, I was once again heading south to join an NHL team.

I couldn't wait to get behind the Sabres' bench. When I was first approached about the position, a number of people pointed out that the team had been struggling, on the ice and with the balance sheet. They weren't sure this was quite the opportunity it appeared. The previous year or two had been a bit tumultuous for the club. The team hadn't performed especially well during the lockout-shortened season, ending the year with a 22–19–7 record and seventh place in the Eastern Conference. John Muckler, who'd been both the coach and the general manager for the last two years, had had a lot to deal with. The franchise had been building a new stadium (which was not yet ready for the start of the 1995–96 season), and there'd been enormous pressure to cut costs, which had fallen largely to him. In the previous spring, he'd traded away one of the team's star players, Alexander Mogilny, while Grant Fuhr and Dale Hawerchuk had left for the St. Louis Blues, upsetting many of the fans. John had drafted a bunch of young and mostly inexpensive players both last season and this one: players like Jason Dawe, Alexei Zhitnik, Brian Holzinger, Mike Peca, Mike Wilson and Jay McKee. Much of the remaining team consisted of seasoned veterans like Garry Galley, Dave Hannan, Randy Burridge, Doug Bodger, Rob Ray and Donald Audette. That said, the team still boasted a couple of bona fide NHL stars: Dominik Hašek, who was, without a doubt, the best goalie in the league, and scoring star Pat LaFontaine. But it was a team in the midst of big changes. And John had stepped away from his coaching duties to focus on managing that transition.

Coaching a team during a rebuilding phase could present significant challenges, not least of which was being the guy people blamed in the likely event that the team did poorly. Hartford had shown me that the pros were a much less collaborative environment than Junior A, where, as a coach, you had a lot of say in which players are brought on. Sherry in particular trusted his coaches to choose their rosters. In the pros, the GMs made the player decisions. Coaches were expected to manage with the players they were given, and yet if things didn't work, the GMs could point to them as the problem rather than look to their player selection. A coach had responsibility without the power.

But I sure wasn't going to turn my back on the opportunity. My time in Hartford had convinced me I wanted a head coach position in the NHL. Granted, since there was less responsibility as an assistant, I had been able to spend more time with the players—especially those who were struggling. Just like I'd found with the Superior State team and my earliest days with the Greyhounds, I enjoyed being the guy who reached out to players making mistakes and who helped them find solutions. As an assistant, you could be more lenient and supportive than the head coach—you could serve as a buffer.

In contrast, the head coach had to have a broader perspective, and when it came to a team's success, the buck always stopped with him. Sure, there was significant pressure in that, but Sherry had shown me that in order to deal with it, you had to be true to yourself and follow your instincts. Accepting the responsibility brought a kind of freedom. As soon as I'd found my own way, I was a better coach and produced better results. I discovered that setting the tone for the club was one of my greatest strengths—and something that was hugely important to me. There just wasn't enough room to have that kind of influence as an assistant.

And while part of my drive to take on a head coaching job in the NHL came from wanting to prove myself to others, this desire felt very different than the need I felt as a player. So much of my ambition back then was about answering all those racial slurs and putdowns that I'd received over the years—code for "You don't belong in the hockey world." But now I wanted to prove that I had what it took in the pros, because coaching was what I loved. I wanted to show I could do it at the highest level.

◆

The border guard might have been the quirkiest welcome I got, but it wasn't the most moving. That happened three days before training camp officially started in September.

A member of the Sabres ownership group, Jean Knox, was deeply interested in Indigenous history and culture. She'd worked with local First Nations groups and the State University of New York at Buffalo (UB) to plan a special welcome ceremony for me at UB's Alumni Arena. The event was open to the public, and it drew a big crowd of Seneca, Mohawk, Onandago and other First Nations folks from across northern New York State, as well as First Nations students from UB, Buffalo State University and Erie Community College, many of whom showed up in traditional dress. It was an extraordinary night. After dinner, I was presented with gifts, and a number of groups took to the stage to sing, dance and play the traditional Iroquois water drums. But perhaps the most meaningful part of the evening was the time I spent with several Elders from the region, listening to their stories about First Nation influence on the city's sports history.

Many people understand that the white buffalo that appears on the Sabres logo is a symbol of good luck, but they may not always understand why. All buffalo are considered sacred to First Nations people. They are often referred to as "medicine," as they once gave our people just about everything needed to sustain life: meat and fat for food; bones for tools and sled runners; hides for clothes, tents and drums; intestines for bow strings, thread and webbing; and on and on. Every part of a buffalo was used. For the First Nations of many parts of North America, if there'd been no buffalo, there would've been no us. The white buffalo, however, is an extreme rarity, and it holds a place of great importance to various First Nations of the prairies and plains, and in particular to the Lakota. In Lakota lore, the white buffalo woman brings tools of faith and guidance from the Creator to his people. And anytime a white buffalo appears, it is said, prosperity comes with it.

Despite the white buffalo symbol, the Sabres hadn't had a great deal of luck since their formation in 1970. They'd made it to the Stanley Cup finals only once in twenty-five years and came away empty-handed. That night at the welcome ceremony the Elders told me why.

Apparently, in the 1930s or 1940s, one of the best First Nations athletes in the area tried out for a Buffalo team, but because he was Indigenous the team wouldn't sign him. Upon hearing of this injustice, some of the Elders put a curse on all sports teams in the area. (The Buffalo Bills had recently lost four Super Bowls in a row, so it seemed as if the curse was still holding up.) Now that I had arrived, however, these Elders told me they were going to remove the curse.

The entire evening felt filled with meaning, as if finally my two worlds were coming together in a really significant way. Not only was Buffalo a city that had adopted a sacred First Nations symbol as its emblem, but my people could see one of their own taking a major role in this much-loved sports club. And maybe, with my help and the help of those First Nations Elders, the white buffalo might bring that promised prosperity to our team. Once again, I couldn't help feel I was right where I was supposed to be.

◆

Sandra and I were in our new Buffalo house less a month when we decided to move back across the border to a rented house in Stevensville, a small town that had become a suburb of Fort Erie, Ontario. Sandra felt the kids would adjust more easily to the move if we kept them in the Canadian school system. But that wasn't a knock against Buffalo. In no time after arriving, I'd fallen in love with the place. It wasn't just my warm welcome at the border, or the embrace of the local Native American community. Every time I walked down the street or entered a grocery store, I'd hear, "Hey, coach!" and be greeted with a wave and a smile. As the year progressed, sometimes people would congratulate me on a recent game, or they'd want to stop and give me a little advice. "You gotta work on that power play, coach." I loved that the fans felt part of the team and had so much affection for the Sabres. But even in the earliest days, before I was widely recognized, I knew that Buffalo suited me. It was a blue-collar town, full of hard-working people who'd faced tough times in recent years as factories were shuttered and industrial jobs disappeared. I felt I understood their struggles—and why their sports teams were so important to them. Sometimes, when I saw them shouting in the stands, I was reminded of my father, leaning against the boards of the Garden River rink on a cold afternoon, cheering for our players, finding a kind of pride and joy there, especially during difficult days.

◆

As training camp got under way, I started to get to know the coaching staff. Despite the clause in my contract that stipulated I could hire my own assistants, I'd been happy to let John Muckler make those calls. He'd selected Don Lever, who he'd worked with the previous year, as associate coach and Terry Martin, who'd been working with the Rochester Americans, as assistant coach. (John Tortorella, who'd been John's other assistant in 1994–95, had taken over as head coach for the Rochester Americans.) John was also very hands-on during camp, which was fine with me, as I needed to get my bearings. It was a great team, I felt, one that filled me with optimism about the future.

That said, perhaps my final interview for the job should have warned me that things were not going to go as smoothly as I had hoped.

That interview had been held in early July in the Buffalo office of Sabres president Doug Moss. Doug struck me as a flashy and high-flying guy, yet he was warm and welcoming at the same time. I'd enjoyed myself, talking with him.

Doug wanted to know about my background—where I was from, what my family was like, how I grew up. He wanted me to describe what kind of coach I was. Then he asked for my thoughts about the game.

"Well, you know, people describe hockey as a contact sport," I'd said. "But ballroom dancing is a contact sport. Hockey is a collision sport."

Doug laughed.

"When I was a kid, we couldn't afford to go to hockey games. So I get it: when people come to a game, it's a really big deal. They want action. They want conflict. No ho-hum playing. They want to be entertained."

At this, Doug was nodding vigorously. Clearly, he wanted a coach who knew how to get bums in seats.

"When I was coaching the Greyhounds," I added, "I was trying to create the hardest-working team in junior hockey. I'd like to build the

Sabres into the hardest-working team in professional sports." I assured Doug that my goal was to compete hard—and to win.

It really seemed like Doug and I were on the same page.

Doug, however, wasn't the only one asking me questions. John was the other half of the interview team. John had coached the Sabres for four years before stepping aside. Before that, he'd had an impressive run with the Edmonton Oilers, coaching at various levels for nine years (two as head coach) and winning three Stanley Cups with the team during Gretzky's glory years.

John's interview approach couldn't have been more different than Doug's easy manner. John was stiff and formal. He didn't seem interested in my coaching philosophy or thoughts about hockey as a spectator sport. Instead, his inquiries were technical and specific. What would I do if this happened in game? How would I handle this kind of situation?

I didn't see a paper in his hand, but I felt like I was being given an oral test and John had a sheet of correct answers stuffed in his jacket pocket. And I had no idea if I was on track for an A or an F. John's expression gave nothing away—except that he wasn't crazy about me. And it wouldn't take long after training camp wrapped up for me to see the first evidence of that.

♦

When I was first offered the job with the Sabres back in July, my brother Steve and I had sat around the campfire talking about what my new job might be like. Steve didn't mince words.

"What are you going to teach someone like Pat LaFontaine?" he asked.

It was a good question. Steve's words had been bouncing around in my head ever since. Just after I'd arrived in Buffalo for training camp,

I'd watched from the observation room as Pat skated around. The Sabres captain was an even more extraordinary player than I'd thought. His skating was so fluid it often seemed as if he was floating across the ice. Yet when he needed speed, he was off like a rocket, his acceleration almost impossibly quick. And then there was his scoring ability. Pat is the first person I ever saw put a puck in the net after switching from his right hand to his left. How in the world was I going to coach someone as talented as this guy?

Almost from the moment we were introduced, however, my fears faded. Patty's personality outshone his on-ice skills. He greeted me with a big smile, his openness and warmth instantly setting me at ease. He appeared genuinely excited about working together to lead the team, and from the very first days of the training camp, I could see what a gift Pat's captaincy was. He had a great rapport with the other players. As the weeks and months went by, I would notice how he checked in with all of them regularly and arranged for dinners out and other social events so the players could relax together and bond. He was supportive of the younger players, and the great trust and affection he'd earned from the veterans was as clear as day. From the start, he helped me get to know everyone, acting as an effective, supportive liaison between the coaching staff and the players.

Shortly after I met Pat, I called Steve.

"He's one of the most down-to-earth guys I've ever met," I said. "You couldn't meet a nicer guy than Pat."

So when John called me into his office one morning during training camp, I was not at all prepared for what he was about to say.

"I think it's time to name a new captain," John said. "Patty's been doing it long enough."

I was speechless. In my short time with the club, I'd been blown away by how well-loved Patty was. And I was a rookie coach—only just getting to know the team. If I'd taken Patty out, the players would have crucified me. The fans would have crucified me. And for good reason.

I finally composed myself and got out a few words. They were a bit blunt.

"No way," I said. "I may have been born at night, but I wasn't born *last* night."

John glared at me. We sat in silence for a while.

Finally, I said, "Well, who made him captain in the first place?"

"I did," John said icily.

"Well, then, maybe you tell him."

John's face was rigid with anger.

"Okay, we're done," he said.

As I left John's office, I had to wonder what he was up to. Did he truly believe naming someone else captain was the best thing for the team? Or was this some kind of test for me—a test to see how willing I would be to follow his every direction, no matter how questionable? Did he want to damage my relationship with the team? That was kind of hard to believe, but it certainly would have been the result of a move like that. Not surprisingly, John made no move to replace Pat.

◆

The season didn't get any easier from there. The home opener, the last one ever to be played at the old Aud arena, was a disaster. At the post-game press conference, I admitted that our play had been inexcusable and said I didn't blame the fans for booing and wouldn't blame them if they didn't come back. When I was hired, the marketing department had launched a big ad campaign with pictures of me standing with a clenched fist and the line "New coach, new team, new attitude." It was on my mind when I admitted that we hadn't exactly gotten off to a "new" start. Doug Moss came to me the next day and high-fived me for the fan-friendly quote.

While I was frustrated by the way we were playing, I was also frustrated with myself for the way I was coaching. For one thing, right from the start, John had been in my ear before every game. He told me who should be in the lineup, how I should put together the lines, who I should play when, how often and how long I should employ each player. I'd winced when I first saw that ad campaign, wondering if it might be a bit hard for the "old" coach to stomach. It may have been, but John clearly wasn't taking it too seriously. He was going to continue making coaching decisions, even if there was a new guy in town.

Yet despite that input, game after game it was obvious the team was struggling. Pat was in a scoring slump, and a lot of the other players seemed sluggish. We were going out each night and getting beat—and the energy level on the ice made it seem like we almost didn't care.

While I was trying to get to know the players and figure out some way to fulfill the promise of a "new attitude," John suggested that the way to go was to come down hard on them, especially the older ones. And I should do that publicly, so that fans knew I was cracking the whip.

I have to admit, I was finding the media scrums a challenge. Speaking in public was still an uphill battle for me—especially when I had to answer unanticipated questions. And as head coach, I was expected to talk to reporters after every game and often several times between games. There was also an hour-long sports radio show I had to do on a local station. A fellow from the Sabres PR department used to meet with me before the post-game interviews to tell me what to say. I knew that the interviews were part of the job, but I always felt they took away valuable time I could be spending with the team.

Maybe John was right: I could do the interview and guide my players at the same time.

In an interview I gave on October 22, I let loose, taking aim in particular at the lack of leadership and effort by the team's veteran players.

The morning after the article appeared in the local paper there was a knock on my office door. Garry Galley asked if he could have a few minutes of my time.

"We veterans have to take our fair share of criticism," he said, "but I'm not sure this is how you want to do this."

As soon as the words were out of Garry's mouth, I knew he was so right. When I was a player, I had never responded well to being yelled at. Nor would I have reacted well if I saw that kind of takedown in print. Humiliation may have made me stick it out so I could prove something, but it didn't make me play any better.

Besides, I didn't like who I was becoming. I wasn't a sergeant-major-type—I'd learned that while coaching the Greyhounds. When I first took on the head coaching job there and was faced with some truly dreadful game results, one of the trainers told me I needed to strike a harsher tone when the team did poorly. I knew what he was talking about: during my playing days, my teammates and I had been on the receiving end of plenty of profanity-laced tirades. I marched into the locker room after a game and tore a strip off the team. I yelled and stomped around and threatened, doing my best to imitate so many of my former coaches. But even as I was doing it, I felt like a complete jackass. First Nations people, or at least my Anishinaabe friends and family, are quiet folk in public. When not with our friends and families, we tend to use words sparingly, speak only when spoken to. And when we are angry or upset, we don't express those feelings at length, if at all. The ranting just wasn't me.

In the hours that followed, I kept seeing how the young Greyhounds players had looked at me while I was screaming. They looked angry, ashamed, defeated, uncomfortable. They didn't look determined or energized or ready to fight for a win. Intimidation and fury weren't me—but even more importantly, they weren't going to work. I was sure of that. The next morning at practice, I apologized. My outburst was uncalled for, I said. We were in this together. I was part of the problem as well, and as long as they were giving their very best every game, I would be behind them.

I knew that my harsh words about the Sabres veterans was another wrong step. I called a closed-door meeting with the team later that day and apologized. I tried to let them know that going forward, I would have their backs. And at the next press interview, I admitted that it had been a mistake to air my frustrations with particular players in public. I wouldn't be doing that again.

And then I got another reminder that my promise was worth keeping.

Just a few days after I made that public apology, on October 27, my dear sister Katie passed away.

Just before we left for Buffalo, I had gone to see her in the hospital. Katie had been battling health problems for many years, and she had been in and out of hospital for months.

Katie had always been a big supporter of mine—even if she didn't understand or care anything about my hockey career. In fact, during my first year in the pros, she'd made the long drive down to Kansas City with my mother so they could see me. I hadn't been surprised about the visit—but I was when they suggested they might come to the rink. When I lived in Garden River, Katie would sometimes give me rides to my games in the Soo, but she never darkened the door of the arena. Instead, she would go to the bingo hall for a few hours and then swing back by the rink to pick me up. In Kansas City, I looked for them in the lobby after the game. I didn't find them. Kansas City, apparently, had a good bingo hall. I was happy they'd spent the evening doing something they so enjoyed, but unfortunately that meant my mother would never see me play hockey.

I'd been visiting Katie all summer, reading her passages from *Keeper'n Me*, written by our good friend Richard Wagamese. It was her favourite novel. Before I left her this last time, she'd grabbed my hand.

"Treat those people down in Pittsburgh good, Ted," she said.

"I'm going to Buffalo," I told her.

She waved my words away. "Doesn't matter where you're going," she said. "Just treat the people good."

I had to smile. Katie may have known nothing about hockey, but she understood what was important.

In the days following her death, I found it hard to believe I had lost sight of her wisdom for even a moment.

◆

My relationship with the players evolved over that first season. While I wasn't going to engage in dramatic diatribes, I wanted to be honest and frank with them at every moment. And I felt they needed to know where they stood in real time. Nothing is worse than warming the bench for weeks with no idea why you aren't being played. Or being called into the coach's office days after the fact to find out what he thought of your last performance on the ice. When players did well, I told them. And when they goofed up, I let them know right away. If I took them out of the game, they always knew why.

I also realized that maybe I'd misjudged the differences between coaching junior and coaching pros. The Soo Greyhounds—they were just kids, really. The guys I was working with now were full-blown adults, many almost as old as I was. They were pros. At first, I thought that meant they had thicker skins than the junior players. But just because you've left your teens behind and are being paid big bucks doesn't mean you can't be demoralized by a few badly chosen words.

I tried to put my criticisms into context whenever possible. Sometimes, in our team meetings, when a comment I made was met with a raised eyebrow or a deep frown, I'd share some of my own history, slipping into stories of my childhood. In those early months, when I was trying to snap the team out its lethargy, I talked about how I never had control of anything when I was a kid—not what went on in my house, or whether I got supper, or how I was treated in school. (Jason Dawe still remembers me saying of some hardship, "It was better than a slap in the face with a wet fish.") What I *did* have control over was how hard I worked. And I discovered just what a powerful force of change hard work could be. It's easy to think you're putting in your very best effort, I would sometimes point out. But even though you're working hard, you might not really be working smart. I once told the team the story of the hungry wolf that had gone five or six days without eating when it spotted a rabbit. It sprang towards the rabbit, chasing it over bushes and under trees, but eventually the rabbit escaped.

"How did the rabbit outrun the wolf?" I asked. "Simple. The wolf was running for a meal. The rabbit was running for its life."

There's effort and then there's *effort*, I pointed out. We needed to bring more passion to the games on a consistent basis. We needed to be proud of the work we were putting into our game. And we needed to work smart as well as hard to really succeed.

I also raised the issue I'd mentioned with Doug Moss in my job interview. When the players weren't working as hard as they could, they were cheating the fans.

"You're getting paid a hell of a lot to play," I said. "The fans out there—most don't have that kind of money. They've had to save to buy a ticket. So when they come to a game, it's a really big deal. So let's give them a big deal."

When they didn't play their best, I added, they were also cheating themselves.

"Life isn't easy. But what we're doing here is. We get to play hockey for a living. Never take that for granted. Go out and do it while you have the chance."

My favourite meetings were always the ones where the inspiration and direction came from the players themselves. After my public blow-up at the team in late fall, I'd had team meetings two days in a row. During the first, I'd invited players to make suggestions for how we could improve our game.

"We can't overextend our shifts," one player volunteered. "We've got to get off the ice when we're tired."

"We can't keep turning the puck over at the blue line," said a second player. "Blue lines are our blood lines. We live or die by them."

A third player said, "We've got to take pride in the last minute of play."

The next day, we sat together and watched some recent game tapes. There was the first player, extending his shift. There was the second player, turning over the puck at the blue line. And there was the third player, skating without enthusiasm as the clock ran down. I wasn't trying to embarrass anyone. Nor was I trying to encourage finger pointing or blame. I was showing them the power of their own words. Now all they needed was to put in the elbow grease to make those adjustments. And if they supported each other, pulled together and always put the team first, those individual changes would contribute to an enormous team improvement.

The players seemed to respond well to my stories and encouragement, and by the end of the fall, their work ethic was on full display. It didn't always result in wins, but my first few years with the Greyhounds had shown me that transforming a club takes time. If effort stays high, the winless seasons can lay a good foundation for future success.

"Mark my words," I told the team, "we'll turn this thing around. We'll start to win."

It wasn't empty motivational talk—I really believed it.

◆

When Steve had asked me what I could possibly do for a player as skilled and as experienced as Pat LaFontaine, he was really pointing to one of the differences between coaching in the major leagues or in junior. In junior, you're guiding young players at what might be the beginning of a long hockey journey. In the pros, you're leading guys who may have played at the top level for many, many years. Unlike me in the minors, they don't usually need to be taught to bend their knees or use their angles. But what I began to see was that seasoned players might face other challenges—like being set in their ways or seeing themselves limited to a certain style of play.

Garry Galley, a twelve-year NHL veteran, was a terrific defenceman and a great leader on the team, but I thought he could do more. After the first couple of weeks of the regular season, I had taken him aside to talk about his game. I told him not to be afraid of doing what he was capable of doing. He was a strong enough defenceman to take a few chances offensively. And if he went out there and did that, I wasn't going to bench him if mistakes were made. I just wanted to see him push himself. That was all Garry needed to hear. By early November, he was the second-highest scoring defenceman in the league.

Fan-favourite Rob Ray was another player who I thought could play a different game. Rob was a tough, boisterous guy, always fun to watch, always willing to go out on the ice and mix it up. But that wasn't all he was. He was a darn good hockey player too. And I thought he should be allowed to exercise that skill more often. I encouraged him to resist dropping his gloves too quickly in his enthusiasm and only engage in penalty-earning moves for good reason.

Rob just needed a few words of support to do that. Other tough teammates needed to be convinced they were good players. Matthew Barnaby was one of those. Matthew often reminded me of myself as a young man, but he was trying to prove he belonged on the ice by fighting. I took him aside one day and told him I loved his work ethic but he needed to keep it under control.

"You can play this game too."

I put him on Patty's line to show him he was a much better winger than he knew. As soon as he gained that insight, his playing got stronger and stronger. (Knowing, like Garry, that he would be allowed to make mistakes without getting sidelined seemed to give him a boost. In the following year, when we were playing a game in Montreal, Matthew made a few major errors. I had to make him sit out the second period. But in the third period, as soon as we got ahead in the game, I put him back out. He came to me after the game with tears in his eyes and thanked me for giving him that second chance.)

We had a number of guys like Rob and Matthew on the team, players for whom fighting had become a habit. We did need men who were aggressive—we had a fairly limited number of skilled centres and wingers, and they needed to protect themselves and be protected. But I thought some of our very physical players were selling themselves short (and drawing too many unnecessary penalties).

I had the same conversation with a number of them.

"Look, you fight a few times in a season. How long do those fights last? A few seconds? A bit longer? Why are you concentrating on that? Why not concentrate on what you're spending the most time doing on the ice—stickhandling, passing and so on?"

I also tried to build the confidence of our rookie players. I noticed how some of the young fellows skated back to the bench looking defeated if they hadn't had a great shift, or would pop their head into my office after every session in the gym, as if to let me know they were putting in the hours, working hard. Their behaviour reminded me of the insecurity I'd felt when I started out, how I'd always tried so hard to win my coach's favour. So I encouraged them—players like Brian Holzinger and Mike Peca—to trust in their own abilities. I'd assure them that I could see they were working hard. If they wanted to spend a lot of the time in the gym, that was great, but they didn't have to do it to please me. And I tried to get them to trust themselves on the ice. "You don't always have to pass to the goal scorer," I might tell them. "If he's not there, you can shoot it yourself."

My way of coaching seemed to work well with most of the players, but maybe it didn't always sit well with the management. John had had great relationships with many of the guys. I know a number of them, like Brad, thought of him as a father figure. But his style was closer to the stern authority figure that was common in the NHL at the time, and occasionally he would say things or give me looks that suggested he thought I was being a bit too lenient with the players.

And maybe my coaching didn't sit well with *all* the players. You can't be the ideal coach for everyone. I've always thought that the game was about emotion, about passion. That was the way I played, and the way I coached. But, of course, some of the players may have felt no need to connect with their coach on a personal level. They might have preferred a more analytical approach to dressing room talks or didn't require a strong sense of camaraderie to ignite their drive. Perhaps there were players who found the stories I told in the locker room tiresome. What's more, despite the encouragement I gave to some players to do less fighting, I do like a scrappy, aggressive game, and some of the newer players, particularly those from Eastern Europe, while hugely skilled, played a different style of hockey. If I was playing Matthew or Rob or Brad, it wasn't because I didn't like other players—it was because they were playing with passion. But I'm sure there were one or two players who bristled at the choices I made about who got to play and for how long. Perhaps the person who bristled the most was John.

◆

It was late October and we were getting ready to meet the St. Louis Blues in Buffalo when my trainer came to me with a message. "Mike Keenan wants to know if you would like to meet him at his hotel for a drink after the game."

The trainer had worked with Keenan years ago and was apparently still in touch. I was thrilled that Keenan had reached out to me. In fact, I was thrilled I was even on his radar. He'd been coaching NHL clubs for over a decade and only two seasons earlier, before moving to St. Louis, he'd led the New York Rangers to a Stanley Cup victory.

When I got to the hotel bar, Mike greeted me warmly. Once our drinks came, he launched into some thoughts about his own coaching philosophy. Keenan explained a mathematical formula he liked to use. Its purpose was to help him decide how much time to give the different lines, but the upshot of it was that he always tried to make sure he made room for his third- and fourth-line guys to get on the ice—and to do that, he needed to cut back on the first line sometimes. I found this encouraging, given my own thoughts on the subject.

After giving me a few more coaching tips, Mike changed his focus.

"Always be ready to be fired, Ted," he said. "And always get fired when you have a year left on your contract, so that when you start somewhere else you're getting two paycheques."

He was already on his fourth NHL franchise as a coach (he'd get to eight during two decades in the league), and I guess his method meant a number of years with great income. But as it turned out, what worked for someone like Mike Keenan wasn't going to work for me.

◆

Trying to figure out how to deal with John's attempts to coach by proxy certainly made my adjustment to being head coach more challenging than it might otherwise have been. And it added to my already fairly high level of discomfort.

Despite my recent half year with the Whalers, the sheer luxury of the NHL world still came as a bit of a shock. I'd invested in some nice suits, and I got the expensive haircuts, but whether it was checking in at a five-star hotel or going up to the "Aud Room," the after-games lounge at the Buffalo Memorial Auditorium, to mingle with the owners and corporate sponsors, I always felt a bit at sea. One day, at the end of a home game, I heard laughter coming from the Zamboni room as I walked past. I popped my head in to see what was going on. The arena staff were all gathered there, unwinding with a beer.

"Buck a beer, coach!" one of them said, inviting me to join them.

After that, I'd popped in as often as I could when we played in Buffalo, buying the guys a round or two, chatting about the game. It didn't take long for the management to figure out why I was so often late to the Aud

Room. They told me that I needed to spend less time in the Zamboni room and more time upstairs. I got it, but it saddened me anyhow.

♦

I loved Buffalo, I loved the work, I loved the team. I could see our potential—and that excited me. But trying to accommodate John was becoming exhausting. (My first win as head coach of an NHL team? Lost in a cloud of anxiety and stress—I formed no memory of it.) That said, I had sympathy for John's desire to continue making coaching decisions. If he loved that work as much as I did, I could imagine how hard it was to give it up. And I sure didn't envy him the difficult work it took to be the GM with a really tight budget.

Despite my frustration, I would never have characterized what was happening between John and me as a feud. In my early weeks in Buffalo, I'd decided to stop paying attention to what sports media was saying about the team. Too often, speculation and rumour seemed to get passed off as news. So I wasn't aware that a number of journalists were dramatizing the tension and regularly using that word, "feud." It may have surprised them—and the many people who have, over the years, commented on our working relationship—that I didn't see the coolness between us as an insurmountable problem.

After all, we weren't yelling at each other or being openly disrespectful. And we did share much common ground. We were in agreement about the need to get the team competing. We occasionally discussed which players should come up and which should be sent down, and more than once found ourselves on the same page. And I really did appreciate much of John's advice and hockey wisdom.

In retrospect, however, I can see why many thought our divide was more significant than I did. Professional hockey is a pretty tight world, and a lot of the coaches and general managers are on very friendly terms, if not downright friends. But at the time, I wasn't fully aware of that.

I was aware, however, that John wasn't a big fan of mine. That didn't feel great, but as far as I was concerned, just because we weren't hanging out after the game or golfing together on our days off, it didn't mean that, once we worked one or two things out, we couldn't combine forces, do our respective jobs and produce positive results.

What I really couldn't manage was the way John continued to issue coaching orders to me. By late December, after night after night of lying sleepless in bed thinking about how I no longer enjoyed my job, I found myself wondering if it was really all worth it.

I didn't want to walk away from a team and a city I loved, but what was the point of being there if the management wouldn't let me do the job the way I saw fit? Not being liked was one thing—being completely hobbled was another.

One evening, I walked through the door and told Sandra I thought it was time to hand in my resignation. Always the pragmatist, Sandra sat me down and talked it through. For one thing, there was the paycheque. On the most practical level, I needed the job and the income. Then there was the fact that I really did love the work. What I didn't like was being pushed to do it in a way that I didn't believe in.

"Why quit?" said Sandra. "Do the job the way you want to do the job, and if they want to fire you, they can. But don't just walk away. Go down fighting!"

I knew she was right. If I hadn't let myself quit in Kenora, why would I allow myself to do it now? I had to stick to my beliefs. If I was correct, the team would show improvement. If I was wrong, I would be happy to accept the consequences. But I needed to see this through.

The next day, I met with John in his office. As respectfully as I could, I told him I could no longer coach his way. I had to coach the only way I knew how.

He leaned back in his chair and stared at me coldly.

"Okay, fine."

The way John spat those words out, I was sure the management would shortly be letting me know my services were no longer needed. They didn't, but their silence didn't erase the suspicion that I'd just had my second strike at bat—the first being my refusal to take the captaincy from Patty. I had a sinking feeling a third strike might be in my future.

◆

Despite John's reaction to my announcement, I started back in the new year with renewed energy and a determination to follow my instincts. Sometimes, this took the team by surprise.

In early February, after we had struggled on the road for the entire month of January, we had a truly disastrous game against the Tampa Bay Lightning. The team seemed listless, making mistake after mistake, as Tampa kept the goals coming. We had at least three games on the road ahead of us, and this lack of energy had to be addressed. In the dressing room after the game, I came down hard on the team. At the end of my remarks, I told them that the following day would no longer be a day off. They would have to show up first thing in the morning for practice.

The next day, when I got to the rink, I could see that the players had gone out after the previous night's game despite expecting a "bag practice"—the usual skate-until-you-drop punishment following a really bad performance. Many of them looked tired. Once everyone had hauled themselves onto the ice, I told them to start skating—at their own pace. After a few laps, some of the players were chatting with each other as they took their leisurely turns past the boards. After about twenty minutes, I called them over to the bench and told them to skate in the other direction. While the first twenty minutes had been an easy skate, I could tell that this next round was getting to them. It wasn't just the monotony. Pushing a stick slowly around the ice can get uncomfortable after a while. A few of them were now shaking out their stiffening shoulders and occasionally straightening up to stretch their backs. I let them go for another twenty minutes, then called them back, only to tell them to head in the opposite direction for a third round. They didn't look too happy. I kept this up for close to two hours. Finally, I called them off the ice. Most of them were clearly mystified and frustrated by the slow, tedious practice. They would rather have skated until they fell over—it would have got them off the ice in half the time.

"Well," I said, "last night you wasted your time, you wasted my time and you wasted the fans' time. And today, I wasted your time— and your day off. Next game, let's get to work instead."

From the expressions on their faces, I knew they'd got the point. The practice had been just as boring as their performance on the ice the night before. And if they felt awful now, the fans must have felt exactly the same way.

To this day, when I talk to the players, this tends to be one of the first memories they raise—and laugh about.

That practice was unusual for a number of reasons. One was that I didn't like using training as punishment. Generally, I wanted the guys to enjoy the practices. I tried to change things up, the way I'd done with the Hounds, so the players weren't moving through the drills on automatic pilot. I'd never forgotten how, as a kid, I used to distract myself from worry and anxiety by running. Pros could be under a lot of pressure, and some of them battled anxiety too. And who could blame them? No matter how good you are, there are always other gifted players coming up through the ranks, dying to take your spot. And even if your stats are great, it just takes a slump to tarnish your record and make you vulnerable to the next cut or trade. No one is ever really secure. Defensive players had even more to be concerned about, it seemed to me. Goal scorers at least had the security of their points ranking. It was harder to quantify a defence-man's performance. On top of that, the tough guys and enforcers always had to worry about the opposition players coming after them. At least one player told me he could never sleep at night before facing certain teams, knowing that the opposing players as well as the fans would be expecting him to get into a brawl. So anything that got players out of their heads and their thoughts could be helpful. That said, while some of our practices were long, if the team didn't seem to be getting anything from the practice, I'd sometimes call it off after fifteen or twenty minutes.

And then there were all the things I didn't make them do. John, like many coaches, felt the way to get the best from the players was to push hard and relentlessly, never taking your foot off the gas pedal. This was before the NHL had introduced the mandatory two days off a month for players, so between games and practices, you could have the team on the ice every single day.

This just didn't make any sense to me. Players could work harder and be more focused if they were rested and refreshed. So I rarely, if ever, made a point after a bad game by imposing a follow-up practice that ran them down further, and I tried to give my players as much time off as we could reasonably afford. (Garry told me that in all his years in the NHL, he'd never had so many days off.) This seemed to drive John crazy.

"Another day off?" he'd sometimes say to me.

I couldn't help feel that while he may have thought I was being too soft on the players, he also thought I wasn't interested in putting in the hours myself. That I was just lazy.

♦

While the team's hard work didn't always produce the results we were all looking for, by mid-February a little string of wins against stronger, better teams really lifted our spirits. In particular, on February 23, we had a remarkable match against the Philadelphia Flyers. They were considered the best defensive team in the Eastern Conference—a big, bad bunch of players with the unstoppable force of Eric Lindros at the centre. There was no point in assigning one or even two guys to cover him—Lindros would just plow right through them, eventually wearing them right down. So we headed into the game with a pack mentality, Mike Peca in the lead. Peca, Rob Ray, Brian Holzinger, Jason Dawe, Brad May, Matthew Barnaby, the guys just bounced off Lindros, but they never got dirty and they never stopped getting in his way. They worked their tails off, hemming in Eric at each turn, frustrating his every move. And it worked. When the game ended in our favour, 7–2, I remember thinking, *Oh man, we're there.* We'd shown everyone we were a winning team. And one that could provide the gutsy, entertaining game I'd promised Doug Moss.

Despite that short flurry of wins, as end of the regular season approached, our chances for the playoffs began to shrink. John then began telling me not to play Dominik Hašek. This wasn't really a new message. All season long, he'd been telling me to use his recently drafted young goalie, Andrei Trefilov, more often. Andrei was talented, and I did want him on the ice. But unfortunately for Andrei, my approach about the importance of playing third- and fourth-line guys didn't extend to goalies. To give your team the best chance of winning, you really have to play your best netminder. And we had the most brilliant goalie in the whole league. I wanted us to win—it went against my nature to play with any other goal in mind, even if coming in last would give us a top pick at the next draft. When the mathematical chance of making the playoffs disappeared, however, I did bend to John's will and played Andrei more often. But the thought of putting the team in a position where they were more likely to lose a game, even a game that wasn't going to get us to the playoffs anyway, didn't fly with me.

I tried not to let a sense of resignation leak into the dressing room. We might not make the playoffs, I told the team, but we still had to compete as hard as we could—we needed to keep up the momentum and then build on it the following year. We could not afford to develop any bad habits or lose our work ethic. I was focused on the future—rethinking lines, rethinking ice time, making mental notes about how I might approach things differently and fine-tune my strategy. I wanted all the players to be doing the same.

At the end of the day, our hard work kept us out of the basement. The Ottawa Senators did us the favour of coming last in the Northeast Division, but we weren't too far ahead of them, with 33 wins, 42 losses and 7 ties. I was incredibly proud of how hard the team had worked to move the needle. There were a lot of games during the season that I thought we'd won, even if the scoreboard didn't reflect that. And we had done it all despite a spate of injuries. I was feeling positive and hopeful for the following year.

When the season was done, however, I received no vote of faith in that future from the management. I had one year left in my contract and was not offered an extension. That raised the eyebrows of some sportswriters and fans—as long as things are going fairly well with a coach, a club usually tries to lock him in for a bit longer than a year.

John explained to reporters that the rumours of friction between us were completely false and that I wasn't getting an extension simply because I hadn't asked for one. When I heard about that later, I wasn't so sure. After all, I did have those two strikes against me.

By the time Sandra, the boys and I headed back to Garden River for the summer, I was wiped out. Probably more exhausted than I'd ever been in my life. I'd been concentrating so hard on getting through each game and each challenge that I hardly got to savour my experiences. It had been a tough year in so many ways, no doubt about it. But my experiences in Buffalo had also lit a fire in my belly. The desire I'd had at the outset to prove I had what it took to turn the team around, that I had what it took to be an NHL coach, hadn't left me. It had gotten stronger, in no small part because of the closeness I felt with so many of the players. The guys, as great a group of men as I've ever met, all wanted to win, and I wanted the chance to be there with them when they did.

11

RISE AND FALL

WHEN I WAS A LITTLE KID, I don't remember seeing any big trophies. As I got older, I received a few soda-bottle-sized individual statuettes, but that was it. Some of the leagues I was in must have had towering silver cups, and I'm sure there was a glass-fronted case in one of the high schools I went to, showing off sizable sporting prizes. But I don't recall anything like that. And sadly, I don't remember seeing the Calder Cup when the Adirondack Red Wings won it—although I must have. The first major trophy that sticks in my mind is the J. Ross Robertson Cup for Ontario Hockey League champions—the trophy the Greyhounds brought home in 1991. When that cup was presented to us, I remember thinking, *Yes, that's what we've been fighting for.* And when I saw the Memorial Cup a year later, the same thought crossed my mind. I'd always wanted to win with any team I coached or played for. But the idea of becoming a *champion*, of winning it all, that took a while to come. By the time I started coaching with the NHL, however, it was firmly on my mind. As I said to Doug Moss before I'd started on my journey with the Sabres, I wanted the club to be a winning team in the NHL. I wanted us to bring home the Stanley Cup. That was what I was thinking about as the team and I embarked on our second year together.

I was feeling optimistic as we began training camp in September 1996. The coaching staff had designed an intense off-season fitness regimen for the players (the previous year, some of the players had arrived a bit under-conditioned). So the guys returned ready to go. And we were now settled into the brand new Marine Midland Arena. We also had some new coaching help.

Before the second season started, I exercised my right to bring in my own assistant coach. I kept Don Lever on—he was extremely good and had helped me immensely in the previous year. I loved working with him. I'd really enjoyed working with Terry Martin too, but felt I needed a really strong technical partner to balance the coaching team, so I'd hired my former coach from my Greyhounds playing days, Paul Theriault. I wanted his skill as a tactician, especially his expertise on defensive zone coverage, but I also valued his calming influence.

John was continuing to struggle with the need to cut costs. His choices for the roster would not have always been mine (although the previous season he'd taken my suggestion to add defenceman Bob Boughner, who'd been such a fearless, hard-working competitor for us in the Soo). But we had a good group of players, and I tried not to think about what-ifs.

Despite all those positives, the season got off to a slow start. Patty was struggling to score, the team wasn't coming together well on the ice and attendance in the stands seemed to be slipping.

Going into our October 17 game, against Pittsburgh, we'd won only one game out of five.

And then disaster struck.

During the game, Patty was blindsided by a high hit to the head from six-foot-six, 250-pound defenceman François Leroux. The blow was so powerful that, despite Pat's helmet being strapped on tight, it came unhooked and flew off as he spun around. When he fell to the ice, his bare head hit with force, knocking him out cold.

It took a few minutes for Pat to come around. When he did, he sat out for the rest of the game. I would later learn that he remembered nothing until after the game was over.

This was Pat's fifth major concussion that he was aware of. Chances are that he'd had more. But Pat made no complaints. He was checked out by the team doctors and was back in the lineup in our next game, a home match against Montreal. Watching him, I could tell something wasn't right. He seemed unfocused and a bit tentative. He wasn't playing like his usual self. A number of games went by, and while I kept asking how he was feeling, Pat assured me again and again that he was okay. But he didn't seem to be doing any better. I benched him several times but would eventually put him back into the game. Even with less ice time, Pat could still make great contributions. Then, in the dressing room after a game against Philadelphia in early November, Pat apologized to the team for his poor performance. He seemed distraught, and there was a strange glaze to his eyes. He didn't look or sound like himself. He didn't seem well. I'd been having my doubts, but now I was certain he shouldn't have been playing all those games.

The next day, I called him into my office.

"Are you feeling okay, Patty?" I asked him.

He began to apologize again. "I have to play better."

"No," I said. "Something's not right. I don't care what the doctors say. Something's not right. I'm not playing you again until you're well."

At that, Pat's face crumpled and he began to sob with relief. I was struck by his reaction, a show of vulnerability that made it crystal clear his suffering had been even more severe than I'd imagined. He would later tell me that since the hit, he'd been battling terrible nonstop headaches, insomnia and confusion. During the Philly game, everything was moving too fast for him—he couldn't keep up and was no longer sure what was happening on the ice, which terrified him. I wasn't surprised he'd pushed himself through all of that, but I was sorry that his dedication to the team had made it so difficult for him to open up about it.

We were heading out to Hartford the following day. I suggested that while we were gone, Pat should rest. Then we called his wife, Mary Beth, to come pick him up.

As soon as word got out that Pat had been scratched for the next game, John called me. He wanted to know why. No one could ever accuse me of coddling injured players—I often encouraged guys to work through their aches and pains. But I explained to John that in this case something was *seriously* wrong.

"You're not a doctor," John barked. "We pay that guy five million dollars. He's been cleared, and he's going to play."

"No," I said, "he's not."

This wasn't something I was going to debate. I said goodbye and hung up.

That night at home, I got a call from one of the owners. We had essentially the same conversation I'd had with John. It was a polite but tense exchange. When I hung up, my resolve hadn't weakened, but I had a sinking feeling I'd just had strike three. I'd refused to follow a directive from the GM, and I'd refused to do what the ownership wanted. The chances I would see another year with the Sabres now seemed pretty slim.

In the team's absence, Pat visited his own doctor, who then referred him to the Mayo Clinic. There, he was examined by six different specialists. They expressed shock that he'd been playing hockey after his hit. He shouldn't have been doing anything at all, they said, given his injury, never mind a contact sport. Significant swelling in his right frontal lobe meant another blow could have resulted in permanent and significant brain damage.

To explain Pat's absence for the Hartford game and the one that followed, the Sabres announced he was receiving a week off to recover from "exhaustion."

By the time Pat was having his tests done at the Mayo Clinic, however, Larry Quinn, the new team president (Doug Moss had been let go at the beginning of November), held a press conference during which he explained that Pat was being examined to determine whether he was suffering from post-concussion syndrome. Anyone could have been forgiven for assuming that the team had sent Pat for the tests, rather than Pat having to undertake his own medical investigation. And while Larry admitted publicly that I'd taken Pat out of the game even though he'd been cleared to play, there was no thank-you coming my way from any of the team ownership or management. Instead, all I got was the cold shoulder from just about everyone in power.

Pat's diagnosis would keep him out of the game for the rest of the year. The loss of our star player was a devastating blow to the team. Of course, we missed his scoring, but even more than that, we missed his positive, supportive friendship on the bench and in the dressing room. I appointed Garry Galley, Rob Ray and Brad May as co-captains. Garry would be a wise, thoughtful guide; Rob would serve with no-nonsense authority; and Brad, ever positive and big-hearted, would bring a calming, brotherly energy to his leadership. While this captaincy team did a terrific job when Patty couldn't be with us, I missed Pat's intuitive, compassionate understanding of the other players and the way he effortlessly created a link between them and the coaching staff. Yet to this day I think pulling Patty was, without a doubt, the best hockey decision I ever made.

◆

The events around Pat's concussion helped reinforce my trust in my own instincts. In the previous season, I'd tried to coach my own way, but it had been a struggle. I'd ended up following John's directions more often than I liked, even after putting my foot down.

But now, after Patty's injury, I committed to doing things my way, thoroughly and completely.

Coaching, I believed then, and still do, is simple. All you need to do is score one more goal than the opposition. A coach's job was to make that happen by inspiring emotion and hard work. One book brought this idea home for me in a powerful way.

When I had first stumbled on *Sacred Hoops* the previous year, I'd thought it was a book about Indigenous spirituality. And it was, but not quite in the way I expected. Famed Chicago Bulls coach Phil Jackson was writing about his coaching philosophy, which included allowing his personal spiritual beliefs to influence his coaching style. In the macho world of professional sport, where war analogies and a kind of military toughness are common, he wrote about the way Buddhism and First Nations culture and spirituality shaped his work. He talked about bringing medicine pouches to the locker room, putting arrows over the doorways and doing stretching circles with the players. He talked about inspiring his players by drawing analogies between sports and the spiritual world.

That book inspired me. But it was a player, Alexei Zhitnik, who gave me the opportunity to put Jackson's spiritual focus into action in the NHL. Around the middle of March, Alexei approached me with an unusual question. He'd just watched *Dances with Wolves* and wanted to know if I was an "Indian" like the ones in that movie. Then he mentioned that he'd heard that some teams had Buddha statues in their dressing rooms.

"Do you think a Medicine Man would be more powerful than Buddha?" he asked.

When I said I didn't know, Alexei asked if we might give it a try.

I checked in with Patty first to see what he thought.

"Why not?" he said.

I called Jake Pine, a traditional healer, who I knew from Garden River. His nephew was one of my best friends. Jake worked the north shore of Lake Superior, providing counselling, holding Sweat Lodges and conducting healing ceremonies. Near the end of March, Jake drove down to Detroit, where we were playing the Red Wings.

This wasn't the first time I'd had a chance to involve one of my people in the Buffalo hockey world. During the previous season, Jean Knox had asked me if I knew anyone who might come down and sing the national anthems in the Ojibway language. I remembered a twelve-year-old girl, Crystal Shawanda, who'd sung beautifully at Katie's funeral. I called her folks on the Wiikwemkoong First Nation, on Manitoulin Island, to see if she'd be interested in coming to Buffalo. Since that time, Crystal has gone on to have a remarkable blues and country recording career, winning a slew of music awards, including a Juno. Yet her Ojibway rendition of the national anthems in Buffalo, when she hadn't even hit her teens yet, was about the best thing I've ever heard her do. It certainly was the most moving anthem singing I ever witnessed. And it had left me bursting with pride. I was excited about the prospect of introducing another bit of Ojibway talent to the team.

In the dressing room before a practice, Jake talked to the players about First Nations culture and spirituality. Then he switched to Ojibway, leading us in a ceremony that asked the spirits to give us guidance and strength and help us walk with a good heart. As he did, he burned sweetgrass, sage, cedar and tobacco. While the fragrant smoke drifted around the room, Jake smudged any player who was interested. It was so quiet, you could have heard a pin drop. When the smudging was finished, Matthew Barnaby came up to Jake. He'd been in a scoring slump for a while. When he asked Jake if he could help him, Jake sprinkled a bit of tobacco on Matthew's stick. We lost that game 2–1, but it was Matthew who scored our single goal.

That ceremony was one of the most powerful moments I've ever had as a coach. In the pros, so many different kinds of experts are brought in to help players: conditioning coaches, physiotherapists, massage therapists, psychologists, doctors. It was an amazing experience to add ancient wisdom and healing to that bounty.

♦

In the second half of the 1996–97 season, despite some injuries and struggles on the road, we seemed to be turning a corner. In particular, the younger players, like Mike Peca, Derek Plante, Jason Dawe, Michal Grošek and Brian Holzinger, were really showing what they could do. In Pat's absence, captains Garry Galley, Brad May and Rob Ray were shining in their leadership roles. Bob Boughner was making our defence even grittier than it had been. Matthew Barnaby, who'd been our penalty leader the previous year, had transformed himself into our points leader by the end of December. And nine of his teammates had seventeen or more points. Truly, every player was showing up each night. And as the new year rang in, we were ranked tenth in the league, with 108 goals. At the end of January, we met with the Pittsburgh Penguins, who were first in the Northeast Division. Facing off against their top scorers, Jaromír Jágr and Mario Lemieux, we came away with a 3–1 win, with two goals scored by our penalty-killing line and Mike Peca putting the winning shot in the net. We followed that with an on-the-road victory over the Islanders. I was impressed, and even a little amazed, at what we were accomplishing.

"Have you ever walked on the train tracks before?" I asked in the locker room after one victory mid-January.

Most of the guys put up their hands.

"When you're walking on those tracks, you see the iron rails, the wooden ties and the gravel," I said. "And then you come upon a weed, growing tall right there in the middle of the tracks. Thriving in unlivable conditions. It has no reason to be there. But it is. That's us, guys. We have no reason to be here, but we are."

And we continued to do it. In fact, between the end of January and the end of February, we'd managed an incredible twelve-game unbeaten streak. And the fans were loving it. The previous year, there were plenty of nights when empty seats left yawning gaps in the stands. A few times, attendance dipped below nine thousand, leaving the stands almost half empty. But during the second season, once we got past our bumpy start, the arena was sold out or near capacity for every home game. In fact, when the regular season ended, we would discover we'd hit the all-time high for attendance in the club's history. The team was in good spirits; the fans were enthusiastic; we'd been playing well.

We'd also been plagued with injuries in the new year. At the end of February, seven of our players had been sitting out, including our backup goalie, Trefilov, and Patty, of course. By March, Patty had begun to join us for non-contact practices, though he was still not ready to play. And then Garry Galley and Richard Šmehlik got hurt, followed by Brad May. Next, Dominik had to sit out with cracked ribs, and Brian Holzinger broke a bone in his hand.

Our roster was getting a little thin. Perhaps not surprisingly, then, by late March, while we'd managed to earn a playoff berth with a 4–1 victory over Washington, with Steve Shields in goal, it looked like our chance to win the Northeast Division title might slip away. And yet, despite the setback, there was no finger pointing, no of loss of confidence, among the players. They were pulling together and feeling confident they could turn things around. But there were, perhaps, signs of trouble to come. Signs I didn't recognize at the time.

♦

Despite the promise I'd made to myself the previous year not to follow what the media were saying about the team or me, now and again friends and family would share something they had read or heard. I was largely able to keep most of the chatter out, which helped me concentrate on my job and probably saved my sanity. But it also made me fundamentally unaware of the story being created. If I'd known, I might have been able to lessen some of the damage it would do me.

Perhaps the most baffling bit of coverage, which I've only recently discovered, was a number of articles about contract offers that supposedly came my way in the early months of 1997, including an apparent three-year deal offered by Larry Quinn and the management team. At least one of the articles, in *The Buffalo News*, quoted Larry directly about an offer that was on the table. But I have no recollection of any of this.

I recently called Larry to ask about my memory of events. He confirmed that he never offered me a contract for any period in the winter of 1997. And he has no clear memory of any interview he gave to the press about offers. To this day, I have no real idea how that story made it into the papers. But what I do know now is that those stories left a certain impression with some people: I was the one turning my back on the franchise, playing games with the management to try to either sweeten the pot or parlay my success into a more lucrative position on another team. Nothing could have been further from the truth. If I'd been offered a multi-year contract, I would've jumped at it. All I wanted to do was stay in Buffalo and see how far the team and I could get in the coming years. I was fully committed to them.

The most persistent stories, however, continued to spin a tale about the tension between John and me, becoming increasingly alarmist as the season wore on. They quoted supposed insiders from John's "camp" and my "camp," although I can't for the life of me say who might have been talking on my behalf. Some of the things I've read recently about the way I was feeling seem to have been manufactured out of thin air. In a nutshell, there were two versions of our dynamic: John was threatened by my popularity with the fans and players and wanted me gone; the other take was that I didn't respect John, wasn't a team player and was trying to curry favour with the team ownership to subvert him. That last accusation is the most baffling to me. At one point, Sabres minority partner John Rigas flew me down to his house in Pennsylvania for lunch. I went because I was invited. We had a pleasant afternoon together, but I thought nothing of it. Jean Knox and I had become friendly after the welcome she'd help organize when I first arrived. When her husband, Seymour Knox III, died in May 1996, we'd met for lunch, and thinking about Jean's interest in First Nations culture, I'd given her an eagle feather. I thought it might give her strength—as it had to me. I certainly didn't see either of these engagements as ways to cozy up to the ownership in order to step over John's head about anything. Frankly, I had too much on my plate to do that, even if I'd understood how to play politics that way.

It really wasn't until after my time with the Sabres that I came to realize that in the suspicious and divisive world of NHL coaching and management, lunch invitations are never seen as just lunch invitations. If I'd understood that in Buffalo, maybe I would have thought more about a dinner Larry Quinn invited John and me to shortly after he became president. *The Buffalo News* apparently ran an article reporting that it was Larry's effort to make peace between us. I do remember the dinner. At one point in the evening, Larry said my job was to coach the team and John's was to build it. I couldn't have agreed more. To me, however, it was a pleasant, comfortable evening during which Larry was just sharing his management philosophy. But now I wonder if John wasn't a good deal more upset than I imagined—and if maybe the media was describing our relationship in inflammatory terms because they were picking up on the seriousness of the situation in a way I wasn't.

Some of those articles apparently mentioned the tension on the bench itself—the feeling some players had that they were expected to "take sides" in the "feud."

Pat LaFontaine was absent for chunks of this time, trying to focus on his post-concussion recovery, but I was in constant contact with the leadership team. They didn't report any trouble between team members. So I was largely unaware that there was any particular drama in the dressing room or backrooms. But in the years after my time in Buffalo, a number of players have mentioned to me and others that John complained to individuals about me or seeded doubts about my support of them and their careers. Other players have talked about the management encouraging players to take sides or criticizing my coaching to the players.

Despite not noticing much change in my relationship with John since the first season, I realize I did get one clear indication that more had been going on than I'd imagined. Sometime late in the season, I got a call from Bill Hughes. Bill, who I'd worked with for two years when he was the goaltending coach for the Greyhounds, was now an assistant coach with the Calgary Flames.

"Hey, Ted," he said. "What the heck is going on down there?"

When I asked him what he meant, he said he'd been told that I was drinking, that I was showing up for practices drunk. He didn't believe a word of it, but he thought he'd better call me just the same.

I was shocked into silence. Eventually I got out a few words.

"Where'd you hear that?"

He said his GM had told him.

I couldn't figure out why his GM would be saying anything about me, never mind something so flagrantly untrue.

"Where'd *he* hear that?" I asked.

The answer was almost more than I could take in.

"Your GM."

I got off the phone truly shaken. Could John have really said this? And even if he hadn't, if the GM of the Calgary Flames had just heard it and was repeating it, how many others were saying it? In the years to come, I'd discover that the answer to that was many, many people. In fact, the following summer, the father of one of Brandon's friends called to tell me he'd heard the rumour repeated on air by a popular Toronto sports radio host. The father had been so incensed by the accusation that he'd called in to say that he knew me and I wasn't a drinker. The radio host replied, "You don't know him the way we do," and then hung up on the guy.

I had no idea, in the winter of 1997, that there were other rumours floating around as well. And I sure didn't anticipate how tenacious the drinking rumour would end up being, but the fact that it even existed and was being repeated by coaches and management of NHL teams was completely devastating. It seemed that powerful people were willing to smear me by invoking an affliction that had ravaged many in my community and in my immediate family. My uncles and my brothers had been broken by alcohol. My mother's death was caused by a drunk driver. I found myself thinking, *Why can't they say I'm doing drugs? That would be easier to hear.*

And then there was the racism that fuelled that choice of slander.

Among the many things that made those first years coaching in the NHL challenging, perhaps the most startling was the fact that I clearly hadn't got away from racism. More than once, as I stood behind the bench, a player from the opposing team would skate by and sneer at me, sometimes dropping insults that I recognized from my playing days: the tomahawk chop, the war cry, the drunken swaying. These weren't young and ignorant Junior A kids. These were pros, many who'd long ago left their teens and early twenties. And I wasn't an on-ice opponent who they might hope to throw off his game with a little racism. It was a genuine shock to realize it made no difference at all that I was now the guy in the fancy suit, standing behind the bench. My position as coach did not leapfrog me past racism. In fact, maybe it made it worse. I was reminded of that by an exchange behind the bench with the coach of an opposing team. Things had gotten heated on the ice, and the coach and I had shouted a few things at each other as well. It was the kind of trash talk that happens all the time during a contentious game. I didn't think anything of it. Then I looked over at the other bench a few minutes later, and the coach raised his hand to his mouth and made the Hollywood Indian war-cry gesture at me. When he lowered his hand, he was smirking.

So, it wasn't as if I thought I'd left racism behind when I became a coach. What made it a shock was that such a cruel stereotype was being used to discredit me and the work I was doing. The rumour that I was showing up to practice drunk was not only nasty and lazy, it was also effective because of the racism it embodied. *Call him a drunken Indian. Everyone will believe that.*

Hearing about that rumour and who might be spreading it was like a sword in the gut. I was deeply and truly shaken, but I had to put the slander out of my mind as much as possible. We were near the end of the season, and I needed to focus all my time and attention on the team.

♦

John was still frustrated that I didn't play Andrei Trefilov more often. Andrei was frustrated too and had opted to have shoulder surgery at the end of December, meaning we had to bring up Steve Shields from Rochester. By the end of the season, however, Andrei had returned.

Before a late-season game, John once again told me to put Andrei in net. Yet the goalie was still recovering from surgery. I didn't want to take the risk. When John heard my thinking, he sneered at me.

"What? You think you're going to win the championship?" he said.

At another point around this time, I discovered that John had been advising Garry Galley to book a needed abdominal surgery right away. Garry was one of our very best defensive players, and losing him just as we headed into the playoffs would have seriously weakened our performance. When I talked with Garry, he said he wanted to see if he could make it through to the end of the season. We agreed to adjust both his game and practice time to make that possible. I didn't hear about it at the time, but apparently John was furious about that.

As the season progressed, it became clearer and clearer to me that the common goal John and I had seemed to share at the outset—the desire to win—was perhaps not so common any more.

I was recently shown a piece Jim Kelley wrote in *The Buffalo News* before the start of my first season as coach. He was reviewing the player departures, the result of trades and free agents leaving for more lucrative deals, between the 1994–95 season and the start of 1995–96 season. Kelley noted that both Muckler and Moss had admitted that the team might have to "take a step backwards for a year or two." Except that we didn't. The first year had been a slog, but we'd become known as the hardest-working team in pro sports. And during our second year, we'd really turned things around, putting ourselves in striking distance of a division championship. In other words, the management had been anticipating a retreat and we gave them an advance. An advance that not everyone seemed happy about.

I have no idea what the thinking was. Maybe, as I often suspected, the decision to show me the door had already been made, and the team's success would make that awkward with the fans and players alike. Certainly, our performance meant we weren't going to get the very top picks in the next draft. But I'd told Doug and John in my initial meetings that I wanted the team to win. And I meant it.

And we were doing just that.

The players and coaching staff, at least, were pumped about our success. The previous year, it had sometimes felt like we were trying, unsuccessfully, to push a boulder up a hill. This year, while we'd been considered a long shot initially to even get close to the playoffs, we'd moved forward steadily, despite injuries and scoring slumps. It was the kind of roller-coaster season that strengthened my confidence— and the team's confidence—instead of weakening it. We'd hit lows and risen from them—we'd faced setbacks and recovered. We'd survived and we'd thrived. Our morale was soaring.

By April 10, we'd made our way into the Northeast Division finals against the Boston Bruins, but no one was taking anything for granted. In our previous eight games, we'd suffered six losses and one tie.

So the focus on the bench in our first game opposite the Bruins was intense. Halfway through the second period, Miroslav Šatan got the first goal of the game, putting us ahead. That ignited a flurry of scoring. In less than a minute and half, Derek Plante, Darryl Shannon and Miroslav all sent pucks in. Dominik Hašek's brilliant netminding kept the Bruins to just one in the third period, when Randy Burridge scored the fifth goal for us. With our lead firmly in place, I decided that the last shift of the game should go to our veteran players, the guys who'd waited longest for this division win. Garry Galley, Rob Ray, Donald Audette, Brad May and Alexei Zhitnik were on the ice when the final buzzer sounded, and the rest of the players charged out to celebrate. The mood in the dressing room was ecstatic. Several players, including Rob and Matthew, had tears in their eyes. It was the first time the team had won a division championship since it had taken the Adams Division title in 1981 (and something the team wouldn't do again for ten years).

We were now the number two seed in the Eastern Conference playoffs, about to face off against the Ottawa Senators. The Senators had been at the bottom of the barrel the previous year (only their fourth in the NHL), but they too had improved steadily this season, with the help of scorers Alexei Yashin and Daniel Alfredsson. Although they ranked just third in the Northeast Division, they'd beaten us in the last game of the regular season to secure their playoff berth. Our hopes, however, were high. As far as I was concerned, we had the best goalie in the league, the stronger roster and a work ethic that no one could rival.

But something was off.

The day before we played Boston for the title, we'd had a light practice. Dominik was apparently upset by that. At the time, we didn't set up one-on-one goalie practices before games like they do now, so perhaps he felt I wasn't giving him the preparation he needed. But he didn't say anything to me, and it wasn't until some time later that I heard he had walked into the dressing room after the game and kicked over a trash can in frustration.

And then, as we entered the playoffs, things started to get really weird.

We played two games against Ottawa on home turf (winning one and losing one). Our third game was in Ottawa. Before the game, Dominik missed the team meeting. Then, during the pre-game warm-up, he seemed uncharacteristically agitated. After missing one shot, he smashed his stick against the goal post, which drew taunts from the Ottawa fans. During the second period, just after the Senators scored their first goal, Dom fell in his crease. When he got up, he skated to the bench, saying that he'd hurt his knee and couldn't finish the game. Then he headed to the dressing room. Brad and Ray followed him into the locker room to talk, but he didn't return. He came back out in street clothes to watch the rest of the game.

In the week that followed, I was told the local press were making a lot of how Hašek's injury was relatively slight, implying something else was going on with our goalie. They noted that he stood to watch the rest of the game. They commented on how quickly he walked when he left the follow-up press conference. They underlined that our team doctor referred to the injury as being minor but that Dominik had said he didn't know if he'd be back before the end of the series. They mentioned other times in the previous weeks when Dominik seemed to lose his temper at practice and in the locker room, and commented on the team meeting the goalie had missed.

The implication was that Dominik was upset about something—perhaps with me—and he was trying to make some kind of point. As the days unfolded, the idea took hold that Dominik and I were embroiled in a feud. I was flabbergasted by that. As far as I could tell, our relationship was exactly the same as it was when I first arrived at the club: professional and positive. I hadn't gotten to know Dominik as well as some of the other players, but I put that down to him being a naturally reserved and private person. I'd never picked up on any unhappiness or disrespect directed my way. And I certainly had none towards him. When he hurt his knee and said it was too painful to play, I was supportive of that decision. (I'd called him the day after the game to find out how he was doing.) And I didn't once question him about the seriousness of his injury, even after I witnessed him effortlessly jumping up and down to celebrate a ping-pong victory during one of our team R&R evenings a few days after that third game against Ottawa. Just as I didn't want Pat LaFontaine to skate when he was clearly struggling after the concussion, just as I had supported other players who got hurt and had to take time to heal, I wasn't going to pressure him to play hurt. In fact, by the time we got to game four with the Senators, the coaching staff and management had agreed that Dominik should go back to Buffalo rather than travel with the team. He needed the time to rest and recuperate, but he also needed to get out of the media spotlight and escape all the suspicious speculation.

But the rumours raged on. They were, apparently, so upsetting to Dominik and the management that the day before game five against the Senators, a press conference was organized. Without informing me first, John called all the players into the locker room and then invited the press in. Dominik read a prepared statement that affirmed his dedication to and pride in the team. John told the assembled journalists that while Dom would not be playing the next day, the management and team would be monitoring his fitness to play. Rob Ray spoke on behalf of the team, denying that there had been player doubts about Hašek's injury or his will to play.

That unfortunately was not going to be the end of the negative press coverage.

After game five, which we lost, putting us one game behind, Dom spotted *Buffalo News* reporter Jim Kelley outside the dressing room and, angered by some of the things Kelley had written, shared a few choice words with him. I wasn't there, and reports vary, but the incident was volcanic enough that the stories about Dominik only heated up again. And he received a three-game suspension, effectively keeping him from the rest of the playoffs.

It wasn't until after the season ended that I would discover that maybe I had misread our relationship—that even if Dominik's decision not to attempt a return to the playoffs and his displays of temper didn't have anything to do with me, his feelings were not quite what I had imagined them to be.

The stress all of this caused affected everyone on the team, including me. During one team meeting, I noticed the team's PR guy lingering around. A lot of what was said in the dressing rooms had made its way upstairs to John, Larry and the ownership over the season, and I'd suspected that this fellow was often the pipeline. I never had anything to hide, but the rumour mill about the Hašek affair had gotten to me, and I felt my trust evaporating. I told the fellow to get out.

"It's the men in this room right now who are going to win this game," I said to the team after the PR rep had left. "Not those guys upstairs."

The tension also showed up on the rink. By game five, players were looking grim as they sat on the bench, holding their sticks in white-knuckle grips. It seemed like some were even losing their confidence. Before game six, I told the team we would even it up, that there *was* going to be a game seven. I had absolute faith in that, and I wanted everyone on the ice to have confidence in it too. If they didn't, they didn't have to suit up.

To their credit, the guys rallied. Despite John's disapproval, I kept Steve in net. Even though Andrei was now able to play, he'd been in so few games since his surgery, it seemed wisest to stick with our rookie. And Steve did not disappoint us. He played his heart out, just like the rest of the team. We came through in game six in Ottawa and then headed back to Buffalo—the first ever playoff game seven for the club.

When the team headed onto the ice for the first period of that final game, things didn't look so promising. Stiff and perhaps a bit anxious, they struggled to make the plays, allowing the Senators a 1–0 lead entering the second period. But as the second period got under way, the team seemed to find their groove. On a power play, with about five minutes left in the period, Brian Holzinger took a shot. Senators goalie Ron Tugnutt knocked it back and Donald Audette put in the rebound to tie it up. Instantly, the energy on the bench ramped up.

Unfortunately, just forty-five seconds into the third period, Senators defender Wade Redden got one past Steve. Matthew Barnaby, Michal Grošek and Derek Plante were working hard to match that. They'd been my top line for most of the season, but Matthew's knee injury meant they hadn't played together for a while. They'd struggled a bit in the first two periods, and now they were gelling again. Our guys were outshooting the Sens, getting off shot after shot, but we couldn't seem to find the net.

Then Derek Plante and Alexei Yashin faced off in front of the Senators' net. It seemed like Derek was attempting to pass to Michal Grošek. Yashin tried to pull the puck back, and when he did, he sent it hurtling towards his own net and right past a surprised Tugnutt.

That bit of good luck gave Matthew, Michal and Derek an extra boost of energy as we headed into overtime. About five and half minutes in, Derek took a forty-foot shot from outside the right faceoff circle. Tugnutt raised his glove, catching an edge of the puck. The puck tripped off the leather and into the net. It was a terrific victory, and perhaps one of the most exciting hockey games of my life.

There was only one sour note that whole evening.

At Derek's goal, the arena exploded. I leaped over the boards along with everyone else on the bench and ran out to throw my arms around player after player. Between backslaps and hugs, I made the mistake of looking up at the jumbotron. On the screen were images of the roaring fans, jumping up and down, cheering and waving. Then the camera cut to the owners' box. There was John and a number of the owners and management, standing motionless, their hands at their sides. There wasn't one smiling face. You would have thought they were at a funeral.

♦

Round two of the playoffs didn't go quite as well as our run with the Senators.

We knew we couldn't out-tough the burly Philadelphia Flyers. Instead, we'd have to rely on the speed of guys like Mike Peca, Brian Holzinger and Derek Plante to face the bruising lineup of Eric Lindros, Mikael Renberg and John LeClair. As another of our quick skaters, Donald Audette, told a *Buffalo News* reporter, "If they can't catch you, they can't hit you."

Our very first match, in particular, was a tough one. While we started off with a two-goal lead, things soon unravelled. The Flyers tied it up, and then, with a few seconds left in the second period, one of our players turned over the puck and Mikael Renberg scored to put them ahead. At one point, tension on the ice was so high that opposing goalies Steve Shields and Garth Snow got into a brawl in front of the Buffalo bench.

In the third period, there was scramble in front of the Flyers' net. One of the Philly players knocked centre Wayne Primeau into the crease just as Rob Ray put the puck in. After reviewing the action on video, officials decided Wayne hadn't tried to get out of the crease fast enough. The goal wasn't counted. In the final minutes of the game, I pulled Shields from the net, but we didn't score—they did, leaving us with a 5–3 loss. Our only consolation was that we had kept Eric Lindros and John LeClair scoreless.

Our second outing was stronger, but we were playing without Mike Peca, who was suffering from back spasms. (And of course Hašek was still out.) We narrowly lost, 2–1. By game three, Donald Audette was also on the injured list, leaving us with no first- or second-line centres.

Game three was also preceded by some strangeness. Our first two games had been in Buffalo, and there'd been some friction between the trainers of the two teams about how cold the Flyers' dressing room was. Then before game three in Philly, some of our players arrived a little early for the pre-game practice skate. Apparently annoyed by that, the Philadelphia arena staff turned the rink lights off on us at the beginning of our skate time. We waited a few minutes, and then I just gave up. I'd held Greyhounds practices in the dark before—on purpose. We could do it again.

"Let's get out there and skate anyhow," I said to the team. "No reason not to warm up a bit."

The first few minutes of the practice were a little tough on Steve, our goalie, but the rest of the players seemed to kind of enjoy the twilight atmosphere on the ice. Jay McKee even taped a penlight to the

LIFE IN TWO WORLDS

top of his helmet. It reminded me of those puckless drills in the Soo—
everyone doing their best despite missing an essential element of the
game. After four or five minutes, the lights came up again, but at the
hour mark they were snapped off.

That night, unfortunately, we didn't play our best and lost, 4–1.

They fooled with the lights again the next day at morning practice.
But if the Philly management were trying to throw us off our game, I
think they did exactly the opposite.

In game four, Dominik Hašek still felt unready to play, but Mike
and Donald were in the lineup again. The entire team dug deep. And
Steve Shields was in top form. That hard work had us ahead 4–3 in the
third period. With just six minutes left, Steve fell on top of a puck that
had entered the crease, trapping it under his pad. But no whistle was
blown to stop the play. With Steve on the ground, Mikael Renberg
dug under the goalie pad with his stick, poking the puck loose and
into the back of the net. I argued with the ref that the goal shouldn't
count, but the scoreboard lit up with the tying goal anyway.

The team went back out and battled until the buzzer sounded, and
then went into overtime with renewed energy. At the 6:24 mark in
overtime, Garry Galley took a long shot from the left point. Flyers
goalie Garth Snow blocked it, but right winger Ed Ronan was ready
for the rebound. Ed had played only eighteen games for us in the
regular season, having spent most of his time with the Rochester
Americans. But he was a seasoned player, a great role player, who was
always a real workhorse, even if he was only on the ice for a shift or
two. And this game, he made a huge contribution. His goal won
Buffalo its first ever playoff game against Philly and our first second-
round win since 1983.

Despite the fact that we had only one win under our belts, bringing
the series back to home ice for game five kept us upbeat.

During that final match, the team gave it their all, half of them pushing through healing injuries or fresh ones received during the game, until every bit of energy was spent. (One reporter described the dressing room as looking like a M A S H unit.)

For the first time, I put Brad, Rob and Matthew on a line together. I'd dubbed it the "Dog Line." Unfortunately, they were not particularly effective offensively, but I knew their aggressive, spirited and highly entertaining play would give the whole team an extra spark.

But we simply weren't a match for the Flyers. The "Legion of Doom" line—Lindros, Renberg and LeClair—had nine shots on goal in the very first period. In the second period, Lindros collided with teammate Alexei Zhitnik and fell on top of Steve Shields, knocking him unconscious for a second of two. After a few minutes' break, Steve insisted on returning to the net, where he faced a barrage of shots from LeClair and Lindros, with three of them finding the net in quick succession. Michal Grošek answered for us, followed by two goals from Randy Burridge. But the Flyers kept scoring,

In the end, Philly retired us for the season, 6–3. Despite the fact that we were underdogs, that none of the journalists or other sports pundits expected us to win against the Flyers, everyone on the team, myself included, was crushed by the loss. More than a few guys broke down in tears in the dressing room.

We'd had quite a year. All season long, the press had been dubbing us "the hardest-working team in the league," just like I'd hoped they would. We'd made it through the first round of the playoffs without Pat LaFontaine, our big scorer, or Dom, our brilliant goalie. We'd been competitive because everyone was contributing. Some of the biggest contributors weren't the most highly skilled players on the team, but they'd made a huge difference. At one team meeting earlier in the year, I'd talked to the players about how Sitting Bull had repeatedly stood up to the encroaching US Army, despite being outgunned and often outmanned. His perseverance had finally led to the defeat of General Custer at the Battle of Little Bighorn. That kind of resolve and faith would see us through. I felt as if the team had really taken the message to heart—we'd accomplished so much more than anyone thought we could.

The evidence of the players' hard work wasn't just in game tallies—it was there in their individual stats too. Many of the guys had a great year. Brian Holzinger not only scored the most goals of his NHL career, he also hit his highest points total (51). Derek Plante scored 27 goals, the highest total he would ever get in the NHL. Brad May had his second-highest goals and points totals in his eighteen-year NHL career. Matthew Barnaby racked up 43 points, the pinnacle of his time in the NHL, with 19 goals by the season's end. (For a guy who spent as much time in the penalty box as he did, that was quite a feat.) We tried desperately to give him enough ice time in our final games so he could get that twentieth, but the goal never happened. Donald Audette posted his third-highest points and goal totals in what would be nineteen years in the majors. Mike Peca improved his total from the previous year by 18 points. Garry Galley posted one of his highest plus/minus totals in his twenty years in the NHL. Darryl Shannon saw his best NHL points number; Mike Wilson posted his best plus/minus; and Alexei Zhitnik his second best. Honestly, I couldn't have been prouder of the guys.

And the team had done all this, had achieved far beyond expectations, despite the fact that their young coach was still on a learning curve when it came to the technical side of the game. All year, I'd struggled with running power plays; my approach to penalty killing could have been more effective; and I was still figuring out the best positioning of my players.

I couldn't help feeling that with the player attitude we'd developed, and some improvement in my own coaching skills, we'd be unstoppable the next season. But I wasn't sure we were going to get the chance.

♦

The first two weeks in May were an emotional seesaw. On May 8, I learned I was one of three nominees for the Jack Adams Award for NHL coach of the year. Three days later, our playoff season ended with that crushing loss. And then, just three days after that, on May 14, John Muckler was fired.

I was shocked when I heard the news. Sure, it had been challenging working with John, but I didn't think he deserved to be let go, and I knew his firing would not work in my favour. Don Cherry was one of the first people to call me a "GM killer," although he certainly wasn't alone. In fact, that label would follow me for the rest of my career. Yet the claim was so absurd it was almost funny. With the exception of bringing in Bob Boughner during the first year, I'd had virtually no influence over which players would be on the team and which wouldn't. I sure didn't have the power to get one of the *management* sent packing—even if I'd tried. And, of course, I never did. Not once did I complain about John to the Knoxes, to Doug Moss or Larry Quinn, to John Rigas. I respected him and his hockey knowledge. I thought he was an asset to the club, even if I couldn't follow his every instruction.

John's firing left me in limbo. Larry Quinn told the press that while he'd like to see me return, it would be up to the new general manager to make that decision. It took almost a month before the person who would apparently decide my future was hired.

♦

Darcy Regier's hiring as the new GM was announced on June 11, 1997. The next day, he invited me to his office to meet for the first time.

When I walked in, Darcy was reclining in his chair, his legs crossed on top of the desk. He didn't straighten up. I sat down, and Darcy began to talk. I'm not entirely sure what he said or how I responded. All I can really remember is the sight of his sock-covered feet and the way he folded his hands behind his head, stretching out as if he was watching TV in his rec room.

One of the Ojibway Seven Grandfather teachings is mnaadendi-mowin: respect. It's represented by the buffalo, which, I have to say, felt a bit ironic in that moment. Now, I'm well aware that different cultures have different ways of showing respect. In many First Nations communities, it's considered disrespectful for a young person to make eye contact with an Elder when the Elder is talking. That has often led to problems when First Nations youth have interactions with settler authorities—their reluctance to look at teachers or police officers can be misinterpreted as indifference or a challenge. But I'd been operating in the white world long enough to know that whatever was meant by the shoeless feet on the desk (at best, a sign of informality), it wasn't a gesture of respect. I left feeling distrustful and even more uncertain of my future than I was going in.

◆

About a week later, on Thursday, June 19, Sandra and I attended the NHL awards ceremony at the Metro Toronto Convention Centre. My brothers Tom and Joe joined us as my guests. Joe was still experiencing hard times in those days, and I'd given him one of my suits and had it tailored for him. I'd also invited them to use the free hotel room that I'd been given. (Joe emptied the mini bar and took the fruit basket. Later, he pawned the suit.) Brandon's elementary school graduation was the very next morning, and Sandra and I wanted to make sure we were back in St. Catharines in time. But even if we hadn't had any other engagements, I don't think I would have wanted to be anywhere other than home after the ceremony. I was anticipating that it was going to be an awkward evening.

And I wasn't wrong.

When Sandra and I entered the reception hall, we could see the Sabres owners, management and other nominees clustered together in one part of the room. Jean Knox pulled away from them to come and say hello, but no one else from the management even looked my way. I spent most of the night chatting with Sandra and my two brothers and feeling like an unwanted visitor at the party.

When the Jack Adams nominees were named, I waited to see which of the other coaches—Jacques Martin of the Senators or Ken Hitchcock of the Dallas Stars—would be called on stage. When my name was announced as the winner, I was genuinely stunned. I took to the stage trembling with emotion. Of course, I knew the award had come to me because of all the Sabres players had done and the incredible help I'd gotten from Don Lever, Paul Theriault, Pat LaFontaine and the rest of the captaincy team. But frankly, as I stood before the microphone, I was mostly thinking of my people: all my First Nations forebears whose spirit and strength had helped me get to this point in my life. I also felt a deep yearning for those who weren't with me but who would have loved to have celebrated this moment: my mom and dad, Rod, Katie. To be honest, I also felt pride in my accomplishment—but it came with no joy.

I hadn't prepared a speech. All I could choke out was, "This is unbelievable," and a thank-you, and then I left the stage.

That wasn't the only award to come the Sabres' way that evening. Mike Peca won the Selke Trophy for best defensive forward and

Dominik won the Hart Memorial Trophy for MVP, the Vezina Trophy for goaltender of the year and the Ted Lindsay Award for outstanding player. It was the most league awards the Sabres franchise had ever won. It should have been one of the most festive nights of my life. But all evening, I sat at the table, just desperate to get out of the place.

Once the hardware had all been given out and all the photos taken, Sandra and I said goodbye to Tom and Joe, and then, still having spoken to no one from the Sabres, we left the conference centre and headed home.

◆

The Tuesday after the awards ceremony, my phone started buzzing. The calls were coming from family and friends who wanted to know if I'd heard about the radio interview Dominik Hašek had given the day before. Asked if he wanted me to return to the Sabres, Dom had said, "To be honest, no. For me, at least, I hope he won't be there."

When pressed to explain, he was blunt: "I cannot respect him. That's my problem. I don't want to play for someone I don't respect."

I felt like I'd been hit by a bus. Those earlier articles about our "feud" had felt so off base that I'd tried not to think about them. I had no idea he was unhappy with me as a coach. Sure, there had been moments when I knew he'd gotten a little upset about a shortened practice or two. Sometime later, I would recall a time during our first season together when I heard Dominik make a disparaging remark about an opposing player, and I had told him I didn't want to hear that kind of talk in the dressing room or on the bench. But I hadn't thought any of that had created any animosity. His heartfelt condemnation in the interview felt as if it had come right out of the blue.

And then, a few days later, on June 25, while I was still reeling from the Hašek interview, I got a phone call at home in the evening. I was already back in Garden River for the summer. The caller was *Buffalo News* sports reporter Jim Kelley.

"Ted," he said, "I hear that Regier is offering you a one-year, no bonuses contract. What do you think of that?"

I didn't know what to think—except to wonder why the first I was hearing about a contract offer was coming from a journalist and not the general manager.

"Jim, for hundreds of years, my people lost their land because they were forced to sign treaties they couldn't read or understand," I said. "But I can read and understand a contract. I should have been given this offer in writing instead of hearing about it from you."

Jim told me that a news conference was being held at nine thirty the next morning at which Darcy Regier would make the announcement about the offer. I told Jim I was disappointed and that I'd hoped the Sabres would show a little more faith in me. Then I got off the phone.

I didn't get the official offer until just minutes before the press conference. Darcy phoned and quickly outlined the deal. He explained that he didn't know me and the one-year contract would allow us to see if we could work together.

That may have been true, but it didn't cancel out the other truth: the offer was an insult. In the world of NHL contracts, it was the weakest possible gesture. It seemed designed to force me to turn it down, a clever way to say to the fans and the team, "See? He turned his back on the Sabres organization, not the other way around."

"I can't accept it," I said.

As I hung up the phone, I wondered why Darcy and the owners hadn't had the guts to fire me.

The following day, there was a rally in front of the Marine Midland Arena. About four hundred protesters chanted things like "We want Nolan" and waved placards with slogans about keeping me in Buffalo. Jean Knox, attending with her daughter-in-law, told reporters that John Rigas had wanted to come as well but couldn't.

Apparently, a second rally was held the next day at City Hall, attended by the president of the Seneca Nation of Indians, Michael Schindler.

Darcy was quoted in the media saying I had rejected the offer but there was still room to negotiate. So when John Rigas called me a day or two later to tell me Darcy was flying up to the Soo on June 30, the day my initial contract expired, I assumed the organization had rethought their position and adjusted the offer. John ended the conversation by saying, "You guys should work this out."

As long as the offer was a good enough that I could return to Buffalo with my head held high, I wanted to do just that.

Darcy had taken a private plane, so when I got to the airport, I was directed to one of the hangars. As I walked up to it, Darcy came out and said hello. Then he got straight to the point.

"Ted, I'm just here to tell you that the offer is now officially off the table. I thought it would be more gentlemanly to tell you that face to face."

I could barely believe my ears.

"It would have only cost you a quarter to tell me that over the phone," I said. "It would have meant the same to me."

12

—

AFTER THE SABRES

THE DAYS THAT FOLLOWED THE END WITH THE SABRES were confusing and sometimes painful. In interviews after the one-year offer was withdrawn, Darcy apparently told a reporter from *The Buffalo News* that he had tried to call me all weekend but I hadn't taken his calls, even though I'd been talking freely with the media during that time. This, he said, convinced him we couldn't work together.

I don't know what to make of that. I was by the phone pretty regularly that weekend. I certainly would have taken a call from him if I'd received one. And I had an answering machine. There were no messages from Darcy.

Shortly after the press conference announcing the one-year offer, I got a call from Pat LaFontaine. Pat had remained an integral part of the team, including during the time when he could no longer take to the ice, and I'd continued to rely on his leadership and friendship. We'd become especially close since I had refused to play him back in November. He let me know repeatedly how grateful he was that I had stood up for him the way I did.

"Teddy," he said, when he called, "this doesn't make any sense at all. It's bizarre." Over the next while, I would hear from other players who voiced their surprise or anger at how things had played out.

John Rigas also called to say he disagreed with the decision. Jean Knox had already voiced her disagreement during televised interviews at the rally, invoking her late husband, who had also been part of the management group. "If Seymour were alive, this never would have happened," she said.

Of course, in the years since, some people have suggested that my rejection of the initial offer was short-sighted. Phil Esposito has even said publicly that I am sometimes my own worst enemy. Maybe he's right. Maybe I should have swallowed my pride and accepted the contract. At least I could have continued doing the work I loved, and had another chance to show I belonged in the league. Maybe, if I'd spent another year with Buffalo, I would have repaired any damage done to my reputation with the NHL power brokers and gone on to entertain big offers for the 1998–99 season. But as difficult as the following years would be, I never for a moment looked back and thought accepting that one-year contract was a real possibility. The insult of it, along with the rumour of my drinking and irresponsibility, had revived such dark memories. Each time I thought about those things, it was as if I was that seventeen-year-old kid in Kenora, confused and bewildered by people's resentful response to my very existence. If I had gone back to Buffalo, I would have questioned every interaction I had with the management, wondering all the time if they were hoping for me to fail, if there were people working against me in ways I couldn't even imagine. Despite the support of players and fans, I would have felt I'd betrayed and belittled myself, that I'd forgotten my father's words: "Ted, always be proud of who you are." If that offer from the Sabres had really been sincere, then I can only conclude that the management completely miscalculated how it would affect me and what it would have cost me to accept.

As the summer slipped by, I tried not to dwell too much on the past, but thinking about my uncertain future wasn't a whole lot easier. I played ball. I hung out with friends. I coached Jordan's peewee hockey team in a tournament. When late August rolled around with no new job on the horizon, we returned to St. Catharines, where we'd relocated during my second year in Buffalo, so the boys could go back to school and rejoin their hockey clubs.

That fall, I discovered that the slander about me being drunk at practices and another stupid rumour I'd heard about my supposed laziness weren't the only ones making the rounds. My Buffalo chiropractor invited me to a Bills football game. At the tailgate party beforehand, he blurted out, "I know why the Sabres didn't want you back, Ted. It's because you slept with Hašek's wife."

I couldn't believe what I was hearing. But my friend was adamant. "It's all over town, Ted."

I called Sandra right away.

"Hey, guess who everyone thinks I was sleeping with."

The idea was so absurd, it was tempting to shrug it off. But another completely innocent person's name was being dragged through the dirt. Dominik's wife, if she was aware of what was being said, must have been angry and humiliated. And what about Dom? Had he heard this rumour before we entered the playoffs? Was he upset that his wife was being slandered, and being slandered in an effort to damage a coach he might not even have liked that much? If so, no wonder he was so agitated at the end of the season. No wonder he took a swing at me in that radio interview. And, of course, there were the racist overtones again. If "drunken Indian" was the most common slur my people faced, the accusation that we were "whores," both men and women, was probably the runner-up. (A number of years later, I would discover there were more rumours, including ones I'm not going to dignify by putting in print.)

♦

Finally, near the end of October, I got a call from Phil Esposito. He was now president, general manager and founding owner of the Tampa Bay Lightning, and he told me that he'd decided to let head coach Terry Crisp go.

"I'd like you to coach the team," he said. "But before I make you an offer, I just want to check. You don't want to be GM, do you?"

He was clearly referring to yet another rumour—that I had wanted to be both coach and GM of the Sabres.

"No way," I said.

Phil outlined the offer and said he wanted an answer in twenty-four hours, as he had other candidates in the wings. I didn't need twenty-four seconds. I wanted in. But I knew I should check with my family, so I told Phil I'd let him know as soon as possible.

When I got off the phone and excitedly told Sandra and the boys about the offer, I was taken aback by their reaction. Sandra was prepared to go wherever my career took me, but she was very concerned that Phil had asked me the GM question. She felt there may be some in the Tampa organization who were willing to believe the falsehoods about my relationship with the Sabres management, and that didn't seem like a good sign. The boys, however, were even more upset.

"Where am I going to play hockey?" Brandon said. He was beside himself. Jordan, seeing how upset Brandon was, started to cry.

Brandon had just turned fourteen, and Jordan eight, and they'd both been playing hockey for years. Brandon had recently moved up to the competitive triple-A ranks. But I knew that the boys' reaction wasn't really about hockey. They were both feeling settled in St. Catharines. They were at a school they liked—they had friends they didn't want to leave.

Any job offer that came my way would likely mean a move for my family, but Tampa did seem very far from home and very foreign. Relocating to another northern US city, or anywhere in Canada, would have sat more comfortably with everyone.

I called Phil and told him Florida was not a great fit for us.

◆

I hadn't wanted to turn down Tampa, but I had done so on the assumption that other teams would be in touch. Sandra was absolutely certain I would get another NHL offer. So I got off the phone, and waited to see what would happen next.

What happened was so much less than I had hoped for.

Over the coming months, a number of tiny carrots were held out, a few calls, a phone interview with the San Jose Sharks, a trip to Atlanta to meet with the Thrashers, but nothing actually offered. I also talked with folks at TSN about being an on-air commentator, and even did a trial as a commentator for NBC for a game in Philly, but I knew that wasn't for me. For starters, while I'd gotten better at interviews and public speaking, talking at length had never been my strong suit. And I was put off by the fact that a steady stream of information and trivia was fed to me through my earpiece during the game. It helped me sound more knowledgeable than I was, but it made me feel like a bit of a fraud.

After that small flurry of interest from various organizations, there was silence.

At the beginning, my agent, Steve Bartlett, had called around to a lot of teams, but he had got nowhere. And I didn't get on the phone myself to chase other positions or network the way some in my position might. Yes, often in the past, being told I couldn't do something had motivated me. But already feeling battered, I didn't want to hear "no" if I could help it. For my people, being told "no" is such a common occurrence, one that triggers so many bad individual and collective memories that it never becomes painless. I wasn't interested in seeking it out. To be honest, the idea that if you really want something you should continue to go after it, despite repeated rejection, strikes me as a belief that only a history of positive experiences with authority can support.

That said, I wasn't shy about letting the world know I wanted to coach again. In fact, when journalist Stephen Rodrick interviewed me for *ESPN* magazine in the spring of 2000 and asked about rumours that I'd turned down assistant coach offers, I quickly let him know that while there had been no such offers, I would have taken any that came my way.

"Tell people I'll wash pucks. I'll do anything," I told him. But nothing changed.

◆

Months of waiting turned into years. I couldn't make sense of it.

I'd won coach of the year, the league's highest honour for anyone behind the bench. I had done what I'd been hired to do. The team's performance had improved dramatically. So many of our players had improved their individual stats, and they had done so while pulling together as a team. We'd moved from the league basement to being serious playoff contenders. And we'd played the kind of exciting, entertaining hockey that I'd promised Moss and Muckler right from the start, filling the arena game after game.

Sure, I'd disagreed with my GM about a number of things, and I'd crossed upper management by pulling Patty from the lineup. But John Muckler and I had got things done in the club, and my disagreement with the owners about Patty wasn't public knowledge, as far I knew. Could the speculation about my working relationship with Muckler truly have scared off other clubs? Did other GMs and management really think that I'd work to get them fired? That I was a "GM killer"? Did the hockey world really think I was irrationally hard-headed and impossible to work with? Did people really believe I'd been drunk at practices?

I just couldn't understand how those bits of misinformation could have ruined my reputation so thoroughly. So many coaches had disagreed with their general managers and owners but gone on to position after position. Even coaches who hadn't gotten along with star players had had long careers in the pros. I knew I was well liked by the men I'd coached. And the two protests, and countless angry letters to the editor in the local papers, were testament to the support I had among the Sabres fans. In the long history of NHL coaches, I could hardly be considered "difficult" or not a team player.

Sandra and I often talked about the strangeness of it all. We were both mystified by the silence.

♦

In the years following my time in Buffalo, I continued to work with Indigenous youth in a variety of ways, including travelling across the country to help out at hockey clinics and talking to kids at rinks, schools and community centres. But I was finding it harder and harder to do.

I knew that my disappointment with my NHL experience was nothing compared to the setbacks and roadblocks many Indigenous people faced all the time. Every trip to an Indigenous community reminded me of those vast challenges. But one visit to Taloyoak, Nunavut, made the point forcefully. Hanging out on the bench with the players as they undressed after getting off the ice, I noticed that when the kids took off their skates, the worn-out boots left rivet marks on their ankles. Yet it wasn't their poverty that most shocked me, but their words. They were all casually talking about siblings who had committed suicide. Not just one or two kids—it seemed to be everyone. And they treated it like it was a simple fact of life.

I was still feeling overwhelmed from everything I had seen and heard when I got to the Taloyoak airport. There, I noticed that one of the teenaged boys from the clinic had followed me. He was a good player, and I could tell he was looking for something.

"Have you ever thought about playing junior hockey?" I asked him.

He nodded shyly.

"I'll pass your name to some coaches," I promised.

As soon as the words were out of my mouth, his eyes filled with tears. He *had* been looking for something. He had been looking for hope.

I could, maybe, do something for this one boy, but what did I have to offer all the others? How could I tell them it was possible to compete in the outside world if I wasn't able to do it myself? How could I keep bringing a message of hope when I didn't believe it anymore?

By the time I got home, I was in a deep, dark place.

◆

I had no work. No opportunity to show what I knew I could do. My whole life, I'd felt compelled to prove people wrong. When they said First Nations kids didn't belong in junior hockey, I showed them. When they said First Nations players didn't deserve to be in the NHL, I answered that too. Now the hockey power brokers were telling me I didn't have what it took to make a championship team. Heck, they were telling me I didn't have what it took to be an NHL coach. And I had no way to prove them wrong.

But what was really making me feel lost was the absence of the job I adored. Ever since I was a boy, I'd imagined my adult self doing some work that made people's lives better. I'd found that in coaching. It was easy to make a difference when coaching Junior A. The players were young and inexperienced enough that there was always some way to help them improve their game. They were also often living far from home and sometimes lonely, often just struggling with the transition to adulthood. If you couldn't see ways to help out or be supportive on a personal level, you just weren't looking. But I'd found that even in the NHL being a coach provided great and varied opportunities to make a difference in players' lives. Of course, I was still attempting to give back through public speaking, hockey clinics and various other efforts, but most of that work was fly-in/fly-out engagements—you never got to really know the people you were addressing or see how things worked out for them. Most of the work boiled down to providing "inspiration," and I'd pretty much run out of that.

Finally, in the spring of 2001, I hit bottom.

For the past twelve months or more, I'd felt completely dead inside. In the early years after leaving Buffalo, I'd been able to find happiness in family time and in some of the work I was still able to do. Now, I continued to enjoy the precious moments I spent with my sons, but everything else was muted. If I wasn't interacting one-on-one with them, it was as if everything faded. I was at home, I was around, and yet in a real way I wasn't there at all.

In the time since my firing, the many empty hours I'd had on my hands had allowed memories of losses and traumas, from both my youth and my adult life, to settle in my mind. Somehow, instead of leaving all those feelings behind the walls I'd built up, I'd become trapped inside the barricades with them. I didn't care enough to move outside again or to pretend any longer. I couldn't do it even for Sandra. One day, out of the blue, I announced to her that I wasn't feeling good about anything—including us. I could see from the look on her face that she couldn't quite believe what she was hearing. I went on to tell her that I hadn't been a faithful husband.

Sandra would later tell me that this news truly blindsided her. She had never once doubted my fidelity. The greater blow, however, was hearing that my heart was numb. And she was devastated—the boys and I were her world. The look of shock on her face eventually, however, turned to one of concern. I suspect she was worried about my mental state as much as about our marriage.

"Why don't you go back to Garden River," she said. "Go home and figure out what you want."

I knew she was right. Our relationship was in tatters, and I was the one shredding it to pieces. I didn't know how to change, how to return to my old self. If I stayed, I would only continue to hurt her. And so I left.

◆

In early May, I arrived in Garden River alone. Despite being a forty-three-year-old father of two, I spent the spring days like a teenager—hanging out with friends, playing pool and being moody. I knew from our brief phone calls that Sandra and the boys were having a difficult time without me, but I was in no state to do anything to help.

When the school year ended, Jordan came to stay with me for about a month, but Sandra and Brandon remained in St. Catharines. And then, on Friday, August 3, 2001, yet another family tragedy hit. My sister Arlene's daughter Lana, Lana's husband, Keon, and two of their daughters—Brianna, aged nine, and Shania, aged five—as well as another granddaughter of Arlene's—Karly-Ann Barry, aged six—were all killed when their car was hit head-on by a truck that crossed the centre line on the highway running through Garden River. Two passengers in the car survived: Lana and Keon's twelve-year-old daughter, Ashley, and her friend Katy Lynn. My sister was shattered, and everyone in the family was sent reeling.

I called Sandra to tell her what happened. She got in her car and drove to Garden River to be with me.

In the days Sandra and I spent together, we talked and talked. Sandra had always shared her feelings this way, but it was new to me. Despite all of Sandra's love and support over the years, I'd never let her into the walled area of my heart, keeping my most difficult feelings to myself. It would take me a few years before I could share the painful memories of my childhood and teen years with Sandra, but our conversations after my niece's death began to help me understand why I had behaved the way I did for so many years. It was finally dawning on me that my life seemed to have become a series of losses, things unexpectedly taken away from me: my parents, my siblings, my career, my reputation. Since Buffalo, I'd been waiting for the next theft, and unable to endure the waiting, I'd made that loss—the loss of my marriage—happen myself.

Despite that revelation, I was still in no shape to return to Sandra or work on fixing what I had broken. Sandra went back to St. Catharines alone.

◆

It would take several more months before I felt ready to return to my family, and several more years for our family to begin to heal. But with Sandra and the boys' patience and forgiveness, and our shared love and prayers, we started the long and continuing process. To this day, I'm shaken by the thought of how a dark episode of my career laid me so low that I almost walked away from the people who were most important to me. And I'll never take for granted how lucky I am to have them still.

My reconciliation with Sandra moved me back into the light. But it was a movie that actually helped me find a way forward. Early in 2002, I went to see the biopic *Ali*, starring Will Smith. Of course, I knew Muhammad Ali's story—how he refused to fight in Vietnam but also refused to flee the States to avoid the draft and the inevitable punishment he'd receive for failure to report for duty. Convicted, stripped of his boxing titles, he managed to stay out of prison but was unable to fight for four years while his conviction was appealed. Four years lost in the prime of his career.

There was something about seeing all that play out onscreen that blew me away. Ali's willingness to sacrifice for what he believed in reminded me of my boyhood heroes. And while I would never have compared my actions or my career to those of Ali, I felt I understood a little of what he'd been through when both his livelihood and the work he was passionate about were taken from him. What stood out for me most, however, was the contrast between the ways we responded to our losses. According to the film, Ali had never quit believing in himself.

I'd made a vow to myself, back in Kenora, that I wasn't going to be a quitter. Yet, in a way, I'd become one. I'd quit believing in myself. I'd quit believing in the power of hard work and dedication. I'd quit believing that my people and I could overcome.

I couldn't stop thinking about the film—and about how I'd been living for the last five years. A few days after seeing the movie, I went into the basement storeroom of our Garden River home. There, shoved into the corner, was a battered and dusty cardboard carton. The Jack Adams trophy. I pulled the box to the edge of the shelf and opened it up. The replica cup had broken off its base. I wasn't ready to repair it. I certainly wasn't ready to display it. But I lifted the pieces out and put them on the shelf. Then I took the box upstairs and threw it away.

◆

Seeing the Ali movie was like having a light bulb go on. During the years I'd been playing pro hockey, my friend Les Couchie and the Union of Ontario Indians (now called the Anishinabek Nation) had helped start the Ted Nolan Golf Tournament. With the proceeds, we awarded education scholarships. After a few years, my late friend Ray Martin and his staff from Southern First Nations Secretariat (SFNS) continued the golf tournament. This kind of charitable work, I realized, could be my future. There were so many more positive things I could do with the celebrity I'd gained from my hockey career.

I began to talk to Ray Martin about how we might expand our efforts. With his help and that of the SFNS, we established the Ted Nolan Foundation in 2004 and assembled an amazing board to oversee the operation. The late Joe Maione became our treasurer. Other members would eventually include my nephew Joe Tice, Cam Campbell (who worked daily on the website), Al Pigram, Robert Irving, my son Brandon, Phil Fontaine, Candice Paul, Kim and Ron Hansell, Juliet Kennedy, Jan Martin, my brother Steve Nolan and Glenn Nolan. (Without Ray Martin, Les Couchie and these amazing board members, our foundation wouldn't have been possible. We also got great help from Gino Cavallo and Dennis Martel, who contributed in the early days of our golf tournaments and then any time we asked for any assistance once the foundation was running.)

This dedicated team decided that the mission of the foundation would be to support the healing process for our young people by promoting a healthy lifestyle that renewed and revitalized the mind, body and spirit. The organization would also provide training for a new cadre of Aboriginal leaders.

But I wanted to add another element to our mission. Since my mother's passing in 1981, I'd been looking for ways to honour her memory. I had never forgotten her influence on my life; I wouldn't have become the person I was without her guidance and love. In my mind, there was no better proof that women were the real strength in our world than my mother, Rose Nolan. A great way to acknowledge this, I decided, was to have the Ted Nolan Foundation provide scholarships for First Nations women who were seeking to improve their lives through education and training. And so the Rose Nolan Scholarship was born. Running it kept Sandra and me busy.

◆

Over the next several years, people would periodically ask me if I wanted to coach again. I always said no. What I'd missed most about coaching was the feeling that I was giving back to people, that my work made a difference. And I'd found another way to do that with the Ted Nolan Foundation. Added to that was the gift of working with the terrific team we assembled to run the foundation.

Attending Sweat Lodges, participating in traditional spiritual ceremonies, I began to talk with God again. I also continued my work with Indigenous hockey schools. My relationship with Sandra deepened and strengthened. And I watched with joy as my sons grew into wonderful, accomplished young men.

I was happy. Happy to be home. Happy to be living a good, purposeful life. And happy with the world I'd finally made for myself.

13

THE UNSPOKEN RULES

WHEN I STARTED WORK ON THE TED NOLAN FOUNDATION, I really believed I was done with league hockey. That turned out to be a little inaccurate. In the spring of 2005, I would be drawn back into the professional coaching world for a stretch that spanned nine years—first to coach with the Quebec Major Junior Hockey League's Moncton Wildcats, then a return to the NHL and the Buffalo Sabres via the New York Islanders, and even a stint as the coach of the Latvian Olympic hockey team in between.

All of those experiences were marked by the highs *and* lows I'd experienced in my previous coaching career, and in many ways they helped me put my earlier career into perspective.

In the years between my first Sabres job and my return to coaching with Moncton, almost every time I met new people—at golf tournaments or speaking engagements or hockey schools—one of the first things they would say to me was, "Hey, Ted, why aren't you coaching?" I would respond with something about bad luck or waiting for the right opportunity and try to move on to another topic. One afternoon, while I was at the airport in Toronto, a little First Nations girl came up to me and pointed to my face.

"I know why you aren't coaching," she said. "You're too brown."

I smiled at her and shook my head. I told her that wasn't right. But I couldn't get her words out of my head. It felt as if they had peeled away the excuses I had used to muffle my own suspicions.

I began to wonder just how deeply racism had affected my career. Did an unconscious bias make it easy for managers and owners to believe that I was drunk or sleeping around? Did deep-seated assumptions about the social hierarchy make my differences of opinion with management particularly unacceptable? Was my desire to coach my way seen as uppitiness?

I mentioned this to Sandra at the time, but she didn't see it that way.

"I don't think racism has anything to do with why you aren't getting called," she insisted, when I mentioned my suspicions.

That response disappointed me. But perhaps I shouldn't have been surprised by it. Sandra has many virtues, but the strongest is her generosity of spirit. She sees the good in everybody, and she will always look at things in a positive light until it's absolutely impossible to do that. So it makes sense that she would be less attuned to subtle or systemic racism—she always gives people the benefit of the doubt.

Sandra's mother, Shirley, was First Nations, of course, and certainly she bore the scars of intergenerational trauma suffered by our people. But Sandra was not aware of Shirley's personal history at the time, since Shirley had seldom talked about her childhood or her own parents' experiences while raising her girls. Having left home when she was so young, Sandra would only learn much later about the names Shirley had been called by white people and the hatred she had experienced because of her heritage. And then there was Sandra's father, Morley. Her white father had fallen in love with and married a Wolastoqey woman. Sandra liked to think that most people were like Morley—they might recognize differences but they didn't see any group of people as less worthy of affection and respect. And finally, Sandra was half white herself. She wasn't raised among her Wolastoqey relatives. She was raised in the city and grew up unaware of all the issues her First Nations family faced.

Sandra and I didn't argue about our differing perspectives. And I didn't really see her position as a lack of support. I knew she didn't want to see me hurting. She thought that if she discouraged me from feeling that racism was a factor, I would be less wounded by the silence I was experiencing.

Yet in the years after that conversation with Sandra, I would return again and again to the question of whether people in the hockey world saw me as an outsider and whether I was being treated differently than if I'd been white. One experience while I was coaching in the Quebec Major Junior Hockey League made it pretty obvious that even if racism had nothing to do with the silence I'd faced from professional hockey after Buffalo, it was still alive and well in some corners of the hockey world.

First, I have to say that the Wildcats was probably the best coaching gig I've ever had. I loved working with Robert Irving, the owner of the club, who gave me extraordinary freedom in putting the team together, assembling the coaching staff and trusting my coaching instincts. My time with the Wildcats renewed my love of the job and allowed me to prove once more that I could excel at it. The season I coached them, 2005–06, the Wildcats won the Quebec Major Junior

League Championship—a first in the club's ten-year history. And while we lost out in the Memorial Cup finals to the Quebec Remparts (whom we'd beaten in the league playoffs), the team earned 107 points in regular-season play, a club high that still stands. We also set attendance records that have yet to be broken. And I won the QMJHL's executive of the year award.

The only shadow over the year I spent with the organization was the reception I received from some of the fans.

During one of our early away games, a Shawinigan reporter asked me what I thought of one of the Shawinigan Cataractes fan traditions. The Cataractes logo features a caricature of a First Nations man in a feather headdress. Apparently, when one of the Cataractes players scored a goal, a mannequin dressed up like a cartoon version of a First Nations warrior would be sent flying across the rink on a wire. I told the reporter that I thought the practice was disrespectful. He countered that it was meant as an honour.

"What if someone made the mannequin look like Jean Chrétien and made him fly across the ice? Would that be respectful?" I said.

I appreciate that it's sometimes hard to distinguish between homage and mockery. A few years later, when I was coaching in Latvia, I was surprised to see Latvians in the stands dressed in First Nations headdresses. At first I wasn't sure what to make of it, although in the absence of war cries, tomahawk chops and jeering calls, the getups didn't seem meant to offend. Eventually, one of the people from the hockey organization explained to me that many Europeans were fascinated by North American Indigenous culture, and many joined clubs to study our stories, traditions and history. One of our Chiefs, who had been invited to talk with one of these clubs, later told me he didn't know whether to laugh or cry.

"Ted," he said, "some of them speak our language better than we do!"

While many folks would still find those Latvian fans guilty of cultural appropriation, if they were accompanying the dressing up with serious, respectful study of our history, beliefs and language, then I'm not even a little bit offended. In fact, I appreciate their interest. But the flying mannequin was a different story.

I'm not sure I convinced the reporter, but when the Cataractes did score during our game, no mannequin appeared, even if there were plenty of tomahawk chops and war cries from the fans that night.

I also told folks I found the "Tomahawk Song" sung by the Gatineau Olympiques to be offensive.

But if the Gatineau song and the Shawinigan cries were unpleasant, much worse was in store for me—and the team—a little later in the season in Chicoutimi, Quebec.

Our December 16 match against the Chicoutimi Saguenéens had barely begun when the air filled with "Indian" war whoops. Things were also being shouted, things I couldn't understand because they were being said in French but that had the unmistakable rhythm of taunts and jeers. I noticed that, along with the tomahawk chop gestures, fans were pretending to shoot arrows in my direction. In fact, none of the words and gestures seemed to be directed at the action or the players, just at me. Finally, I asked one of our players what was being said.

"Oh, coach," he responded, "you don't want to know."

The commotion in the stands seemed to infect the action on the ice, and before long the Chicoutimi players also began to shout things in my direction, upsetting the Wildcat players, who responded with words of their own.

Eventually, the refs managed to turn down the temperature on the ice, but nothing could quiet the fans. Verbal assaults turned into physical ones. The father of one of our players got roughed up pretty good when he jumped to my defence. The game had to be stopped several times to address the chaos.

Throughout the whole game, I bit my lip, trying to stay calm, trying to set an example for my players, trying not to fuel the fans any further or give them any excuse to say, "You see, those people can't control themselves."

The crowd didn't stop, even when the game was over. When I exited the arena, guided by a police escort, a group of adults was waiting for me, and they hurled insults as I walked to the team bus. By the time I took my seat, I was trembling with fear and rage and the effort not to respond.

When I was finally alone later that night, I called my brother.

"Steve, you're not going to believe what happened," I said. "It made Kenora look like child's play."

The incident hit the papers, and the Saguenéens management issued a formal apology to me a few days later. My experience apparently also prompted the QMJHL to develop an anti-discrimination policy for players, teams, league officials and fans that year.

But it wasn't enough to make me feel much better about an evening that was, without a doubt, the most humiliating experience of my life. I've never gotten over seeing those grown adults with their faces twisted in loathing or the fact that a parent got hurt trying to defend me. It was all agonizing. And it proved that as much as times seemed to be changing, they hadn't changed enough and they hadn't changed everywhere.

◆

Nothing like the Chicoutimi incident ever happened again, but over the years there have been events that made me feel as if my character was doubted by those in positions of power in hockey. And there have been others that made me feel like I was trying to walk through the door of a private club where I wasn't a member.

After the Tampa offer, I waited four years to hear anything from an NHL franchise. Then I received three interviews in two years, each odd in its own way.

In the winter of 2001, the Islanders were looking for a mid-season replacement for head coach Butch Goring. Apparently, in early February, during an open meeting with season ticketholders, Islanders owner Charles Wang had thrown my name out as a possible option. A few weeks later, the GM, Mike Milbury, called me to talk about the position. Then he offered to fly me to Long Island for an interview.

When Mike and I met at his office at the arena, things seemed to go well, and yet there was something about our conversation and the topics Mike brought up that left me uncomfortable. When we'd finished talking, Mike said that two of his staff would be taking me out for dinner. Not Mike, just two fellows I hadn't met. I tried to shrug off the strangeness of that, but when my two dinner partners drove me out to a bar—not a restaurant—my unease mounted. When we got into the bar, it didn't seem like one of those places where people go because it has surprisingly decent burgers or something. It was just a bar. *Why'd they bring me here?* I asked myself. I couldn't think of any good reason. I was tired. I was hungry. I had no desire for a drink. I excused myself and grabbed a cab back to my hotel room. I didn't hear from anyone from the Islanders after that. Now, I can't say exactly what was happening there, but it did feel like a test, and not one that I expect many other coaching candidates were given.

Then, in the spring of 2002, Glen Sather, famed former head coach of the Oilers in their Stanley Cup–winning heyday and then general manager of the New York Rangers, asked me to come down to Manhattan to talk about a possible coaching position. It wasn't much of an interview. Chewing on a cigar and leaning back in his chair, with his feet propped up on the desk, Sather clicked through a few generic questions about coaching, asked me nothing about myself and then thanked me for coming. I knew before we had even finished talking that I'd flown over a thousand kilometres for nothing. I suspect someone had suggested that he interview me, and Sather, an old pal of John Muckler, was just going through the motions. In the end, he hired Bryan Trottier, only to fire him midway through the season.

More promising, however, was a call later that spring from George McPhee, general manager of the Washington Capitals. He was thinking of making some changes to his coaching staff and wanted to know if I was interested in a position with the club. In mid-June, after several long conversations over the phone, George suggested I meet him the day before the NHL draft in Toronto, which began on June 22. He gave me his room number on the tenth floor of a hotel overlooking the lake and asked that I not take the elevator. He didn't want any other hockey personnel or reporters spotting me.

After I'd walked up ten long flights of stairs and into George's room, we exchanged a few general greetings. George got off the couch and walked over to me, hand extended.

"Ted, it's time you started coaching again," he said. "Congratulations."

And then he told me to go out and buy myself a new suit.

"We're going to introduce you as our new head coach at the draft table tomorrow morning."

I was buzzing as I drove back to St. Catharines to tell Sandra. After five long years, I was once again getting the chance to do what I loved doing. As soon as I broke the news to her, we raced out to the mall and bought that new suit. Once we got home, Sandra, still bursting with excitement, decided to run out and do a few more errands. So I was alone when I got a call from George at about six that evening.

"I'm sorry," he said, "Leonsis has overruled me. We're giving the job to Bruce Cassidy."

Ted Leonsis was the owner of the Capitals.

I'm not sure if I asked George for an explanation or if my silence prompted him to give one.

"He just likes Cassidy's name better," George offered.

He didn't explain what that meant.

When Sandra got home a while later, she found me in our bedroom, lying down with my face buried in a pillow.

I was devastated, completely devastated. Something wonderful had just been put in front of me and then snatched away, as if someone was playing a cruel joke. After I told Sandra what had happened, we sat together in silence for a long time, both lost for words.

In the coming years, I would deal with that crushing disappointment by pretending the whole thing never happened at all. In fact, until now, I've never mentioned the offer or its sudden withdrawal to a soul. It was one of the things that convinced me to let go of my coaching hopes for good and embrace my new life with the Ted Nolan Foundation.

Years later, Leonsis would give me a vague apology along the lines of "We decided to go in another direction." His true motivation will remain a mystery to me, but the withdrawn offer certainly cemented my feeling that there was an inner circle and I wasn't in it.

There was one more far less devastating but nonetheless strange interview in my future. After my successful run in Moncton and my two years with the Islanders, during a period when I was living in Rochester, New York, and working with Curt Styres, from the Grand River First Nation, on his newly acquired sports franchises, the Rochester Americans hockey club and the Rochester Knighthawks lacrosse team, I heard that the Soo Greyhounds were looking for a new coach.

"Hey, Sandra, do you want to go home?" I said. "See me coaching the Greyhounds again?"

I had such great memories of the staff, the fans and the players from my earlier Greyhound coaching days.

"What do you think?" she answered.

I called up someone in the ownership group and said I was interested in the position.

I should send in my resumé, he instructed me. There wasn't a flicker of interest in his voice.

I was knocked back on my heels. Apparently, winning three junior league championships and a Memorial Cup for the Greyhounds, not to mention my performance with the Wildcats and four years of NHL coaching experience with the Sabres and the Islanders, wasn't enough to get me an interview.

I sent in my resumé.

A few days later, I called the Greyhounds management again and asked if they were interested in interviewing me. The fellow I spoke to offered only one appointment time. I told him I wouldn't be able to make it unless I flew. "We don't fly anyone up for interviews," he snapped back. That's when the conversation more or less ended. I got off the phone, stunned.

Once again, it's difficult to know what the management was thinking, but it was hard to escape the thought that the hockey world is a place where people are not necessarily judged on their merits, where rumours flourish, where assumptions are made and where minds often close and stay closed.

♦

My return to the Buffalo Sabres for two seasons, starting in 2013, reinforced another truth I'd come to see during my first round with Buffalo: the goal of the players and coaches—to win games—isn't always shared by the ownership and management. And when business considerations clash with the spirit of competition, it can create a destructive divide, challenging team morale and creating terrible stress for those who are actually playing the game.

My second stint with the Sabres, however, wasn't my initial return to the NHL. That had happened in 2006. I hadn't been looking to return to the pros. As a matter of fact, when I was coaching in Moncton, I'd turned down a mid-season offer from Charles Wang, owner of the New York Islanders, to join the club as head coach. I was enjoying my time with the Wildcats, who were on a tear, performing better than anyone could have expected. I didn't want to miss out on what was shaping up to be an extraordinary year, nor did I want to abandon the team mid-season—even if there was never another NHL offer. I was happy with the thought of staying with the Wildcats for the next year and beyond. But the following spring, I heard from Pat LaFontaine, who was consulting for the Islanders. Charles Wang had asked him for coaching recommendations, and he said I was the man for the job. I loved the prospect of working with Patty and trusted him completely. And I had to admit that as much as I'd been happy focusing on my foundation and happy again in the junior hockey world, a small part of me still hungered to prove that I belonged behind an NHL bench. I hadn't been seeking out the chance to do that, but now it was in front of me, I couldn't walk away. I accepted the renewed offer from the Islanders.

That summer, not long after I'd started working for the club, Wang fired his newly hired GM, Neil Smith, and replaced him with Garth Snow, most recently goalie for the Islanders. Patty then left his new position as director of hockey operations. I was very disappointed to lose the chance to work with Patty, but I developed a comfortable working relationship with Garth. Unfortunately, the club's performance over the following two years was less than hoped for, and at the end of the 2007–08 season, Garth decided he needed to bring on a new coach. Unlike my departure from the Sabres, my exit from the Islanders was civil and straightforward—the way transitions should be, as far as I'm concerned.

My third round with the NHL, a return to the Buffalo Sabres five years after the Islanders, was rockier.

◆

In mid-November 2013, I was coaching the Latvian national team in the hopes of qualifying for a spot in the 2014 Olympics. I was in Germany, where the team had just finished an exhibition series against Russia. I was getting ready to go home, hoping to pack up again a few days later so that Sandra and I could head to New York City for a little holiday. I'd called Patty earlier to see if he might be able to pick up some tickets to a Broadway play—I'd asked if there were seats left for *The Book of Mormon*. When I saw that Patty was calling me, I assumed he was following up on that request.

"You're not going to see *The Book of Mormon*," he said, when I answered. I thought he meant they were sold out. I was going to ask him what else was available.

"As a matter of fact, you aren't going to New York at all. You're flying to Buffalo."

Patty told me that the Sabres general manager, Darcy Regier, and the head coach, Ron Rolston, had just been let go. Patty had been hired as head of hockey operations and tasked with finding the new coach. He wanted me in the position.

I was speechless.

The idea of returning to a franchise where my reputation had taken such a beating would have been almost unthinkable if the offer wasn't coming from someone I trusted as much as Patty. But when I heard the excitement in Patty's voice, it sparked a hope that things might be different this time. I loved Buffalo. Perhaps I'd get the chance to do what I'd wanted to do fifteen years earlier—help the Sabres become a winning franchise. And Patty would be there, working with me to make that happen. As nervous as I was about rejoining a club that had caused me so much unhappiness, I couldn't say no.

Of course, despite the ownership group and Darcy's recent tenure, at the player level it was an entirely new team from the one I'd coached. After my departure sixteen years earlier, the franchise had continued to improve. Under head coach Lindy Ruff, they made it to round two of the finals in 1998, and right through to the finals the following year. After 1999, however, it had been a bit of a roller coaster. The Sabres failed to make the playoffs seven out of the next fifteen years, including two years in a row before I started back with them.

By the time I was hired, on November 16, it was pretty clear Patty and I had our work cut out for us. The team had lost seventeen of their twenty-two regular-season games. By early January, it seemed we were turning things around, having got a few more wins under our belt through December and the first week of the new year.

On January 9, Pat announced the hiring of Tim Murray as general manager. (Tim had been GM of the Binghamton Senators, an AHL affiliate of the Ottawa Senators.) Once again, I was in a position of working for a GM who had not hired me himself. But given that we were both Patty's picks, I was optimistic. It wasn't going to be an easy year, for sure, but I felt we were all committed to securing as many wins as we could as we tried to reinvigorate the club.

LIFE IN TWO WORLDS

At the end of February, Tim traded our starting goalie, Ryan Miller, and our talented team captain, Steve Ott, delivering a blow to our lineup.

But worse things were happening, as far as I was concerned. The upper management seemed to have turned against Patty and were, apparently, making ridiculous accusations about the way he was doing business. On March 1, Patty reluctantly resigned.

A few days after that, Tim made another flurry of trades. During my time with the Islanders, Garth Snow had been rebuilding the team, and I'd found the frequently changing roster a challenge, but I could see what he was trying to do. With the Sabres, it seemed different, as if a significant shift in approach was taking place. I was overcome with a deep sense of foreboding, which made the decision about my future with the Sabres especially difficult.

Around the time Tim had traded Miller and Ott, the management offered me a three-year contract. The move confused me. I knew Patty was likely on his way out, and I'd assumed that if he left, I'd be gone too. I couldn't shake the suspicion that accepting the contract was a bad idea.

When I coached my last season in Buffalo in the nineties, I'd heard a few people say that maybe they had hired me to be the fall guy. That, as a newbie coach, I could be pointed to as the culprit for a losing team instead of any weakness in their scouting and drafting operation. I'd never believed that. Now, however, adjusted a little for the current circumstances, this theory didn't seem that far-fetched. Was the club retooling in a way that would almost certainly guarantee we'd finish in the basement? Tim had talked publicly about a five-year rebuilding plan. Connor McDavid and Jack Eichel, two young players everyone in hockey was excited about, would be coming up in the 2015 draft. Did the management hope to see the team at the bottom so they could get top draft picks for the next few years? While I had no doubt Patty offered me the job so we could build a winning franchise together, perhaps now those in power believed my long shutout from the NHL and my damaged reputation made me the perfect guy to wear a losing track record.

I didn't sign the contract. Instead, I called everyone I could think of—family, friends, my agent, various pals from the hockey world—to ask what I should do. Everyone said the same thing: "Are you crazy? Sign the damn contract." If they didn't fire me, people reminded me, I'd have a job for three years. If they did fire me, I'd walk away with cash in my pocket. In other words, I should follow Mike Keenan's advice from all those years ago.

I was persuaded. I had a family to support and no other obvious job prospects. And besides, if I turned down a three-year NHL contract for no apparent reason, what other franchise would want me? Wouldn't that confirm the suspicion some seemed to have that I was a difficult guy? I couldn't help thinking of my old friends back in Garden River, my family members, the hundreds of struggling Indigenous folks I'd met over the years. What they wouldn't give for a contract like this. Who was I to walk away from a solid job, a decent salary? Finally, at the very end of March, I signed the contract. But I didn't feel good about it.

♦

On the ice, March was a mess. As we slid lower and lower in the rankings, our player injuries mounted. By April 7, we had thirteen players out of an already diminished lineup on the disabled list. By the end of the 2013–14 regular season, the Sabres were sitting at the very bottom of the league with only 52 points.

The summer would see more trades, more "rebuilding," more team adjustments. The Sabres got the number two draft pick, choosing centre Sam Reinhart in the first round and Brendan Lemieux in the second. I was looking forward to meeting the challenges. But my uncertainty about the management's goals for the team made me feel as if I was walking into a daunting year with a dark storm cloud hanging over my head. And I wasn't wrong.

There's no real point in recounting the Sabres' performance during the 2014–15 season except to say that we struggled from the very beginning to the bitter end. And that's hardly surprising. We'd started "rebuilding" the previous year and continued over the summer, but it felt as if we'd no sooner get a lineup established than it was taken apart and reassembled. Our locker room that year was one big revolving door. And I never had much warning who would be passing through it. Half the time, I'd only find out that a player was being traded or sent down when he showed up in my office to say goodbye. And more often than not, the trade would be so counterintuitive, despite what I knew to be going on, that it took me completely by surprise. It was nerve-racking realizing that any player who was performing well, like our tenacious defenceman Tyler Myers, or our number three scorer, Drew Stafford, was in danger of being traded away, their spot filled by some young hopeful from our AHL franchise. I swear, by mid-season, almost every game started with the announcement, "And now give a big welcome to so-and-so, playing his first game in the NHL . . ."

And while the players we got in return sometimes showed potential, some of the picks were downright frustrating. In the Myers and Stafford trade in February, we signed Evander Kane. A heck of a player—except he was still recovering from a shoulder injury that everyone knew would keep him out for the rest of the season and who knew how long after that.

The pattern of trading well-performing players was never more obvious, however, than with our goaltenders.

After my first season, I'd hired Artūrs Irbe, the tremendously talented goaltending coach who'd spent two years training the Washington Capitals goalies before bringing his considerable skills to the Latvian Olympic team. Artūrs was able to get the very best from the Sabres netminders, helping them improve their save percentages in every instance. But his reward was seeing them traded away when they began to hit their stride.

I couldn't help feel that the young goalies who were called up to fill the empty net, as well as all the other young faces who showed up on the bench that year, were being given a raw deal. They might have been thrilled at first, but all of us on the coaching staff could see that most weren't ready. But that wasn't the worst of it. Putting green players on a team that is foundering, that goes out on the ice, night after night, to suffer crushing losses, makes it almost impossible for those players to improve. They don't get the confidence bump that allows them to push past what they perceive as their limits. They can't take risks, tending to blow their mistakes out of proportion. With no one winning, they can't see how it's done or how they might make a contribution to the team's success. And it's just damn hard to play good hockey on a team that is struggling to maintain its morale and camaraderie.

If I'd had any doubts about the management's strategy (and now I sure didn't), Sabres owner Terry Pegula made it crystal clear after one mid-season game.

"Rebuilding is all about the draft, Ted," he said to me. "As Jimmy Devellano once told me, if you're going to be bad, you might as well be f——ing bad."

That approach would never sit well with me.

My assistant coaches Danny Flynn and Bryan Trottier and I tried as hard as we could to keep the team's spirits up. I did what I'd always done, spending time trying to get to know players, giving locker room chats that put our challenges into context, stressing the importance of hard work, optimism and resilience. The coaching staff and I organized plenty of off-hours events so the players got to know each other and bond, but the musical-chairs feel to our club made those kinds of efforts almost useless.

In the locker room, I often reminded the players that if they worked as hard as they could, they'd never really lose a game in their lives. Winning was about giving your best. But I knew finding inspiration in that way of thinking was a challenge for many players when they were hearing constant media chatter about how the franchise *didn't* want them to do their best and was, in fact, trying to lose in order to nab Connor McDavid or Jack Eichel. And keeping morale in positive territory was even harder when the players could see that many of the fans were hoping that too.

Frankly, no other fan base has ever impressed me more with its stalwart loyalty than the hockey crowd in Buffalo. During my first term with the club, I learned of the deep commitment Buffalo had for their team. On my second stint, I was just as awed by how devoted they were. Despite several seasons of truly awful results, they kept coming, filling the arena to near capacity, night after night.

Yet by the time the second half of the 2014–15 season was under way, it was clear that some people in the stands were, like the management, rooting for victory in the upcoming draft rather than in the game before them.

The Buffalo News repeatedly wrote about this "pro-tank" fan faction. (It also referred to the season as "Tankapalooza 2015.") During a home game against the Arizona Coyotes—our rival for last place—in late

March, loud cheers could be heard every time Arizona scored. Likewise, when the Arizona goalie, Mike Smith, made a number of saves late in the game, Sabres fans let out cries of relief. And when Sabres captain Brian Gionta tied up the game with a power play goal with 3:37 minutes left in the third period, the arena rumbled with groans and boos.

In some ways, I could hardly blame the fans—they were hoping for the best of a bad situation. But their reaction was devastating for the players, none of whom was trying to do anything but win, and all of whom were crushed to hear the fans rooting for their failure. I came away more convinced than ever that any process that results in fans hoping for a loss is working counter to the true spirit of sport.

The organization got its wish a few weeks after that game against Arizona. When the regular season wrapped up, we'd finished dead last.

◆

I've had a lot of painful experiences during my hockey days. But my last two years with the Sabres were the most excruciating. Hands down.

While my time with the Sabres in the nineties had dealt my reputation a blow from which it still hasn't recovered, I left my second term with the franchise feeling as if my time there might have further tarnished my name. I knew people were saying that I'd lost my touch, that I wasn't a very good coach anymore.

It wasn't as if my abilities hadn't been questioned before. Over the years, I've heard people say that the reason my coaching career has been so patchy is that I wasn't very skilled at my job, that any success I had was the result of good luck. When the Greyhounds won the Memorial Cup, I heard that people were saying I was fortunate to have Danny Flynn at my side. And apparently Larry Quinn, when he first joined the Sabres as team president, was quoted in the media wondering if I had what it took. (Later that year, he denied having said this, but just like those other bits of misinformation, the quote would have a life of its own.) All of that hurt. So, too, did this new criticism. And I felt it was unfair.

Danny has said that in the seven years we coached together, he never saw me coach better than I did with the Sabres in my last two seasons with them. I don't know about that, but I do know that I coached the way I always had, working as hard as I was able, supporting the players in any way I could. And, honestly, no one—I don't care if he was Toe Blake or Al Arbour or Scotty Bowman—could have won under the circumstances Danny, Bryan, Artūrs and I found ourselves in.

I don't want anyone to think I'm blaming the players. Far from it. Those guys impressed the hell out of me. They went out and did their jobs the very best they could. And the evidence of that is in our scores. You'll find few blowouts in that season, few complete embarrassments.

There were many, many games that we lost by a single point. There were many I felt we should have won. Facing teams that seemed unstoppable, our guys never gave up—even when it was clear that making the playoffs was impossible. At the end of the season, I was incredibly proud of them all, and incredibly sad that they had been put in such an impossible position. In fact, the knowledge of what those players went through was far, far more painful to me than my dented reputation. It was gut-wrenching to see young new players struggling, especially knowing the part I played in all of it. I'd suspected what was to come, and I'd signed that contract anyhow.

◆

I knew very well I'd be gone once the season was done. I was now a coach with an abysmal recent record, even if it was a record that the ownership seemed quite content with. But the way I was fired was yet another reminder that the hockey world is a private club, with its own rules to be followed. And I'd broken them.

At the end of the previous season with the Sabres, I had been thinking about the coaching ranks for the next year. Since my first NHL coaching contract, I'd insisted on a clause that would allow me to hire my own assistants. And since both GM Tim Murray and I had come in mid-season and worked with the existing staff, everyone expected a changeover.

Tim had clearly been thinking about it too.

"You should talk with my uncle Terry about an assistant position," he'd suggested.

I was certainly aware of Terry Murray and his considerable coaching chops. His NHL career had started over thirty years before. He'd served as head coach for the Washington Capitals, the Philadelphia Flyers, the Florida Panthers and the Los Angeles Kings. For the last couple of years, he'd been coaching the Adirondack Phantoms, an AHL affiliate of the Flyers. But my understanding was that the NHL did not allow you to approach any staff that was already under an NHL contract.

"You should talk with him," was all Tim said in response to my concerns.

Aside from the iffy ethical issue, and despite Terry's impressive resumé, I wasn't keen to interview him. I already had my picks in mind: Danny Flynn, Bryan Trottier and the amazing goalie coach Artūrs Irbe. All men I'd coached with before, all men whose skill set would complement my own.

But I'd called Terry anyway and explained to him that the only position I had left was the "eye in the sky," the assistant who sat in the press box to analyze the game play from there. If he was interested, he should let me know. It was clear from his reaction that, without meaning to, I'd deeply insulted the man.

A few days later, Tim took me aside. He too was upset.

"How dare you make him an offer like that," he said.

I tried to point out that it was the only position that would be open after I installed the assistant coaches I had my eye on. And besides, I had just been feeling Terry out. I didn't think I was free to make him an offer of any kind.

There wasn't anything more to say, but when I left Tim, I had the sense that the matter would not be forgotten.

Now, at the end of the 2014–15 season, on April 12, Tim called me into his office. I knew exactly what was going to happen. And I thought I knew why. But Tim would surprise me.

"I'm sorry, Ted, but—"

"I understand," I said, and turned to leave. "Thanks for the opportunity, and good luck."

"Wait!" said Tim. "Don't you want to know why you're being let go?"

"Not really," I replied.

Tim kept talking anyhow. "You're losing your job because your coaching staff let you down."

I was taken aback. Danny? Artūrs? Bryan? That was so obviously untrue, I almost laughed. I was sure Tim knew it was untrue too. He was saying it to make a point. Once again, I hadn't followed the rules—in this case, I hadn't hired the people he wanted me to hire. I left the room without saying another word.

14

—

PLAYING WITH HEART

THE SECOND HALF OF MY COACHING CAREER shone a light on the weaknesses of pro hockey, no doubt. But amid the disappointments there were also personal triumphs and plenty of examples of what the sport can and should be. My time with the Moncton Wildcats, the Latvian national team and Team Indigenous reminded me of the ways I coach best and of what's really important about team sports.

One of the things I loved about coaching the Greyhounds years earlier was the opportunity that Sherry gave me to help choose players for the team. Robert Irving, having given me the titles of head coach, general manager and director of hockey operations for his Moncton Wildcats, allowed me the same freedom.

While I'd never had any wish to be an NHL general manager, in the smaller arena of junior hockey, the wide responsibilities I had with the Wildcats turned out to be hugely satisfying. Danny Flynn was the first guy I'd called, asking him to join me as my associate coach. Daniel Lacroix, who'd been with the club the previous year, stayed on as an assistant coach, and I kept Frantz Bergevin-Jean, our goalie coach, as well. I also lined up a number of unofficial scouts, including Bob Beatty, who'd been the coach for the Humboldt Broncos, a Tier 2 junior team. I asked him to search the Saskatchewan junior hockey leagues for talented players who might have been overlooked. I arranged for several others to scout the other junior leagues as well. I hadn't forgotten that many of the great players on the Greyhounds teams had been talented yet undrafted guys, like Denny Lambert and Steve Sullivan (Sullivan went on to have a sixteen-year career in the NHL).

Scouts study players on the ice and consider their stats, but they don't usually have the opportunity to get to know them in the dressing room. They don't get to see how they interact with their teammates or how they respond to adversity. Knowing who players are as people is crucial to understanding their true potential and how they might contribute to your team.

Frankly, the players who make it to tryouts or training camps come with essentially the same set of skills. Or, put another way, the skill range really isn't that great. What makes the biggest difference, then, when you are looking to build a team, is the character of the players.

From my Greyhound coaching days, to my time with the Wildcats, to my work with the Latvian national team, what I was looking for was players with heart.

I love to see a player who fills every moment on the ice with passion. Who refuses to give up. Who goes to the wall—whether he's on the ice for one shift or every shift.

So many players I've worked with over the years were like this. I remember one game shortly after Bob Boughner arrived in Buffalo in 1996. He ended up on his back on the ice after losing a fight with an opponent. When Rob Ray saw that, he turned to me and said, "Hey, I thought you said that guy was tough!"

"Nope," I said, laughing, "I said he had game."

I knew that despite the beating, Bob was going to dive back into play with every bit of energy he'd had when the puck first dropped. That kind of spirit trumps toughness or skill when it comes to a player's value, as far as I'm concerned. And it's infectious. When someone embraces the game with that enthusiasm, you can see other players pushing a little harder, staying a bit more positive. Even your star players shine a bit more brightly when they see a third-line guy busting his ass every second on the ice.

As far as I can tell, playing with that kind of heart comes from appreciating the opportunity to play rather than feeling you are owed time on centre stage. It comes from knowing that even if you scored fifty goals last season, you aren't entitled to skate every shift. Stats are just stats, after all—players need to be trying and working at every moment, always earning their time in the game.

Playing with heart also means responding to adversity with resilience and grace. Both in junior and in the pros, I'd sometimes create little setbacks, like benching a first-line player for making a mistake. If that fellow came by my office later to apologize for messing up, I'd know he was a player we could win with. If he came to complain, it was clear he was not going to help us build a successful team.

Players with heart always put the team's interests ahead of their own. I don't care how talented you are, if you won't pass, if you overextend your shifts, if you complain every time you warm the bench, then you aren't focused on the team. No cares if you score the fifth goal in a 5–0 game, except you and maybe your agent. But it makes a huge difference to the team if other players get a chance to work on their game when your side is ahead. Simply put, you have to be willing to share.

That kind of heart, the key to a successful team, is found in the very best players in the league, as well as in so many journeymen. In fact, it's what makes certain hockey figures legends. Bobby Orr, Wayne Gretzky, Mario Lemieux, Mike Bossy, Sidney Crosby—they all had phenomenal skill, but they were true stars because that skill was accompanied by heart. They were team players with a spirit that inspired others. And when your team has players with incredible skill, players with great heart, and players with both, then you've got a winning franchise.

Let's be honest, exceptional players are going to find their place in the hockey world, regardless. But their numbers are small. Most hockey players out there aren't going to be legends. So when it comes to building a winning team, the trick is to find those players with a great attitude who aren't going to walk straight into the lineup because of their phenomenal scoring abilities or other outsized talent. I think of those players as the "blue collar" element. While they needn't have been raised in scarcity, like I was, some part of their upbringing has taught them that hard work, perseverance, accountability and the ability to leave their egos at the door are traits they need to succeed in life.

Those are the players I always look for: individuals who deserve an opportunity.

Once in a while, you get an intuitive sense of a player's character or catch a twinkle in their eyes that tells you they have that spark. But usually you have to do a bit of research to get to know your young prospects. With the Greyhounds and the Wildcats, since so many young men are shy, we didn't talk with just them when trying to find out what kind of people they were. We sat down with their parents.

We interviewed their teachers. We asked how the boys reacted to set-backs and disappointments. How they behaved with their friends and classmates. We found out about their hobbies and interests and what they wanted to do in the future other than play hockey. And we asked questions to find out what they might need in order to have a positive experience on the team. Could they use some academic tutoring? Was there anything else they might want or need? We used to joke that if a kid had been dropped on his head as a baby, we'd find out about it.

I imagine it's already pretty clear that I think this kind of player selection works best if the coach is involved. There are a couple of reasons for that. First, coaches have a sense of the kind of guidance they and the rest of their coaching team can give to players. I was pretty sure I could reach Chris Simon and Denny Lambert, for exam-ple. Coaches may also be more aware of what kinds of players will respond well to their coaching style and their approach to team build-ing. They may also know what kind of players won't respond. Dominik Hašek certainly didn't need my help to play to his full potential, but another player with his personality and fewer skills, well, my style of motivation and encouragement might not have moved the needle for him the way it did for some players.

A coach can also consider how a player might fit in with the exist-ing team. Scouts might consider if a candidate's skills fill a gap. Coaches can think about whether a player's personality will mesh well with the team culture—if he is likely to form bonds with other play-ers, become a mentor, respond to the mentorship of veterans on the team or embrace the existing team ethos.

In the end, with the Wildcats, Danny, Daniel, the scouts and I brought in and kept about fifteen new players, some undrafted, from various leagues from across North America. And that turned out to be a formula for a winning franchise.

♦

In North America, lots of solid players with great attitudes haven't made it up to the higher ranks of minor hockey and therefore haven't made it onto Junior A draft lists, either because they couldn't afford the hockey clinics and league fees or because of where they live. The same difficulty accessing elite sport is true in other parts of the world, including Europe, as I would learn during my time coaching in Latvia. Yet if coaches and scouts are willing to do a bit of legwork, they can pull together great teams even in the most unlikely places.

My road to coaching an Olympic team started with a fellow named Tom Coolen. He and I had met at Danny Flynn's wedding. A teacher and long-time hockey coach for the Acadia University and University of New Brunswick hockey teams, as well as several minor league teams and a number of European hockey clubs, Tom was one of those fellows who seemed in the know about everything going on in the world of hockey. In the summer of 2011, he called me.

"Any interest in coaching for Latvia?" he asked. "I hear they're looking for someone."

"Whose team is that?" I asked, showing just how much attention I'd paid to world geography in school.

"It's a country, Ted," Tom said, "in Europe."

He explained that the national team was looking for a coach who would help them qualify for the 2014 Winter Olympics in Sochi.

The Olympics host twelve men's hockey teams. The top nine teams from the Ice Hockey World Championships receive an automatic place at the competition. Any other interested countries are divided into three groups, which each play a round robin qualifying tournament in the winter before the Olympics. The winners of each group secure a berth at the Olympic games the following February. Tom was hoping that we might put ourselves forward as a team: me as head coach, him as an assistant.

Not long after that phone call, Tom and I were making our first trip to Riga to meet the Latvian team management and discuss strategy. We already knew our positions would be like permanent part-time jobs. We'd go over to Europe for two or three weeks and then return home for a month or more. The Latvian national hockey organization couldn't afford scouts. With the help of an interpreter, Tom and I would be building the team—finding Latvian players from across North America and Europe, players who could take time from their regular hockey schedules to practise and participate in tournaments for their national team, and, if everything went right, represent their country in the 2014 Olympics.

It would be a challenge, no doubt. With a population of only two million, and only seventeen indoor rinks in the whole country (no outdoor ones), Latvia wasn't exactly known as a hockey stronghold. Yet I soon discovered it was a country with a deep and abiding love of the sport and an enthusiasm and optimism that was striking. Right from the start, my work in Latvia was a terrific experience. Just like with the Wildcats, I loved the process of searching for the unsung heroes and the raw, overlooked talent that was sometimes hidden in plain sight.

It would take our coaching team almost two years to find our team. We had only one active NHL player on the roster, nineteen-year-old Buffalo Sabres rookie forward Zemgus Girgensons, and one Latvian superstar, Lauris Dārziņš. But we found some other terrific players. We discovered Kristers Gudļevskis playing goal in a Junior B league—without the proper equipment. (In short order, and with the help of our goalie coach Artūrs Irbe, he'd make it into the NHL with the Tampa Bay Lightning.) Forward Miks Indrašis was another player who joined us from his Junior B club.

LIFE IN TWO WORLDS

We found brothers Koba and Māris Jass playing in a Slovak hockey league. From the start, I felt a special connection with those two. One day, just after the brothers had been named to the national team, we were met at the airport by a large group of their relatives. We were about to head off to a tournament, and the family wanted to thank me in person for putting the boys on the team. At first, I was a little surprised by their effusive gratitude, but then I remembered that the Jasses were Roma and therefore outsiders among the wider European population. I got the sense that they hadn't had the same opportunities as others. Koba, Māris and I never talked about our shared "outsider" status, but I think we recognized it in each other. Koba would turn out to be one of my favourite players to coach—probably the hardest-working player I've ever met.

We invited another player we'd spotted in a Latvian senior league. And we added three players who weren't on any sort of elite team— they were playing essentially beer league hockey.

While Tom and I were on the hunt for young talent, we kept hearing the same thing: "Too bad Sandis isn't playing for you."

Sandis Ozoliņš was a Latvian-born defenceman with a golden hockey pedigree. He'd spent sixteen years in the NHL, playing for the San Jose Sharks, the Colorado Avalanche, the Carolina Hurricanes, the Florida Panthers, the Anaheim Mighty Ducks and the New York Rangers. He'd been named to seven NHL all-star teams, earned a Stanley Cup with the Avalanche, and was a Norris Trophy finalist before returning to Europe in 2008. A brilliant offensive defenceman, he was, no question, the most famous Latvian hockey player ever, with NHL franchise records that stand to this day. No wonder everyone wished he could be on the team.

While Sandis was still playing in the KHL (the Russian-run Kontinental Hockey League), he seemed to be working his way towards retirement. But I wondered if there was a chance he would join us.

I called everyone I knew who had played with him in the NHL, including Chris Simon, to learn what I could about the man. And then I called Sandis himself. He was as clear as could be: he wasn't interested in joining the Latvian national team.

Over the next year or so, I called him over and over again, trying to get him to go for coffee, explaining to him why I felt he was so important to the team. Finally, in early 2013, just as we were starting in on our final practices before the qualifying tournament in February, Sandis agreed to join us.

That was a turning point. The team was a collection of unlikely Olympians, but Sandis became a true hero to those players, his intense competitiveness setting an example for them all. A sage elder whose wisdom and attitude inspired everyone, he was especially supportive of the younger players, sharing his hockey knowledge and helping them see their own importance to the team.

Working with the team as we began our practices and then headed into all the tournaments leading up to the final qualifier was unbelievably rewarding. The team spirit was strong, and the players learned to work together in a powerful way, engaging in style of play that was a mix of European and North American approaches and produced great results for us. What I enjoyed most about my time with the Latvian team, however, was the attitude of the European hockey world. The competition on the ice was always intense, but no friction remained when the final buzzer sounded. At the end of each game, the teams would shake hands with their opponents and, more often than not, head out for a beer together at a local bar. It felt as if the players, coaches and management had not forgotten we were all playing a game. A competitive game, sure—everyone wanted to win—but not one that money had turned into an enterprise stripped of spirited fun and friendliness. Sport the way it should be.

◆

The final qualifying tournament in February 2013 was a time of high excitement. All along, the Latvian fans had been like the seventh man on the team, packing the arena in Riga every time we played there. Many followed us to attend all our road games, including the tournament. We beat out Great Britain and Kazakhstan. Our final match was against France. That game turned out to be a real comeback story. France scored two goals in the first period, and we battled back with a goal in the second and then another in the third. Finally, with a goal in overtime, we won ourselves a spot in the Olympics.

A year later, in early February 2014, when the NHL and the Sabres were on break, I returned to Europe to join the Olympic team in Sochi. We were, of course, the underdogs. After the first round, Norway held twelfth place, and we squeaked in above them. Yet all our games were tight matches—we never lost by more than two points, and there was only one game where we failed to put one in the net. On top of that, we managed an upset victory over Switzerland to make our way into the quarter-finals—a first ever for Latvia. We would be playing the best hockey team in the world, Canada.

That quarter-final against Canada was a game I'll never forget. It was unquestionably a David and Goliath match. Here we were, playing against a collection of true hockey greats—Carey Price, John Tavares, Jonathan Toews, Shea Weber, Sidney Crosby, the list could go on and on—yet half our team wouldn't even be considered for a spot on a struggling AHL franchise.

In the dressing room before the game, I told the guys that Team Canada no doubt thought we were a bunch of country bumpkins. We could use that to our advantage. The Canadians weren't expecting to work too much for a win, so if we pressed hard and pressed consistently, we might be able to take them by surprise and even force them into mistakes.

"It's like trying to take down a huge oak tree in your backyard. You aren't going to do it all at once. You're going to do it one chop at a time. Just keep at it, guys," I told them.

And to maximize the element of surprise, why not play into their assumptions about us? I knew that Koba Jass was a huge Sidney Crosby fan. "How about skating up to him at the beginning of the game and asking for an autographed stick?" I suggested. (Koba did, and Crosby, always a nice guy, brought one to our dressing room after the game.)

The team hit the ice with energy. But when Canada scored a little more than thirteen minutes into the first period, we decided to try an unusual play. I'd learned it years earlier from Mike Zuke, and we'd used it with success in an earlier game in the series. Mike used to call it the "old number seven," but in Latvia we'd renamed it the "Tommy gun," since Tom Coolen was such a big fan of it. During a faceoff near the Latvian bench, our centre shot the puck off the boards. Just as he did, one winger stepped off the ice, and our best scorer, Lauris Dārziņš, stepped on. A winger picked the puck off the boards and made a breakaway, getting it to Lauris, who fired it into the net, raising a roar from the crowd.

The guys took the "keep chopping" approach to heart, holding onto that tie for the rest of the first and throughout the second period, and Kristers Gudļevskis outdid himself, batting away puck after puck. (Team Canada would outshoot us 57 to 11.) During our nail-biter third period, we managed to get off a number of close shots. The crowd grew increasingly raucous after each miss, everyone, it seemed, thrilled at the thought that tiny Latvia might just beat the Canadian hockey greats.

Then, with only about ten minutes left in the game, we got a slashing penalty. During the power play, with just under seven minutes left, Shea Weber managed to fire one past Kristers. We did our best to come up with a goal to tie, but the clock ran out on us.

After the game, a number of the Canadian players claimed they hadn't been worried about the outcome. But a *National Post* headline said it all: "Canada Breathes a Sigh of Relief." More than one Canadian hockey fan would tell me they'd found themselves on the edge of their seat. Some, like Brad May, were unable to resist the urge to root for the little country that was making the Canadian team scramble.

I was bursting with joy for the Latvian team. Not only had we made Canada work, *really* work, for the win, but we ended up being the only team to score a goal against Canada in the playoffs—the United States lost 1–0 in the semi-finals, and Sweden lost 3–0 in the finals.

The Latvian team's performance certainly proved to me, once again, that good hockey players don't necessarily rise like cream to the top of the hockey world—and that a team made up of players with heart can be a winning one, even if it doesn't have a lot of star power.

Latvia's Olympic success also suggested something about my own coaching aptitude. While I've never had the chance to work with a big-budget, star-packed team, perhaps I'd be out of my element working in that environment. Having to make do with what I had was something I was good at.

♦

While junior hockey and my Latvian experience are good examples of what a coach can bring to player recruitment and selection, when I was working with NHL teams, I could see the point in a division of labour between the general managers and the coaches. Frankly, I had my hands full coaching, the first time especially. But even with seasoned NHL coaches, the way the NHL is organized and run makes it impossible for them to be really involved in player selection. Training camp is generally set up by management, with the prospective players chosen by the GM. The schedules are tight—there certainly isn't enough time for the coaching staff to hang out with the recruits to try to get to know them, even if the coaches are allowed some input into the final selection. That always bothered me. I'd watch some poor guy struggling on the ice and think, *No one has a bad game for no reason. I wonder what's going on with him?* But I'd never have the opportunity to find an answer to that, and there were no second chances for a wannabe player who didn't shine in their brief time at camp. I found it frustrating, like being a carpenter who can't choose his own tools.

Of course, there are times when a coach gets to put in his two cents' worth, as I did with Bob Boughner. The Islanders gave me another chance to use my player knowledge to help a deserving guy make an NHL career for himself.

Charles Wang, the owner of the Islanders, who hired me as head coach, was interested in building a more collaborative model for player selection. He wanted to introduce a group interview system for prospective players—if they didn't get a thumbs-up from everyone, they wouldn't even be considered. We never fully embraced this, and I'm not sure how it would have worked if we did. But his out-of-box approach did provide one young man with a great run in the NHL.

The team management was at the NHL draft in June 2006. At the start of the sixth round, Charles turned to me and insisted I pick a player. Of course, I'd joined the new management team at the draft that year, but I hadn't expected to play a role. I looked over at the scouts and at Neil Smith, who was still the GM at the time. This was their territory—and their area of expertise. I shook my head. Charles told me again to choose. I again declined. This went on for several more minutes, until it was clear that Charles was getting agitated.

"Okay," I finally said, "I pick Andrew MacDonald."

Andrew MacDonald was a defenceman who'd played for me on the Wildcats. During my pre-season work in Moncton, I'd heard of him but discovered he was planning to join the NCAA for the 2005–06 season. Robert Irving and I had convinced him to play junior instead, and he'd been a terrific addition to the team.

As soon as I mentioned his name to Charles, the scouts began to flip through the scouting lists.

"He's not on here," one of them said.

"I know," I replied. "But that doesn't mean we can't draft him."

Charles agreed.

Andrew spent the next two years on our AHL team, the Bridgeport Sound Tigers. In 2009, he would move up to the Islanders, beginning a twelve-year stint in the NHL, playing for both the Islanders and the Flyers. Only three of our choices that year landed in the NHL for more than a couple of trial games, and only one, Kyle Okposo, our number one pick, had a longer NHL career than Andrew did.

◆

Another belief my Latvia experience confirmed for me is that almost nothing is as important for motivating players as a sense of belonging. The Latvian team, like all the Olympic teams, had nationality drawing them together in a tight bond. Indeed, whatever the Jass brothers had experienced in the past, once they were on the Latvian national team, those differences seemed to evaporate. You couldn't have asked for a closer bunch of guys.

But perhaps the clearest example of the power of belonging that I've ever seen was Team Indigenous.

After my contract had ended with the Sabres in 1997, I was invited to meet with NHL commissioner Gary Bettman. For a number of years, the NHL/USA Hockey Diversity Task Force, founded in 1994 by Bryant McBride, had supported a wonderful program called Ice Hockey in Harlem, which taught boys and girls to play hockey but also supported their education and community involvement. I'd helped out with the program a little earlier in the year, and Bettman seemed interested in having me work with the diversity task force to support and promote the Indigenous presence in the NHL. But after our meeting, talk about my involvement with the task force or any other NHL-sponsored projects trailed off.

I'd travelled to that meeting with Chief Phil Fontaine of the Assembly of First Nations and his partner, lawyer and professor Kathleen Mahoney. Phil had been incensed when he'd heard I had been effectively let go from the Sabres and was disappointed that the NHL task force didn't lead anywhere for us.

"Well, if they aren't going to hire you, I will," he said.

That prompted a number of conversations about how we might develop our own hockey organization for First Nations, Inuit and Métis youth. As with the Ice Hockey in Harlem program, we wanted to support educational goals, provide social support and improve the quality of life for Indigenous players. We decided to form an under-twenty team, called Team Indigenous, to enter in the Universal Players Tournament in Tampere, Finland, in August 2000. I would be the coach, and Danny Flynn would join me behind the bench, along with First Nations coaches Albert Louie Jock and Kenneth Kane. First Nations OHL scouts Donnie Chrysler and Derek Fontaine would help us assemble the team. Chief Billy Two Rivers would serve as our Elder and spiritual adviser, and our management team included Chief Bill Erasmus and Chief Charles Fox.

In the fall of 1999, we began reaching out to our contacts in the OHL, the WHL and the QMJHL, who identified potential players for us in those junior leagues as well as in the midget leagues below them. In the end, three of our players would become future professional players: my son Brandon, Cody McCormick and Jonathan Cheechoo, who would light up the NHL and become the second First Nations player (after Reggie Leach) to score 50 goals in a season.

The tournament was a fantastic experience for all of us, and we fared well, winning four games to two and coming fifth out of twelve teams, included ones from Russia, Sweden, Finland, Norway, Germany and the United States.

We'd hoped to expand the program in years to come, with teams for younger players and a women's team as well, but we hadn't been able to secure funding commitments from Hockey Canada for the original team, so even getting that one team on the ice had been a huge challenge. And then, about a month before the team left for Finland, Phil Fontaine was replaced as National Chief of the Assembly of First Nations, and by the time he won the next election for Chief, the program was pretty much mothballed.

Yet the experience of playing together on an international stage was, I think, a deeply important and incredibly meaningful one for all of us. For some of the players, being part of an all-Indigenous team meant they could escape the subtle biases that had them pigeonholed on other teams. Indigenous players are frequently used as enforcers and tough guys rather than the finesse players they often are. For everyone, our shared history and culture gave us a baseline for under-standing each other and connecting. After all, First Nations folks have learned the strength that comes from sticking together. Indeed, it's the only way we can move forward. And our pride in showing the world who we were drove Team Indigenous on the ice with a kind of intensity few of us had ever felt before. It wasn't just the world we were showing—it was our own people. We knew our community was watching, sitting up a little taller with every minute we spent on the world stage. Honestly, whenever I've seen Indigenous teams in action, I feel as if I am watching players hit their very top form—because of their sense of belonging and the powerful bond they feel with their teammates.

I should pause here and make it clear I'm not suggesting that sports should be segregated in any way. In fact, I feel passionately that we need to work harder to have our teams reflect the diversity of the societies they represent. Yet a coach can build an environment in which belonging can take root. He can create experiences on and off the ice that encourage a sense of camaraderie and a group dynamic in which everyone feels like a valued part of the collective. This is especially true with young players.

When I first got to Moncton, I talked with Robert Irving about how we might create opportunities to help our young players gain life experience and engage in team-building and bonding activities. Robert agreed immediately to the idea of investing in the kids.

During that season, we took the whole team to Boston to see a Red Sox game (and also to the place where the TV show *Cheers* was filmed). After Christmas, the team travelled to New York City. We saw a Broadway play and went out for a steak dinner. We had the young guys play tourist, but with a purpose. We divided them into small teams that had to research some aspect of New York's culture and history and then present what they'd learned to the rest of us on our return. Of course, there was hockey too. I'd called Glen Sather to ask about getting the team tickets to see a Rangers game. He said he would and then generously offered to let us practise in Madison

Square Garden. But no doubt the highlight of the whole adventure for most of the players was the afternoon we spent at Pat LaFontaine's house, playing three-on-three on his backyard rink. Like I'd hoped, those team-building activities seemed to produce a remarkable team spirit in which everyone supported each other, shared on-ice opportunities and showed accountability to the team by giving every game their maximum effort.

But even in the pros, engendering this sense of belonging is possible. When I first got to Buffalo in 1995, it's what I noticed about Pat LaFontaine—the way he took his position as captain as an ongoing opportunity to bring the guys together. And it was what I continued to try to do as coach with that team, with the Islanders and with the later Sabres team.

◆

When it comes right down to it, the biggest thing a coach can do to inspire his players and bring his team members together is also the simplest: "Just treat the guys like human beings."

Those words, an uncanny echo of my sister Katie's instructions, are the best hockey advice I've ever gotten. And they came from one of the sport's coaching legends: Al Arbour.

My opportunity to meet Al came about after my usual Monday morning meeting with Charles Wang sometime late in the first season I was coaching the New York Islanders. We'd been talking about how we might raise attendance. As I walked down the Coliseum hallway, past the locker room, I stopped at the big board that listed the franchise's award winners and milestones. I'd looked at it dozens and dozens of times in the past year, and one stat always jumped out at me: Al Arbour's record number of regular-season games coached, 1,499.

Al Arbour was one of my heroes. When I'd coached for the Sabres, and then for the Islanders, I dreamed of one day becoming not just a good coach but a great coach. A coach like Toe Blake, Scotty Bowman or Al Arbour. Al had won four consecutive Stanley Cups for the Islanders. And for eleven seasons, he helped the team to regular-season winning records. He followed only Scotty Bowman in regular-season wins and playoff games coached, held a record for the most playoff victories for one team and set another, which still stands today, of nineteen consecutive playoff series wins. And from what I understood about the man, his records weren't his only accomplishments. Players, apparently, loved playing for him—many saw him as a father figure. And pretty much everyone praised his decency and fairness.

Of all Al's records posted on that board, the one that always nagged at me was the 1,499 games coached. It seemed a shame that Al hadn't got a nice round 1,500. And then it occurred to me: there was no reason it couldn't still happen. We could invite Al back to officially coach one more regular-season game so he could hit 1,500. It would be a wonderful way to honour a legendary coach, but it would also be a great inspiration for the players, giving them the opportunity to be coached by an icon and reminded of their team's amazing legacy. And it sure would fill the stands.

Al was delighted when we suggested it to him in the summer of 2007. So the game would count in the record books, the management then had to create a one-day contract making him the head coach. (It was the shortest contract in NHL history, another record for Al.) We settled on a November 3 match against the highly touted Pittsburgh Penguins, with their superstar, Sidney Crosby.

Two days before the game, Al came to a practice and then watched our home game against Tampa Bay. He was friendly and surprisingly humble. I could tell he was a little nervous too. Perhaps it was because it was his birthday. He was turning seventy-five, making him the oldest man ever to coach an NHL game. But more likely it was simply that he wasn't familiar with the team.

"Ted," he said at one point, "I don't know anyone's name anymore."

"Don't worry, Al," I told him. "Just call them by the lines."

Al's 1,500th game was a thrilling night, with plenty of fanfare and hockey glitz. When the team walked out from the dressing room, I could see that the stands were packed. The whole arena seemed to vibrate with anticipation. As Al and I watched from behind the bench, Scotty Bowman and Islanders former GM Bill Torrey walked out onto the ice for the ceremonial faceoff.

As the game started and Al began to send the lines out and give instructions, I found myself marvelling that I was standing shoulder to shoulder with a true hockey great.

And, boy, was it an exciting game. I wanted us to win for Al. But there were times when it looked like that might not happen. In the second period, Sidney Crosby's stick struck the face of our goalie, Rick DiPietro, resulting in a cut to his eye that required several stitches and interfered with his vision. He had to sit out the rest of the game. Heading into the third period, we were down 2–1, without our star goalie. And then, five minutes in, Miroslav Šatan scored to tie it up.

As the clock ran down, the tension in the arena was intense. And then Miroslav came through once again, putting the last one in the net with only two minutes and forty-one seconds left in the game.

Al had got his 740th regular-season win with the Islanders and the magic 1,500 games coached. During the post-game ceremony, he was joined on the ice by Bryan Trottier, Mike Bossy, Ed Westfall, Clark Gillies, Pat LaFontaine, Gerry Hart, Jean Potvin and Benoît Hogue as the banner that hung over the rink commemorating Al's 739th win was taken down and replaced with a banner with the number 1,500.

Over the couple of days Al and I spent together, I tried to pick his brains whenever we had a quiet moment. The piece of advice that struck me the hardest—"Just treat the guys like human beings, Ted"—seemed in keeping with everything I'd heard about him. And if I had to boil my own coaching philosophy down to just seven words, that would be it.

15

—

THE THREE NOLANS

I ALWAYS EMPHASIZED TO MY NHL PLAYERS how lucky we were to be paid to play a game we loved. Of course, that's true, but pro hockey comes with stresses. The frequent trades and the relocations, among other things, can be hard on players, but also really hard on families.

My choice not to take the Tampa job involved a number of factors, but my concerns about the relocation for my family were tops. I've never regretted my decision. My family loved the time we spent in the St. Catharines area and in Garden River. And if we'd moved to Florida at that point in the boys' lives, chances are they wouldn't have had the hockey careers they did.

While I'd never wanted either of my boys to pursue a career in pro hockey, by the time Brandon had hit his teens, he had his eye on the

NHL. Perhaps I should've predicted that would happen. I'd put both boys in skates as soon as they could walk. And every winter, I'd built a rink outside our Garden River home or in the backyard in St. Catharines. We'd also had them in recreational league hockey from the start. I bought them decent equipment and skates that fit properly. But I knew those weren't the things they really needed, so I spent hours and hours with them, teaching them the skills I'd picked up from other players. All the things Jody and Bill and Rick had shared with me. (The one thing I didn't teach them was how to fight. I always assumed that by the time they were old enough to enter the contact leagues, the hockey powers that be would have outlawed fighting on the ice. Unfortunately, in the coming years I would realize I'd been badly mistaken. Eventually, I'd have to teach Brandon and then Jordan what they needed to know to take care of themselves on the ice.)

Sandra and I both tried to make sure they were always playing for fun, just like my dad had with me. Once, we even pulled one of them off a team, because the coach had been yelling at the players and refs, throwing f-bombs around and ratcheting up the intensity to a level we felt wasn't at all appropriate for kids. But despite our cautious approach, both boys were immersed in the world of hockey, hanging out at the arenas when I coached, sometimes taking a turn on the ice when the games were done. They even accompanied me on some of the road trips with the Greyhounds and the Sabres. So I suppose it wasn't surprising that they were both crazy about playing competitive hockey. And they did well at it.

In June 1999, Brandon was drafted in the first round of the OHL draft. He was only sixteen, however, and not ready to start. But in the fall of 2000, he moved into a spot on a Major Junior A team: the Oshawa Generals, Sherry Bassin's old stomping grounds. At seventeen, he'd be leaving home to play hockey, just like I'd done.

Sandra and I were excited for him and relieved that he would be just a two-hour drive from our St. Catharines home. We were also encouraged that the OHL provided scholarships for players to go to college or university if they chose to. At fifteen, Brandon had been offered several NCAA hockey scholarships, including one from Harvard, but by the time the wait period was over, he had opted for the OHL. His education, however, was still important to him—and to us.

My years in Glens Falls and my friendships with my teammates taught me a lot about hockey, but they also taught me a lot about how the middle-class and upper-middle-class white world operated—and how other parents did things. One day back then, I was at a buddy's house in the early evening. My friend's young daughter was at the kitchen table. She had school books in front of her but was asking to watch TV.

"Not until after homework," her dad said. "Got to do your homework or you won't go to university."

It seemed like such an odd thing to say to a girl who was probably only in grade three.

"How do you know she'll go to university?" I asked my friend.

He looked puzzled. "Why wouldn't she?"

I could barely wait to tell Sandra when I got home that night.

"I know how they do it!"

I felt like I was holding the key to a locked door, that I had uncovered the secret to educational success. "They talk about university when the kids are young!"

While my mother had always emphasized the importance of education, neither of my parents had much of it themselves, and we never talked about how someone would go about getting any post-secondary education, or all the things you could study. In other words, higher education was an abstract concept to me—and a bit of a mystery. Now I understood that you could put your kid on the path in grade school.

That didn't strike me as putting pressure on a child. My friend's attitude suggested confidence in his daughter, as if he was telling her, right from the start, "You can do it. It is there for you, if you want it." It was not a message I or my siblings had ever heard. While my parents had stressed the importance of having pride and self-respect, they didn't tell us we could do whatever we set our minds to. I suspect few First Nations parents of their generation did. That wasn't their reality. But it seemed to be the reality of others, and I could see the power in that.

So as the boys grew up, Sandra and I talked with them about schooling—not about hockey careers. Yet, here was Brandon, determined like I never was to make it to the big leagues and truly excited about this next big step. And we were thrilled to support him. In the next year or two, there would be many afternoons when Sandra would pack a dinner in a cooler so she, Jordan and I could eat on the road as we travelled to various towns to watch Brandon and the Oshawa Generals play. Jordan was a real trooper, never once complaining about all the long drives. (One night, we made the four-and-a-half-hour trip to Sudbury and back to see a game.) Jordan, like us, was just excited to see Brandon play the game he loved.

Brandon's pro career started in 2003, when he was picked up by the Vancouver Canucks in the fourth round of the draft. (He'd actually been drafted in 2001 by the New Jersey Devils in the third round but couldn't agree on a contract, so he didn't join the franchise.) After signing with Vancouver, he began a three-year run with the Manitoba Moose, an AHL farm team for the Canucks, followed by a stint in the East Coast Hockey League with the Columbia Inferno. The following year, he began the season playing in the Swedish Hockey League before joining the Bridgeport Sound Tigers, the AHL team affiliated with the New York Islanders. At that time, I was head coach of the Islanders, and while it seemed unlikely that Brandon would be moved up to play for me, it was fun to think about. In 2007–08, Brandon signed with the Carolina Hurricanes, and on December 22, he was called up to play his first NHL game, against the Tampa Bay Lightning. Sandra was able to be there, along with some family members who spent part of their winters in Florida. I have to say, of we three Nolan boys, Brandon was probably the most passionate about playing the game, and watching that enthusiasm and devotion, we all thought he was destined for a long, long NHL career.

Brandon went on to play five more games with the Hurricanes before being sent back to Carolina's AHL franchise, the Albany River Rats, just three days before the Islanders were due to meet the Hurricanes on December 31. Brandon continued to play well for Albany, leading the River Rats in goals. And then, in a game on February 22, he received an elbow to the head. It was a devastating blow, literally and figuratively. Brandon went down, blacking out for several seconds. Once he came around and got to the bench, he was keen to go back out, but the coach, wisely, wouldn't let him. The next morning, he woke up dizzy and vomiting. His concussion, it turned out, was severe—career-ending, in fact. Brandon's playing days were done. He was only twenty-four, three years younger than I'd been when my back injury sidelined me for good.

Brandon's brain injury turned out to be so bad, it took the next two years for him to recover enough to be able to work or go to school. By the fall of 2010, however, he was able to start a business administration program at Durham College, graduating two years later at the very top of his class and winning several awards. Shortly after that, he began his ongoing career in marketing and administrative work for various Indigenous businesses and organizations.

Jordan, luckily, had a much longer run in the pros. After playing minor hockey in St. Catharines, in May 2005 he was drafted by the Erie

Otters of the OHL in the third round. We were thrilled for him and relieved that Erie wasn't too far away. But when the Otters took their Christmas break, Jordan decided he wasn't ready to live away from home. He didn't return to Erie, and the following summer he was traded to the Windsor Spitfires. Two years after that, he requested another trade and was sent to the Soo Greyhounds. When Sandra and I returned from Long Island, Jordan moved in with us in Garden River.

Then, one day in the spring of 2009, I came home from a visit with my brother. When I walked into kitchen, I could see that Sandra had tears in her eyes. They were tears of joy. She'd just heard that Jordan had been drafted in the seventh round by the Los Angeles Kings. When Jordan walked through the door a short time later, the three of us fell into a huge hug. Sandra was as excited as she'd been the day he was born, and I was overcome with pride.

Jordan played the 2009–10 season for the Greyhounds before moving in the fall of 2010 to New Hampshire to join the Kings' farm team, the AHL's Manchester Monarchs. And then in mid-February 2012, during his second season in the pros, he was called up to the Kings.

Jordan's move to the NHL was a huge thrill for all of us, of course. (I think Brandon was more excited than he'd been when he was called up himself.) And, in a sideways sort of way, it fulfilled a promise that had been made to me.

In the summer of 2011, while on a speaking engagement to a First Nations community in Manitoba, I was invited to a Sweat Lodge for a Sunrise ceremony. At the end of our sweat, the Medicine Man who was conducting the ceremony asked the drummers to do a special song for me, to bring me a Stanley Cup.

I couldn't help chuckle at that. That spring, Curt Styres had sold the Rochester Americans, and I'd returned to Garden River. I had no job, never mind a coaching position.

"Well, you'll have to get me a team first," I said to the Medicine Man.

"Don't worry," he said, as the drummers started, "we'll get you that cup."

So, in the latter half of the 2011–12 NHL season, I felt an extraordinary First Nations presence as I sat in the stands and watched my son advance through the NHL playoffs with the Kings, making it eventually to the championship game against the New Jersey Devils. It was wonderful to see the way Jordan contributed throughout those matches, but I was more nervous watching those games than I had ever been playing or coaching. When the LA Kings beat the New Jersey Devils 6–1 in the final game to win the cup, it was a greater thrill than if I'd been behind the bench or on the ice myself. I was too choked up to even cheer, watching Jordan hoist the cup as he skated around the Staples Center. At twenty-two, and in his very first year in the NHL, Jordan had won the biggest prize in hockey. A Manitoba Elder had promised me the Stanley Cup, and that promise had come true—but in a way that was even more rewarding than if I'd won the thing myself. I could have kissed that Medicine Man.

Jordan continued to thrive with the Kings. During his second year with the team, he made a life-changing decision that improved his hockey career but more importantly his life. Like so many others who are trying to find balance, Jordan looked within himself and decided to abstain from alcohol. Sandra and I were incredibly proud of his self-awareness and resolve.

The LA Kings continued to do well too after that 2012 Stanley Cup.

So well, in fact, that in 2014 they won the cup again. During both of my later seasons with the Sabres, since the team was out of the playoffs, Sandra and I were able to attend a number of Jordan's playoff games, as well at the 2014 cup victory.

In 2017, Jordan was traded to the Sabres. The season after that, he played with the St. Louis Blues and their AHL franchise, the San Antonio Rampage. That year, 2018, the Blues won the Stanley Cup, and while Jordan wasn't on the bench for the playoffs this time, he still had his third day with the Stanley Cup.

Jordan signed with the Pittsburgh Penguins' AHL affiliate, the Wilkes-Barre/Scranton Penguins, in 2020, but the COVID-19 pandemic delayed the season, so he played only two games before deciding in March 2021 to wrap up his on-ice career. The following fall, he joined the LA Kings front office as a community relations ambassador.

◆

Over the years, Brandon, Jordan and I have talked about the differences in our upbringings and our hockey careers. The boys never felt they were split between two worlds. They are immensely proud of their First Nations heritage and feel a true sense of belonging in Garden River. Yet the world outside the reserve is a place that feels like home to them as well. They tell me they have never felt divided the way I did, never been targeted with racist slurs while on the ice or made to feel they were not welcome on a team, in a school or at a workplace. I am enormously grateful for that.

But my boys also realize they grew up with so many advantages that many other First Nations children don't have—on and off the ice. And they've always wanted to do more to help those young people.

In 2013, once Brandon had finished his college program, he, Jordan and I joined forces to offer youth hockey camps in the off-season to Indigenous communities across the country, dubbing our new enterprise "3Nolans." In the past, I'd spent a great deal of time participating in hockey clinics, but the boys and I could see plenty more that we could do.

One of the big barriers for less-advantaged kids who want to play hockey is the expense. The further you go past rec league hockey, the more expensive it gets. To keep their kids competitive today, parents are forking out six hundred dollars for skates, two hundred dollars for sticks and thousands for hockey clinics and league fees. That alone keeps many talented kids out.

Of course, the challenges for our youth go beyond money.

Recently, a friend told me about a podcast Malcolm Gladwell did about barriers to education for the lowest economic classes in the United States, a population in which African Americans and Hispanic Americans are vastly overrepresented. One of the striking things he pointed out was that simply giving poor students scholarships was often not enough to keep them in school. He told the story of a very talented teenager who received free tuition and money for living expenses but had to drop out of the private academy he was attending because his mother died and he was the only family member who could take care of the young children left at home. In other words, there are many barriers that prevent poor or marginalized people from taking advantage of opportunities that might present themselves.

Indeed, if you come from a remote community, or a community where few have experience with the hockey development system, money is just one barrier. My boys may be First Nations, but they had the benefit of parents who could afford to keep them in good equipment and pay for their league fees, and they lived in areas where those leagues existed and where they could easily commute to other teams and leagues as they moved up the ranks. They also had a former pro coach helping them develop their playing skills and their ability to navigate the system. If a young Ted Nolan were trying out today for any of the competitive leagues, he simply wouldn't make it.

There isn't a lot Jordan, Brandon and I can do to address those large systemic problems—or even to address the financial challenges so many of our young athletes face—but what we can do is share our knowledge of the sports system.

The skills clinics we offer always include sessions for parents about how the youth hockey world works and what they can expect if their children move outside the community to play competitive hockey. We also try to show young people in remote communities that while they may not experience a level playing field, they can still succeed and have the ability to compete with anyone, in any area of life.

And, of course, the hockey clinics are always, first and foremost, about coming together to have fun on the ice.

While our efforts are focused on Indigenous children, we recognize that the inaccessibility of hockey for a huge number of kids—because they don't have the financial resources or they live someplace where it's difficult to access the world of organized hockey—is a real loss, both for the kids and, frankly, for the sport itself.

The famed science historian Stephen Jay Gould said about the efforts to discover the secrets of Albert Einstein's genius, "I am, somehow, less interested in the weight and convolutions of Einstein's brain than in the near certainty that people of equal talent have lived and died in cotton fields and sweatshops." When I read that quotation, it really struck a nerve. It can so obviously apply to talent of all kinds, including physical brilliance. How many wonderful athletes never get the chance to even experience a sport that they might shine in? How many potential Wayne Gretzkys or Connor McDavids can't afford a pair of skates or the fees to join a hockey league? How many of them are floating around in rec leagues, hoping to be plucked out and given a chance? I know that organizations like Hockey Canada and the NHL, with their Hockey Is for Everyone campaign, are trying to reach out to those sidelined communities, but I can't help think that challenges to those communities remain frustratingly high.

◆

Both boys are now navigating through their post-hockey careers. As co-founders of the 3Nolans, they work hard on delivering a great program to First Nations youth across Canada and always talk with the kids about their own experiences growing up and the importance of school, education, health and wellness. Jordan also tells them how much his decision to refrain from drinking has helped his overall health and career.

Jordan continues to work with the LA Kings organization and also has received his firefighter certification. And both boys have roles in the Canadian sitcom *Shoresy*. Created by the team behind the TV hit *Letterkenny*, the show focuses on a triple-A hockey team, the Sudbury Bulldogs. Along with former pro hockey player Jon Mirasty, Brandon and Jordan play Hanson brothers–style hockey tough guys, and they're having a ball doing it.

My sons have married wonderful women, Stephanie (Brandon) and Laura (Jordan), and Sandra and I have been blessed with five amazing grandchildren: Hunter, Ryder, Sadie, Quinn and Harper. Since Jordan lives in St. Catharines with his family and Brandon lives in Whitby, Sandra and I bought a townhouse in St. Davids, in Niagara-on-the-Lake, and spend a good part of the year shuttling between there and Whitby to spend time with everyone. Every summer, and as often as we can throughout the rest of year, we return to Garden River, the place I always think of as home.

And in 2022, I began work as an adviser for the Chiefs of Ontario (COO), an organization that supports the self-determination of the

Anishinaabe, Mushkegowuk, Onkwehonwe and Lenape peoples. In working to exercise and protect inherent and treaty rights, the Chiefs of Ontario meetings are often a stark reminder of the issues that continue to plague our people. In fact, while public awareness of our history and of current living conditions in many of our communities has been raised by the attention focused on the unmarked graves on residential school properties, I'm saddened by the lack of progress for Indigenous communities. At the COO, we continue to talk about things I remember my Elders discussing at our kitchen table, issues Alex Akewense and members of the American Indian Movement discussed around the campfire during their many visits to Garden River: lack of decent housing, lack of drinking water, lack of medical care in northern communities, lack of schools in our remote reservations, lack of opportunity.

I find it heartbreaking to listen to the struggles and tragedies of our community. Sometimes unbearably so. But I'm grateful for the chance to work with this inspiring bunch of leaders and to help their important work in whatever way I can. And it feels right and good to be spending my time connecting with my community and my heritage in this way, working in a political environment to improve the lives of my people and in a manner that is helping me to learn and grow.

The Chiefs of Ontario work has given me ways to do that professionally. Life has given me ways to do that on an emotional level.

The last number of years have been marked by periods of profound sadness. On September 26, 2007, while I was in Long Island, my brother Rick passed away at the age of sixty-two. Rick was not only like a second father to me my whole life, he was also a role model. A true and caring leader whose influence helped me at every step of my life. I may not have taken any professional coaching clinics, but I learned from Rick, so I learned from the best.

On March 17, 2010, my feisty brother Terry passed away. He was three months shy of his fifty-eighth birthday. On November 22, 2012, during a time when I was moving back and forth between Canada and Latvia, fierce and loving Rita, sixty-nine years old, passed. Then, in the summer between my last Sabres seasons, on August 5, 2014, Arlene, my nurturing second mother, died. She was just sixty-six. Gentle and wise Tom made it to sixty-nine years old, dying on March 17, 2016, six years to the day after Terry left the world.

Every two years, a deadly drumbeat.

By the fall of 2021, Joe, Steve, Janice, Barb and I were the only ones left of Rose and Stan's twelve children. And then, on October 27 that year, Joe suddenly passed away at the age of sixty-six.

Ever since I first left home at seventeen, I'd missed my siblings. Whenever I played or coached in Montreal, I'd think of Rod and his passion for the Canadiens (he'd even painted a huge rock outside his home with the Habs logo). At every big moment, like standing behind the bench at the Olympics, I'd felt a pang that my parents or my brothers and sisters couldn't be there with me. And at the oddest moments, the sense of homesickness and loss would sweep over me. One day, during my last days coaching with the Sabres, I was walking the streets of Philly before a game. I was struggling with the sense that I was missing somebody. Then I glanced up at a street sign: Rita Street. I was missing Rita.

In my most conflicted moments, I'd find myself resenting hockey and my career in it, because it had taken me away from my family. If I hadn't played, I would think, I would have spent precious years in Garden River, drinking cups of coffee around the kitchen table with my sisters or playing softball with my brothers.

With every passing, I'd been revisited by that feeling, had been overcome with what-ifs. It had been part of how I mourned all my siblings' deaths. But the way I reacted to Joe's exit was different. His death knocked me flat, leaving me crying like I've never cried in my life. For days, it felt as if I couldn't get through a single hour without breaking down.

It was strange. I'd always had a difficult relationship with Joe. For most of my life, I'd been angry with him. One of my clearest early memories, in fact, was the moment he took the watch away from me after my father died. A loss following a loss. When the tears finally stopped, I realized that although I'd done a lot of grieving in my life, perhaps I'd never *fully* grieved the string of losses that began with the death of my father. The family deaths. The evaporation of my career for nearly ten years. The destruction of my reputation. Joe's passing somehow allowed me to finally do that. And when I emerged from that darkness, I felt lighter. The bitterness that had never left me suddenly seem to vanish. The anger softened. In the year since his death, I feel as if I've gained some new clarity and been able to embrace the many joys in my life in a way I perhaps wasn't able to before.

One of those joys, of course, is coaching.

Most recently, I've been working with the Wiikwemkoong women's hockey team as they play in various Indigenous tournaments, including the 2022 "Chief Thunderstick" National Hockey Championship, in Saskatoon, an annual event founded by the late Fred Sasakamoose, the first full-treaty Indian to play in the NHL, and his family. Coaching this team has been an extraordinary experience, a chance to work with some amazingly talented athletes in a fun, supportive and competitive environment. And it's brought me some fresh insight into my career.

After leaving Buffalo in 2015, I realized I no longer felt the need to prove myself in the NHL. And while I enjoyed a short stint coaching in Poland from 2017 to 2018, it didn't ignite any burning desire to return to the international hockey world. If my coaching had stopped there, I might have felt I was done with it. But joining the women's team has been a powerful reminder of the sheer magic of coaching.

Team sports can have many benefits to society, including drawing diverse groups of people together. When I was coaching the Greyhounds, all you had to do was look at the stands to see fans who came from every walk of life and a wide range of cultural and ethnic backgrounds. It was hard to imagine too many other places where all these people would find themselves sitting down to enjoy time together.

Team sports also shows us the power of working collectively. It seems to me that it's becoming increasingly difficult to do this. In our modern world, so many have embraced the importance of the individual over the welfare of the larger group. You combine that with the gig economy, the trend to work from home and the independence that technology can give us, and it's easy to see why so many of us can get caught in our own little bubbles. In many ways, I get the appeal of that. When there's such a huge gap between the haves and the have-nots, when many companies and organizations are hierarchies where power is so concentrated that everyone other than the top guns is left out of the decision-making, working and living alone can look like freedom rather than isolation.

Team sports, then, can be one of the few places where it's possible to find the joy and power of working together. Granted, they don't always function that way. But I think a coach can help make that happen. On a great team, everyone supports each other, everyone gets better at what they do and everyone plays an important part. Leaders are born on a good team. When it works, when you are involved in a group where those things are happening, it's the best feeling in the world. And it's a great model for all of life.

Working with the Wiikwemkoong women's team has reminded me that coaching is coaching. You can do it anywhere, with any sort of group. Awards or paycheques or national attention aren't necessary to make it unbelievably satisfying work. I've found, in fact, the absence of those things is freeing, allowing me to coach the way I know best, focusing on helping players. And the absence of those things has reminded me that coaching isn't really a job for me. It's a gift—a gift of work I truly love.

CONCLUSION

MY DECISION TO WRITE THIS BOOK, to tell my story fully for the first time, came about in early 2020 with the killing of George Floyd and the rise in prominence of the Black Lives Matter movement.

Like so many other people, I was horrified about what happened to Floyd. But not surprised. The stories about Black men and boys being assaulted and killed by police had been in the news for years. His murder also echoed some of my people's experience with the police—the Indigenous population in Canada is ten times more likely to be shot and killed by police than white people, according to a 2020 analysis by CTV News. Once in custody, we represent 16 percent of the deaths, CBC News's "Deadly Force" investigation tells us, although we represent only 4 percent of Canada's population. And those statistics don't include what the First Nations community in Saskatoon calls "starlight tours," the 1990 to 2000s police practice of driving Indigenous men they'd detained into the countryside and leaving them to freeze to death during sub-zero winter nights.

Yet Darnella Frazier, the young woman who took the video of Floyd's murder, changed the way these stories are so often told. Here was one brutal crime that no one could skim over in the newspaper or could second guess. I couldn't stop thinking about what she had done and how important her documentation had been.

Over the last few years, I've been pretty open about my feeling that racism had something to do with my being kept out of the NHL for such long periods of time. But the shock that reverberated throughout the white population after the video of George Floyd's murder made it clear how difficult it's been for folks to see the racism that's right in front of their eyes, to truly understand the things people of colour have been trying to tell them for years. And I realized that all of us who have experienced some form of it need to tell our stories, especially if we have some name recognition that will bring attention to them. (I'd never compare what I've been through to what Floyd or many other Black and First Nations folks suffered, but that's not the point.) Telling our stories, in detail, is the only way more people can understand the sometimes subtle but insistent way racism operates in this world.

In the early years after Buffalo, when the boys were still playing hockey, I mostly kept silent about what I went through and what I witnessed. I didn't want to ruin things for my sons. I didn't want men in positions of power in the hockey world to sour on the boys because they thought their father was a whiner and complainer. But in thinking about George Floyd and the thousands of men, women and children whose experiences with the police preceded his, I realized that in protecting my own children I was perhaps letting other people's children be hurt. I was perhaps contributing to the silence and denial about racism in the hockey world. I was perhaps letting other people's children be kept out of the sport.

I know, I know. Times have changed since I played and coached. My sons' careers, after all, were very different than my own. But I have to point out that while my sons didn't experience racism from teammates, coaches or owners—and only very occasionally by fans—there are plenty of other players their age and younger who've had terrible experiences. If you don't believe me, take a look at the Hockey Canada report that identified nine hundred documented or alleged incidents of discrimination involving taunting, insults and intimidation across all levels and age groups of organized hockey during the 2021–22 season. Or check out what Akim Aliu had to say in the September 2020 *Maclean's* magazine article "Black Hockey Players on Loving a Sport That Doesn't Love Them Back," or read about incidents with Ethan Bear, K'Andre Miller or Jonathan-Ismaël Diaby. And so often, the discrimination is not perpetrated by the players but by parents and hockey authorities. In recent years, I've seen and heard of so many incidents, from the pros to the youngest leagues. Parents who grumble about some "Native" kid taking their child's spot. Indigenous players being repeatedly called out for penalties they haven't earned. First Nations players being pressured to be tough guys instead of finesse players. I've been told of coaches who've passed over First Nations kids because they thought they couldn't be relied on to show up. And I've heard of Indigenous teams that had to be escorted out of arenas during tournaments. Hockey and the NHL are not isolated spheres where the dark forces of the outside world don't creep in. And sport is not some magic balm that erases hateful feelings and prejudices.

A few months ago, I was at my grandson's baseball game. Out in the field, the little guy misjudged a fly ball and it hit him on the head. He cried a bit and then continued playing. After the inning was over, another player, a white boy, rushed over to ask my grandson if he was okay. It struck me, watching this unfold, that I couldn't imagine that happening when I was my grandson's age. What I remember from that age is sitting in the Soo arena lobby with my hand wrapped in a wad of bloody paper towels. Steve and I waiting there, hour after hour, as parents, kids and coaches walked past us, barely glancing our way. I'm relieved to think that my grandchildren will likely never experience anything like that. It gives me hope for the future.

Things do seem to be changing. But we shouldn't be complacent about that. As Cyrus Mehri, the civil rights lawyer whose research and advocacy led to the formation of the NFL's diversity committee and the creation of the Rooney Rule, has recently said, "Racial progress is fragile, and you can lose it in a heartbeat." Besides, I think it's important that we don't let our hope for the future obscure the fact that racism is alive and well. And that there are thousands upon thousands of men and women who have already been deeply scarred by racist acts and attitudes and feel the effects of those scars every day.

Someone recently showed me an article with the title "Nolan's Sullen Act Is Getting Tiresome." It was, as you can imagine, both highly critical of my career and of the way I've voiced disappointment and dissatisfaction in the past. And it repeated a lot of false rumours and misinformation about me. I wasn't surprised by any of that. The author's general message, that I should just get over it, is something people have been saying to me—and to the entire Indigenous community—my whole life. But how do you just get over it? Even if the taunts, the persecution, the bias disappeared overnight, you can't simply forget it. It takes time to deal with pain. And so often, when you think you've faced it, managed it, moved past it, the wounds reopen at unexpected moments.

And besides, saying that someone needs to get over it always carries the implication that whatever "it" is, it's in the past. This is not true for the injustices that Indigenous people face—we continue to struggle against them every day. And on a personal level, it isn't true for the reputational damage I contend with. Nine years after the rumours about me started, Sandra was sitting in the stands in Finland, watching one of the Latvian team games, when she overheard a conversation from folks sitting behind her. They were talking about our team's performance and my role as coach.

"Yeah, he's a good coach, but you know why he doesn't coach for the NHL, right?" one of them said. "In Buffalo, he used to show up to the practices drunk. That's why they had to can him."

And just the other day, twenty-five years after I left the Sabres the first time, someone working on this book told me they'd mentioned my name to an acquaintance who is the son of a long-time NHL player of John Muckler's generation.

"Ted Nolan?" the son said. "Yeah, I don't know about that guy. Did you hear about the affair he had with a player's wife?"

The rumours cling to me like an inky stain. For some people, they are all they know about me. The passage of time has done nothing to soften that sting.

Over the years, I've attempted to find out how those rumours started. Not surprisingly, I've found no answers. One nagging mystery was clarified, however, a little more than a year ago. While watching the 2021 TSN documentary about my career, *The Unwanted Visitor*, I was shocked to see it contained a 2005 video clip of an interview with one the Sabres' founders, Bob Swados. When asked what the thinking was behind the one-year contract I was offered in 1998, Bob said, "I think the original discussions were to make an offer that he would certainly reject." It's what I'd always believed. The only surprise was hearing one of the owners say it out loud.

In all of this, I don't mean to say I was let go from Buffalo in 1998, or that I wasn't hired by the NHL for almost ten years, because I was First Nations. I think I was let go because I didn't fit the mould. And one of the reasons I didn't fit the mould was my heritage, my history. I truly believe that the nasty rumours from my Buffalo days, the remarks about my successes being just a series of lucky breaks, the fact that I was never asked to coach the World Juniors and never received any coaching award from the junior leagues, despite winning five championships—all of that was, in one way or another, because I was different.

A number of people who have been involved in the NHL have commented that they don't think I was blackballed. Usually, they follow this by raising the idea that the upper ranks of the NHL is just an "old boys' club." My exclusion, they are implying, wasn't caused by someone expressly saying, "Don't hire Ted Nolan. He's a GM killer," and wasn't conscious or official in any way. But by talking about an old boys' club, they are suggesting that the closed nature of the organization might have contributed in some way to the lack of opportunities I had after Buffalo.

During my years in the NHL, I *did* feel that there was an exclusive circle and I wasn't in it. I'm always a little frustrated by the way people offer up this explanation, as if I shouldn't take it personally. As if it's no big deal. But what is an old boys' club except a structure that keeps certain kinds of people out? Women, for instance. People with different backgrounds, experiences or affiliations. People who you might do business with occasionally but who you aren't friends with in the after hours? As far as I'm concerned, it's delusional to think that an old boys' club is a benign thing.

In writing this book, I've had a chance to talk with many people from my hockey past. Sometimes, our memories differ strongly. But I can only tell you how I experienced the events. Most of the people I worked with are good people, and when they say there was no racism involved in decisions that were made about employment, I understand that they truly feel this to be true. Perhaps because so many people were unaware of the First Nations experience in Canada or of how other racialized people have been treated in North America, they couldn't understand where I was coming from. They couldn't put themselves in my shoes. They expected trust when I had none to give. And because of my own past, I sometimes couldn't understand them either.

◆

As I've said, sometimes I wish I'd never played hockey, because then I wouldn't have left home for all those years and missed so much time with family who passed away so early. And if I hadn't become a pro, I would still be playing beer league hockey, battling it out with my brother and friends, enjoying a game, having fun. That just doesn't feel possible anymore. A few years back, I was convinced to join a First Nations hockey tournament. As soon as I got on the ice, another player speared me hard. He clearly wanted to start a fight. I shook my head.

"I beat you, or you beat me. Either way, I lose."

After the game, the fellow came up to me and told me he just wanted to take on the pro. I eventually got to know him. He's a nice guy. But I recognize that even nice guys sometimes can't resist trying to show up an ex-NHLer, and that just takes the joy right out of the game for me.

That said, I'm grateful for everything my hockey career gave me. I've met wonderful people and made terrific friends. I've travelled all over the world. I made enough money to provide for my family. And I've had the honour of playing and coaching with some of the greatest players and greatest franchises in hockey. Even in my darkest days, I recognized the extraordinary privilege in that.

One of my fondest memories of this gift was the last time I was at the Montreal Forum. It was January 1996, and the Sabres were playing our final game in the Forum before the Habs moved out in March. I left my hotel room early in the morning, picked up a coffee and got to the building before the rest of the team arrived for the morning skate. In the near-deserted arena, I sat on the bench, looked at all the banners hanging from the rafters and drank in its history. I thought of Toe Blake, Maurice Richard, Jean Béliveau.

And I thought about Rod and his devotion to the Canadiens. How he would have loved to come here as often as I had. How lucky was I? As a player, I'd played in four of the original six arenas. As coach, I got to revisit them. It gave me the feeling of being part of hockey history, being part of the very best of this world.

Of course, hockey has also given me work I felt I was meant to do—coaching. And it's given me the best job in the world—working with my sons on the 3Nolans. (Spending time with them is a joy. Hearing them tell the stories of their lives to the young players we are working with reminds me over and over again of their hard work and what wonderful men they have turned out to be.) Hockey has also given me a public profile that's allowed me to connect with my heritage in a powerful way. When I was a kid doing the Pow Wow circuit with my mother, I thought nothing would be better than visiting every corner of this country and every First Nation and Indigenous community that is rooted in this land. I haven't managed to do that entirely, but I'm close. And every place I go, every person I meet, brings me some new appreciation of the beauty and strength of our people.

Finally, hockey has afforded me the opportunity to build something I truly believe will be my most important contribution: the Ted Nolan Foundation and the Rose Nolan Scholarship.

Despite the fact that I've spent most of my career helping young men, I truly believe that the real strength in our world comes from women. I can't overstate the influence the women in my life have had on me: my mother, my five sisters and my wife and best friend, Sandra. While my mother's death was the pivotal moment in my life, I would not be the person I am today without the unwavering support and love I received from all of them.

I was reminded of that during a dinner Sandra and I had with the Wiikwemkoong women's team when we were at that "Chief Thunderstick" tournament in Saskatoon. The team general manager, Walter Manitowabi, invited the players to tell us a bit about themselves, including the universities and colleges they were attending. Sandra and I were blown away by these accomplished young women. I couldn't help thinking of my three granddaughters, Sadie, Quinn and Harper, and the futures that lie ahead of them. And I couldn't help thinking about my mother. I was sure she was looking down on this room of extraordinary young women and smiling.

Over the years, the Ted Nolan Foundation evolved. In January 2009, for example, we formed a five-year partnership with the Tim Horton Children's Foundation to send children to first-class summer camps at Onondaga Farms in St. George, Ontario, and in Tatamagouche, Nova Scotia. (Sandra and I are so grateful to all our donors and generous sponsors, including the Bank of Montreal, CN Employees' and Pensioners' Community Fund, the Tim Horton Children's Foundation, Midland Transport, Robert and Jill Irving, and Fritz Construction.) By 2019, however, I knew I wanted to focus on 3Nolans, and Sandra and I decided it was time for the foundation to wind down. But we didn't let the Rose Nolan Scholarship disappear.

Since its inception in 2004, the Rose Nolan Memorial Scholarship has raised close to two million dollars and awarded scholarships to over 130 woman across Canada. (I'll never forget one of our winners,

Jennifer Katherine Beaucage, who has gone on to become a medical doctor in Northern Ontario. But there are many such remarkable and deserving recipients.) When the Ted Nolan Foundation ceased operations, the remaining Rose Nolan Scholarship funds were transferred to a number of colleges, training institutes and universities. Cape Breton University, Sault College, First Nations University, Indigenous Institutes Consortium, University of Winnipeg and Algoma University will continue to grant Rose Nolan Scholarships for years to come.

◆

In recent years, my siblings and I have begun talking more and more about our experiences. I come from a generation of First Nations kids whose parents didn't speak openly about what they went through. So we often didn't understand the things our Elders did or the choices they made. Steve, Barb, Janice and I find ourselves wishing that those who have already passed had had the chance to connect and work on healing the way we are continuing to do. And the understanding that is growing out of our conversations makes me appreciate, just as Darnella Frazier's video did, that silence is rarely a positive thing—for individuals and families or for our wider society.

In one of the interviews I did for Canada's very first National Day for Truth and Reconciliation, on September 30, 2021, I was asked what I thought we needed to do to move towards reconciliation. It's certainly a big challenge to meaningfully address so many injustices of the past, including the residential and day schools, the Sixties Scoop, the missing and murdered Indigenous women. But I said that, more than anything, I wanted Indigenous and non-Indigenous folks to work with open hearts on understanding each other. That may sound like a simple solution, but it's not. It takes effort, real effort. You have to get to know others to gain understanding. You have to *ask*. You have to listen when folks answer. And you've got to keep at it. As Stan Nolan always said, "If things aren't working, you're not working hard enough."

We have to work harder.

Hope is a good thing. And my hope for the future is that we all do that labour, that we make the effort, over and over again, to understand each other. Perhaps this book can play a small part in that.

—Ted Nolan, January 2023

ACKNOWLEDGMENTS

Nick Garrison, I want to thank you for reaching out and for feeling that my story is worth sharing, that it could both entertain and educate. Meg, thank you for telling that story. You made me feel comfortable when subjects were difficult to talk about. Never once did you question my behaviour. Your understanding and compassion helped me open up even more. Your commitment and passion didn't go unnoticed, and I am thankful for you! Chi-miigwetch!

Thanks also to Matthew Flute for the beautiful cover, to Alex Schultz for his careful and sensitive copyediting and to Zainab Mirza for your thoughtful assistance with choosing the right photos to help tell my story. A special thank-you to Joe Corbiere and family for help in collecting those photos. A shout-out also to everyone on the Penguin team for their hard work and support of this project.

A big, big thank-you goes to the hearts that helped me along my journey: the late Bill LeClair, the late Morris Martin, Bill Bailey, the late Jim McAuley, Mrs. Forbes, Mrs. Payette, Danny Flynn, the late Mike Zuke, Bill Hughes, Paul Theriault, Sherry Bassin, the Knox family, Artūrs Irbe, Tom Coolen, Māris Baldonieks, Kārlis Zirnis, Olivier Chouc, Nada Ristich, the late Paul House, Jody Gage, Dave Hanson, Bill Hogaboam, Stan Pesner, the late Keith Rogers, the late Ken Hill, Phil Fontaine, Pat Madahbee, Nick Javor, Pat LaFontaine, Robert and Jill Irving and my late aunt Fanny.

Mom, Dad, Rod, Katie, Rick, Rita, Arlene, Tom, Terry and Joey, I miss you everyday.

I am so very grateful for my parents. They made each of their twelve children feel special. Life was hard, yet together they made it work, creating a family bond that was unbreakable. Dad, thank you for showing me you don't need the best in order to be your best. Learn to work with what you have and not to wish for things you haven't got. Mom, miigwetch for giving me a valuable lesson about who I am as an Anishinaabe man and for sharing the beautiful teachings of our people. You showed me how much we have and how to be proud and thankful for family.

Barb, Steve and Janice, I will never take for granted your unconditional love and support. I'm so grateful to have you here, to know you are only a phone call away. I love you.

To all my nieces and nephews, I see so much of my brothers and sisters in you and that fills my heart. And to my family members that have moved to the spirit world, baamaapii miinwaall kaanbmin (later again, I will see you).

To my Anishinaabe Nation, thank you for all your love and support. It matters!

Brandon, Jordan, I am so proud of you. And working together on the 3Nolans has been a true blessing. I love you both with all my heart and soul. Now with your families and our precious grandchildren, Hunter, Ryder, Sadie, Quinn and Harper, the blessings continue.

And finally, Sandra. When I first saw you, I felt I was looking at an angel. But by that time, I'd forgotten how to love, how to open up my feelings. Then when my mother followed my father to the next life, I put up even more walls, not wanting to feel that pain again. But you didn't give up on me. You never once wavered when I had only little to give. I have lost so much; the only consistent thing in my life has been you. We will celebrate forty-three years of marriage this coming spring. During our time together you showed me what unconditional love really is and what love really means. You helped me, piece by piece, to begin the process of loving again. (Thank you, Morley and Shirley Howe, for raising a such wonderful daughter.) And you gave us our two beautiful sons, Brandon and Jordan—the most precious gifts I have ever received. Watching them crawl, walk, run, smile, talk and grow into the men they are today couldn't have brought me more joy.

Sandra, I will be forever grateful. This life would not have been possible or even imaginable without you.